The New York Times
Home

BOOK OF MODERN DESIGN STYLES, PROBLEMS, AND SOLUTIONS

BY SUZANNE SLESIN
DESIGNED BY TOM BODKIN

EDITED BY WENDY SCLIGHT
RESEARCH ASSISTANT: INDA SCHAENEN
ART ASSISTANT: LAURIE BAKER

Times
BOOKS

Published by TIMES BOOKS, a division of Quadrangle/The New York Times
Book Co., Inc., Three Park Avenue, New York, N.Y. 10016

Published simultaneously in Canada by Fitzhenry & Whiteside, Ltd., Toronto

Copyright © 1982 by Suzanne Slesin

Library of Congress Catalog Card Number: 82-50040

ISBN: 0-8129-1027-3

Typography by Typogram

Color separations by Color Associates, Inc.

Printed and bound by W.A. Krueger Company

Manufactured in the United States of America

10 9 8 7 6 5 4 3 2 1

Acknowledgments

This book is based almost entirely on articles that appeared in *The New York Times'* Home Section and *The New York Times Magazine* over the last three and a half years.

I am indebted and grateful:

To my editors and colleagues at *The New York Times* with whom I have been privileged to work during that period. Their advice and support have been instrumental in helping me develop as a journalist and reporter. They include A.M. Rosenthal, Arthur Gelb, James L. Greenfield, and Louis Silverstein; Nancy Newhouse, Living/Style editor; Dona Guimaraes, editor of The Home Section; Ed Klein, editor; and Carrie Donovan, senior editor of *The New York Times Magazine,* whose sound advice on every aspect of these stories has been invaluable.

To Wendy Sclight, Maryann Bird, and John Montorio, past and present deputy editors of The Home Section, and to Marilyn Pelo, formerly of *The New York Times Magazine,* who shepherded and coaxed most of the pieces in this book into their original journalistic form.

There is little reporting on interior design that is not dependent on good photography. In this area, I am forever indebted to Mort Stone, assistant picture editor of *The New York Times* and diplomat extraordinaire, for his continual help. A special thank-you also to Edwin Gross, manager of *The New York Times'* Studio, and to *The New York Times'* staff photographers whose work is shown here, especially Gene Maggio, Edward Hausner, and Bill Aller.

I am indebted as well to Norman McGrath, Gilles de Chabaneix, and Jaime Ardiles-Arce; and especially to Robert Levin, who contributed the majority of the photographs in this book.

Many thanks also to the other photographers whose work is included: James J.C. Andrews, Rick Barnes, Roger Bester, Peter Fine, Raeanne Giovanni, Mark Golderman, Michael Halsband, David Kelley, Nathaniel Lieberman, Chris Mead, Jean Pagliuso, Bo Parker, Robert Perron, E. Stoecklein, and Paul Warchol.

To all the people who live in the houses and apartments shown here, many thanks for letting us come and photograph, often on inopportune days and in disruptive circumstances.

To all the designers and architects whose work is illustrated and credited throughout the book. Their ideas and solutions make up the content of this book, and it is their work that shaped my thinking about modern interior design trends. Without them, there would simply not have been anything to write about or report.

To Times Books and Leonard Schwartz, whose initiative and perseverance convinced me to undertake this project in the first place. To Patrick Filley, my first editor there, who helped me shape the contents of this book; to Joseph Consolino, president of Times Books, whose continued support was also crucial; and special thanks to Marge Anderson and Pam Lyons, who extended themselves beyond the limits of their jobs. Thanks also to Hugh Howard, Bill Zirinsky, Bernadette Hackett, and Dorothy Desha, all of whom displayed a professionalism, enthusiasm, and patience that made this project possible.

To Wendy Sclight, currently the editor of The Westchester Weekly section of *The New York Times,* who expertly and tirelessly molded the original material into its final book form. Her understanding, expertise, and sound editing advice were invaluable to this project.

To Inda Schaenen, my research assistant, who put together the catalog, typed, telephoned, and never said no to extra work.

To Laurie Baker, art assistant, whose high standards and meticulousness matched those of a demanding art director.

Thanks also to Fran Rothenberg and Toni Ross for their extra researching help.

To Tom Burke, Nestor Delgado, Ray Downing, Manolo Guevara, Jr., Paul Hacker, Al Hawkins, Lora Holbrook, Alfred Lugo, John Palmer, Mark Pieper, Michael Shiffrin, Jack Taromina, all of whom were indispensable to the production of this project.

To Howard Angione, Bill Young, and Jed Stephenson of the Systems Support department of *The New York Times,* for their advice and expertise.

To Greg Ryan for the illustrations in the catalog and for his continued support and patience.

To Mike Leahy, Nora Kerr, and the other editors of the Travel section of *The New York Times* for graciously sharing their art director.

To the many people who have been generous with their time and were helpful in many, many ways. They include Robert Bray, Alan Buchsbaum, Charles Churchward, Stafford Cliff, Tina Cohoe, Noel Corbett, Gary Cosimini, Ron Couture, Joan Deneen, Marion Donnelly, Joseph Paul D'Urso, Mary Emmerling, Carl Fischer, Robert Green, Steve Heller, Marny Hurst, Nikki Kalish, Peter Katz, Diana LaGuardia, Bridget Leicester, Timothy Litzinger, Elaine Louie, Chris Mead, Derek Miller, Juan Montoya, Thom O'Brien, Wendy Palitz, Al Roberts, Daniel Rozensztroch, Michael Schaible, William Sclight, Paul Segal, Erica Stoller, Mike Todd, Gregory Turpan, Michael Valenti, Pam Vassil, Carol Vogel, Jeffrey Weiss, and Yann Weymouth.

To my agent, Lucy Kroll, whose optimism and encouragement were among my greatest supports.

And finally, to Tom Bodkin, who designed this book, but whose contributions went beyond art direction. His dedication and perfectionism were inspirational.

Suzanne Slesin
August 2, 1982

To Michael Steinberg
with love and thanks

Contents

4

10

34

Choices

36

For most of us, whether prompted by a simple need to freshen up our surroundings or by the more ambitious goal of rectifying unfunctional floor plans, decorating, redesigning, or renovating a home is a major undertaking.

As we no longer live in a world where one stylistic viewpoint predominates, this book, in reporting on what is being done in modern interiors, reflects a range of styles and attitudes. And underlying this visual diversity are the varied lifestyles that were at the basis of their creation. Diversity of expression is one of the hallmarks of contemporary design, with architects, designers, and clients each confidently choosing to express their preferences.

The choices indeed span a wide vocabulary. Modern design includes the minimalist esthetic, which has come to be synonymous with a spare look—glossy white walls and floors, and platforms covered in charcoal-gray commercial carpeting; the high-tech interior, where the functional lessons of the factory or warehouse space and no-nonsense industrial paraphernalia and materials have been applied to residential spaces; the complex postmodern form of expression, with architectural and historical references and a soft palette of pinks, pale blues, and celadon; the country-style home, incorporating the wares and furnishings of the recent, seductively simple past; and the enduring attraction of the Bauhaus era, for those who remain faithful to that design school's direct philosophy as the ultimate design statement.

Whatever the look, there is little doubt that modern urban life has influenced our expectations of how a home should work, and that today's financial constraints encourage improving one's present living space over moving to a new one. Because of this, renovation has become a major part of the design business: from lofts to brownstones, from suburban family houses to studio apartments, the goal is to make these spaces more flexible for the changing needs of their occupants.

We no longer enjoy the luxury of "special rooms"— the Victorian parlor, for example, kept pristine and out-of-bounds except for visiting guests; or a small but private study, where one could retreat to think or read. Instead, every corner and closet in the modern home is at a premium. Kitchens have come out into the open to be used simultaneously as living and dining spaces, maid's rooms have been converted into nurseries, and living rooms double as family rooms. Foyers, pantries, hallways, attics, even guest rooms have all but disappeared as rooms of their own. They are in the process of being converted into extra storage or sleeping areas or incorporated into the functions of adjacent rooms. The modern house or apartment is a compromise in terms of space. But these renovations and conversions not only can be successful in terms of design but also allow their occupants to make the most of what they have.

If these ventures can be exciting, they can also prove a frustrating task. How to decide what style one truly prefers? What will make a livable interior? How is a compatible designer or architect chosen? And, perhaps most importantly, how much will all of this cost? It is hoped this book will help guide the reader through such decisions, by offering an overview of the options and an illustration of some of the results.

Crucial to the design process are the interior designer and architect, whose roles have been changing in recent years as living spaces have become more diversified. Where once the image of interior decorators centered mostly on cosmetic style, they are now appreciated as well for the problem-solving, structural aspects of their work. At the same time, architects have become more involved in decisions about interior furnishings and color schemes.

The loft revolution has had its influence here. While once it might have been assumed that additional space could solve all the problems faced in an efficiency apartment, the cavernous loft spaces proved as problematic as tiny, boxlike rooms and underlined the need for professional design advice to create functional living spaces. Visual privacy and sound control are essential aspects of modern life. Putting up partitions is as important to the modern interior as tearing down walls. Each requires its own special expertise.

Many large cities—New York, in particular—offer a range of resources and a diverse talent in interior design. The two initial questions when choosing an interior designer or architect are "What style?" and "How much?" Although their styles can range from minimal to traditional, from high-tech to country, designers do tend to fall into those two increasingly important divisions: the lavish spenders and the more budget-minded. There are those one wouldn't dare call unless willing to spend a small fortune, and others who cheerfully list themselves in the "no-job-is-too-small" category.

In the shadow of the established and acclaimed maestros, a multitude of energetic but as yet unheralded designers exist. Problem-solvers or stylistic innovators, their interiors range from conservative to avant-garde. Because they are just starting out, they will accept projects under $10,000, which more established designers tend to turn down. Generally, fees of $25 an hour are not unusual for design and construction supervision, with some designers adopting the architect's practice of passing on trade discounts on furnishings and materials to clients. On a small but time-consuming project, charging on an hourly basis is often preferred; from drafting to design this can range from $10 to $70 an hour. On projects costing more than $20,000, a percentage is usually charged, with 25 percent of the budget the most common fee.

There are, of course, those who without any kind of professional help manage to "pull a place together"—often with panache. They tend to have a distinct point of view, often backed up by years of collecting and reflecting about their homes. They are not afraid of making mistakes, and are often perfectionists. On pages 10 and 11 are two examples of this intensely personal approach.

But for most of us, professional design help is not only necessary but can make the difference between an ordinary interior and one that functions well. Most raw spaces are far from perfect, and often seem overwhelming to confront. There are myriad tricks of the trade—each the best solution in a particular situation. A strip of well-placed mirror, custom-built seating or cabinetry, an unusual furniture configuration, or an imaginative lighting scheme can contribute to the success of a striking and livable interior. And while there is little doubt that it is the famous and trend-setting designers who pave the way for the next generation, the design profession as a whole seems to be enjoying a revival. "Everyone copies someone," admits Doug Frank, a designer who has been influenced by the minimalists, including Joseph Paul D'Urso, Michael Schaible, and Robert Bray. His work appears on pages 116 to 119. "The relationship of forms is what's important," he explains. "The job may look like someone else's but each space is different."

One approach that is seldom mistaken for anyone else's is that of Diana Phipps, an interior decorator who works in London but travels to the United States frequently. She is known for a kind of do-it-yourself style, executed with flair. Instead of interior decorating, she calls her craft "house arrangements."

"I rather like nineteenth-century things," Mrs. Phipps said. "Some people, the lucky ones, are sufficient unto themselves and not dependent on their surroundings. They can wake up in a modern plastic box and not feel like ending it all. I can't. I'm totally dependent on my backdrop for my state of well being." Her backdrop is definitely the period room. Although usually Victorian, her choices are sometimes of an indeterminate time.

While designers and architects have ideas and know how to implement them, their ideas won't always knock you over. They can be understated, but cleverly so. "If the solution feels strained, I just don't do it," says Kevin Walz, a young New York designer. "They're not gimmicks." Often a designer's idea can inspire someone else, or the idea itself can be applied in another situation. Walz's movable walls, shown on pages 104 and 105, were not only the right solution for that apartment, but may well strike other apartment dwellers as the perfect solution to their needs.

The main challenge for designers is the creation of versatile, usable spaces. But clients who are reluctant to embark on expensive and time-consuming decorating projects are forcing designers to come up with quick and upbeat design schemes that are not too costly. In an apartment by Robert Hart, for example, the windows are absolutely bare, an old sofa has been slipcovered in striped linen, the chairs are wicker, the modern sideboard is chrome and glass, the table lamp has a galvanized steel shade. Nothing matches, yet it all fits together. This approach, exemplifying a younger and often more budget-conscious outlook, has become a noticeable modern trend.

The rigidity associated with many decorating schemes of the past has been deemed no longer necessary, and even in interiors where the final effect is frankly luxurious, an underlying creative freedom takes the most lavish decor out of the realm of simply grand. The success of an interior, no matter what its cost, ultimately depends on a mix of textures, a sense of scale, and perhaps a striking use of a dramatic architectural element. Eric Bernard, a designer whose work appears on pages 26 to 29, often opts for slick, all-black rooms. Yet he is able to achieve a range of expression within that esthetic—from a sophisticated art-deco living room to a computerized, high-tech environment.

In nearly every design scheme, a part of it is fantasy, a part is practicality, a part is whimsy. Traditionally, interior design books either celebrate the more glamorous aspects or tend to the how-to school of decorating. This book hopes to combine a bit of both approaches. Interior design is a creative expression. It should be practical as well as entertaining, inspirational as well as eminently livable.

Future space: lavish for today

A decade ago, it was easy to conjure up the image of a modern interior: streamlined, open space, shiny surfaces, and glossy walls. The design goal was to attain a bare, clean look synonymous with industrial sophistication, and it supposed a willingness to eliminate most of one's possessions.

If the glistening minimal look was not widely adopted, this "modern" look did create an attitude toward design that had a more lasting effect: the taste for open loft spaces. In the case of a Park Avenue apartment, it prompted the owner, Iris Kaplan, to tear down walls and adopt a relaxed style more associated with less traditional neighborhoods in New York.

Robin Jacobsen and Scott Bromley of Bromley-Jacobsen Architecture and Design were called in by Mrs. Kaplan, a painter who often shows her work at home for charity benefits. "What I really had wanted was a loft downtown," she said. "And this is, of course, a compromise." Her eight-room apartment became a three-room space, with structural elements dictating the design and the degree of openness. After taking down the walls, the designers found that they would have to deal with three major structural columns.

"We started by pivoting the main dining area around one of the columns," Bromley said. That also meant designing three cantilevered tables at different heights—one for dining, one as a coffee table, and the third for displaying sculpture. The dining table determined the placement of the kitchen—a gleaming series of elliptical cabinets and counter tops, open and accessible to the main living area and encircled by a wall of glass block. Her studio, although connected to the living room, juts out from the building and has a glass-block roof. Throughout the apartment, lighting is concealed in the ceiling, along with the stereo speakers, and the stereo equipment is stored under the window.

Three metallic surfaces are used throughout the space: anodized aluminum on the cabinetry and stainless steel, slightly polished for the counter tops and highly polished for the columns. One thing Kaplan discovered was that the stainless steel, marble, mirror, glass, and wood need a lot of maintenance. Someone comes in every day to clean and polish. "It's just a bit more elegant than what I bargained for," she said.

Scott Bromley and Robin Jacobsen focused the design of an apartment on a stainless steel column, opposite left. In the kitchen, left, the oval counter tops are stainless steel, the cabinets anodized aluminum.

The guest bathroom, far left, has a stainless steel sink and shower for the artist's models. The living room, left, features cantilevered marble tables and sliding panels to display paintings.

The loft: to each his own

Robert Levin

In an all-white loft, right top, architect Stephen Levine has kept the kitchen open to the main living space. Mary Emmerling's loft is used as a neutral background for her collection of American folk art, right. Peter Stamberg helped actor Michael Wager create an old-world quality in a Manhattan loft, opposite top, while the furnishings in Joseph Lembo's tiny loft, opposite bottom, have been kept to a minimum.

Chris Mead

Lofts—those adaptable, mostly open spaces in what were once commercial or factory buildings—are the chameleons of modern design. Once the working and living spaces for artists, they have become over the past few years one of the most economical and functional alternatives for many urban residents.

The clean, large spaces offer many design choices. Lofts are shells that often include impressive square footage, big windows, and an uncluttered floor space in which residents can arrange their living requirements as they please.

The way a loft will look once renovated and inhabited is, to a large degree, a question of personal choice. The existence and placement of structural columns often form the basis for the layout of the loft and provide its esthetic impetus. But after that, a "raw" loft offers a myriad of stylistic possibilities. There are those who prefer to emphasize its industrial or high-tech antecedents; others ignore its factorylike features and choose a more lavish decorated scheme. Some focus on a dramatic view, while others emphasize a detail of the interior as a point of reference.

There are loft dwellers who opt for keeping wide open spaces, but others prefer to fill their new homes with the objects they have collected over the years. And while loft living has helped to bring the open kitchen into new prominence, it has also afforded a greater privacy for many families. In most lofts, it is as easy to put up partitions as not, and to adjust the configuration of the living space as one's needs change.

A collection of antique frames in the dining room, right, holds Len and Mickey Sirowitz's family portraits. The paneling in the Gothic-style dining room, opposite left, was restored. A wide doorway frames a view of the tiled fireplace in Beni Montresor's classically simple and serene apartment, far right.

For those whose sense of home is inextricably linked with their perceptions of interior design, every decision made about decor is intensely personal. The feeling and look of their homes are the result of years of thought and the slow accumulation of possessions.

Len and Mickey Sirowitz have lived in the same rambling apartment for eleven years. The neo-Gothic rooms, with their dark paneling, arched doorways, and leaded windows, seem particularly suited to house the couple's extensive collection of Art Nouveau and neo-Gothic antiques and objects.

The Sirowitzes have been collec-tors since high school and each object has a special meaning. The hall is filled with personal memen-tos and artwork; each plate dis-played on the rail in the paneled dining room recalls a vacation or trip. The pièce de résistance is Mrs. Sirowitz's collection of antique frames, which are used to display family portraits.

Beni Montresor has lived in a Greenwich Village landmark build-ing for nearly twenty years. The high-ceiling apartment, with its angled rooms and floor-to-ceiling doors, has plenty of old-world charm. Yet, he has brought his own personal style to the space. The rooms are sparsely furnished, the windows bare, the parquet floors polished and uncarpeted, the walls gleaming. The uncluttered rooms contribute to the appeal of the apartment, as do his choice and placement of objects. "There's not a thing here that comes from a store," he said. "Instead, I go around, I put things together." That includes two early-twentieth-cen-tury chairs from Cleveland, a num-ber of glass objects from Toulouse, France, white ceramic vases from Venice, a piece of pottery from Rio de Janeiro. "My philosophy is that what's valuable is not what is expensive, but what one likes."

Purely personal points of view

In a room with a curved ceiling and huge window, far right, Juan Montoya chose platforms and overscaled accessories. The fireplace, right, has a monumental mantel. In the railroad-type apartment, below, Barbara Ross and Barbara Schwartz lined the living room window with a long banquette.

Mark Golderman

The New York Times/Gene Maggio

Dealing with odd spaces

Today's residential spaces in the city—often found in renovated factories and modern high rises—are smaller and more angular than their older counterparts. Their inadequate storage, tiny kitchens, windowless bathrooms, and nonexistent dining spaces seem almost standard. "They're strange spaces, typical of the 1980s," said Barbara Schwartz of Dexter Design.

"Interesting proportions, yet very awkward," was how Juan Montoya assessed one such apartment. "It had a dark living room, a viewless window, and an old-fashioned brick fireplace," he said. But the coved plaster ceiling and the room's height and huge window encouraged Montoya to rethink its potential.

He used a system of platforms to create different levels as well as a place to dine. For window treatment, Montoya had the frame painted a pale turquoise. "Like oxidized copper," he said. "I wanted to give the feeling of looking at the roofs of New York." Gauzy curtains diffuse both the light and the color. Montoya made the massive fireplace the center of attention. "I wanted it to be of stone," he said, "but that was too expensive." He settled on Sheetrock, framed in metal and covered with cement. The fireproof plaster was then painted to look like stone. To make the two niches that flank the fireplace appear larger, he removed the bookshelves and installed lighting.

Sometimes extensive renovation is required, as Schwartz and her partner, Barbara Ross, learned in a railroadlike apartment in a former hotel. "There was no entrance, and you had to walk through the ten-by-twenty-two-foot-long living room to get to the bedroom and bathroom," said Schwartz. As any usual arrangement of furniture would create an obstacle course, they had banquette seating installed along one wall, facing the apartment's best feature—a striking skyline view. A plastic-laminate-topped counter under the windows provides twenty-two feet of storage. Granite-topped tables by the banquette double as dining tables.

With Bob Cole, the firm also renovated a small duplex penthouse. "There was essentially a sixteen-by-sixteen-foot room with a bathroom at the center, a tiny kitchen, and a terrace, but no dining room and no storage," Schwartz said. The renovation included converting the bathroom into a service bar, adding a greenhouse to the terrace, and turning the main room into a flexible living room.

In another apartment—a one-bedroom in a converted factory—the problems could be quickly summarized. "No definition of an entrance foyer, a kitchen at one end and a bathroom on the other, both exposed to the living room, as well as a space, six feet at its widest point, that was supposed to be the bedroom," said Ross, who worked with Michael Byron on the project. Two freestanding walls, one rectangular, the other curved, were devised. One hides the kitchen and defines the foyer; the other separates the bathroom and living area. A three-section bedroom was created. A six-foot-wide area near the door includes a banquette, a television set, a closet, and a dressing area. The bed is on a platform and next to it is a mirror image of the banquette area. The raised bed became a vantage point for the view. "God forbid you should miss a minute of it," said Ross. "That's why the clients took the apartment."

In a narrow and awkward bedroom, far left, the bed was placed on a platform and a mirror reflects the view. A curved partition in the living room shields the bathroom entrance from the living room, left. In a small penthouse, below, the terrace was enclosed to provide an alternate dining area.

Second life for a city house

The exterior of the five-story 1890 mansard-roofed brownstone, above. In the top floor duplex, the living room, right, has been kept fairly sparse. On some floors, the original wainscoting and moldings around the windows were restored, opposite right.

The renovation of an 1890 building in Manhattan by Sassoon Shahmoon, an architect, and his wife, Barbara Schwartz, attests to the enduring attraction of the small but eminently livable brownstone spaces. Following the lead of many families who have bought dilapidated brownstones on tree-lined urban streets, the couple restored the older details of the original brickwork, woodwork, and fireplaces, which contributed to the charm of the late-nineteenth-century house. At the same time, they created modern, efficient living areas in the five-story building with an English basement.

"Our main problem was that the building is only forty feet deep," Shahmoon said. Another concern was, while a lot of light enters from the front, he had to get light into the back of the three floor-through and two duplex apartments into which the structure was divided. He had a series of bay windows installed on the second and third floors, a sky-light on the fifth floor, and a green-house extension in the basement. The layout of the upper duplex is unusual in the placement of the kitchen and dining area upstairs and the living room and bedrooms on the lower level. "This way we can take advantage of the terrace for eating," Schwartz said.

Unlike many other modern renovations, the stark angularity of the all-white interior has been tempered by the reuse of the original brick and the care taken in finishing the wood. New oak was used for the stair railings, the balcony, the floors, and the window sills.

The smallness of the building turned out to be a boon for the renovator. "That's one of the reasons brownstones are attractive," Shahmoon said. "They're of a size that someone starting out for the first time can grasp."

Jaime Ardiles-Arce

Ups and downs in a design career

In December 1974, he felt miserable and had $242.22 in his checking account. But Mario Locicero, a designer, went out to a plant store and bought four of the tallest Douglas firs that would fit into his apartment. He sprayed them with white snow and put them into his airbrushed cloud environment. "I was overdrawn by eight dollars, but I had a winter fantasy in my house," said Locicero. He also called one of the shelter magazines. "They came, they photographed, but they didn't publish them on the cover until the following December," he said. "It didn't make any difference anyway," he added, recalling his clientless days.

After many years of small projects, his dream job materialized. The project was an East Side duplex with a forty-foot-long living room. He based the overall concept on the design of the *Normandie,* the luxury liner, with a ribbonlike steel staircase as the focus. The stairs have no risers, making the carpeted steps look as if they are floating. Everything in the co-op, from the light switches to door hardware to the soap dishes, was custom designed. The $7,000 tables were on order for months, the chairs upholstered in glove leather. Metals, chrome, stainless steel, and brass were used throughout—with the huge columns sheathed in polished aluminum.

The "dream" project took two years, during which time Locicero paid off his debts and had an admittedly extravagantly good time. But the shiny finished apartment is now simply a reminder of that luxurious time, and he is once again directing his energies into his own place. He bought some army surplus parachutes, sewed them together, and, to create a shifting pattern, he placed fans behind them. "I call it upholstering the room," he said. "Fortunately I had taken dressmaking in school, because I had to do it all myself."

Main features of an apartment designed by Mario Locicero, left, include a gleaming curved staircase, shiny columns, and custom-furnishings.

Creating a new sense of Europe

Photographs by Norman McGrath

For a graciously proportioned living room, Richard Knapple and Eileen Joyce opted for neutral walls and modern seating to set off antique boiseries and art, right. The dining room, above, has a chrome-based table and antique chairs.

European interiors often have a certain drama, crispness, and stylishness that are lacking in the United States. One reason is that late Renaissance and baroque buildings provide startling and extravagant frameworks for modern interiors, and American designers rarely get a chance to try their hands at such spaces.

An exception was the renovation of a 2,000-square-foot space for Valentina-Cidat, a fashion concern, in a building originally designed as a residence in 1873. "There's actually nothing European here," said the designer, Robert Currie, explaining that his clients wanted the interior to reflect European taste. "It's mostly a look." The goal of the design was to take the classically proportioned rooms back to their original, grand condition by restoring the wood floors, fireplaces, and doors. In the main room, the designer opted for black drafting stools, with the casters removed for normal seating height, placed around black plastic laminate-topped tables. In another room, he had the wall mirrored above the carved wood fireplace. And what at first appears to be wood kindling spills out of the fireplace opening. "They're not just thrown in," said Currie, "but wood sculptures by Larry Arfield."

Another example of international stylishness that pairs a contemporary look and an old world background is an apartment designed by Richard Knapple and his partner, Eileen Joyce. In the living room, eighteenth-century Venetian chairs are placed around a modern table. The antique Italian celadon-green boiserie is framed in chrome and an eighteenth-century Buddha sits on the Italian modern coffee table. In the dining room, a new glass-topped table is encircled with antique painted chairs, upholstered in embroidered fabric. "It reflects a traditional, rather European taste," Knapple said.

Black drafting stools stand out against ornate moldings, in a room by Robert Currie, far left. Mirrored wall, overscale sofas, and wood spilling out of the fireplace are details meant to contrast with the grandness of the room, left.

The Oriental new wave

Toshiya and Eme Takahashi have forged a personal design style that combines many of the traditions of Japan with an enthusiastic view of the American new wave style. The result is an approach that is at once surprisingly avant-garde and budget-conscious.

But there are few elements of Japanese design in their apartment. Takahashi, a clothing exporter, has been collecting furniture and accessories from the 1950s, and his home is almost completely furnished with wrought-iron pieces from the 1950s and 1960s—side tables with plastic laminate marble tops, a small geometric settee, a

glass-topped free-form coffee table, and a number of chairs by Charles Eames. "The simple lines are what appeal to me," he said.

The apartment of Yasushi and Kiyoko Suzuki also reflects more conventional Japanese elements—there are large pillows on the floor, a low table, and not much other furniture. But the table is covered with a black-and-white checkerboard pattern that is, by design, "a little bit off." And the new wave wall decorations recall the colorful surface patterns of design in the 1950s.

"That's what we love," said the couple. "It's a new feeling and a point of view we never saw before."

Photographs by Robert Levin

Yasushi and Kiyoko Suzuki's loft has avant-garde and traditionally Japanese elements, left. Nylon stocking, cotton handkerchiefs, and crushed cellophane paper are part of Kiyoko Suzuki's collages, above.

Toshiya and Eme Takahashi's living room, far left above, acts as a background for his collection of 40s and 50s wrought-iron furniture. A metal chair was upholstered in zebra-printed vinyl, far left, below.

Basic all-black rooms

For Richard Assatly's apartment, Eric Bernard chose an all-black scheme to set off the view.

"People think black is depressing," said Eric Bernard, a designer. "They're wrong. Black is serene, relaxing, dramatic—a perfect background." Like many other contemporary designers, Bernard favors a monochromatic scheme. There have of course been black rooms before. In the 1920s and 1930s, during the glamorous Art Deco period, a black marble bathroom was synonymous with luxury. And in the 1970s, minimalists championed the starkness of the black-floored, white-walled room.

In Bernard's small, twelve-by-fifteen-foot bedroom, the mattress is on a black-tiled platform, the bedcover is quilted black silk, the floor is black slate, and the walls are lacquered in black. The color scheme makes the room seem larger by letting it look undefined. In the sunny living room, there is black leather seating and a black slate floor. Treating the room as a stage set, he routinely changes the accessories, rugs, and flowers. "Many people can't think of daylight and black rooms," said Bernard. "To me it's like a black bathing suit in the sun. I wanted a room where I could display art from any period."

He admitted one major inconvenience: "You can't keep a black room clean enough," he said. "Surfaces, especially horizontal ones, have to be dusted twice a day. Black is an outrageous extravagance and not for everybody. I would never do a black apartment for a family."

Richard Assatly, the fashion designer, was the first of Bernard's clients to be enthusiastic about the color scheme. In his apartment, Bernard had the walls painted in seven coats of black lacquer, covered the floors with black slate tiles, and used black glass lavishly.

"Because I hated it when people used to come here and go straight to the window to admire the view," Assatly said, "I felt I had to make the apartment as dramatic as possible."

Art Deco objects are highlighted in Eric Bernard's all-black living room, right.

Modern collages of times past

Confronting us are crumbling arches, cutout columns, fake neoclassical pediments, and pastel-hued rooms full of puzzling architectural allusions. It's a postmodern interior, the cognoscenti explain, dropping the names of such architects as Robert Venturi, Michael Graves, and Robert A.M. Stern, who rather than interior designers are the main exponents of the style—which ranges from the serious intellectual approach to the fanciful. Some of the movement's most successful applications are in the home—where the postmodernist interior proves surprisingly livable. Instead of treating space as a black canvas, the postmodernist makes a collage of architectural details always evocative of the past and sometimes functional.

"It's avant-garde because it represents the latest thinking, and is a reaction against the spare minimal look of the last ten years," Stern said. "It's for people who have personal histories and are not trying to escape them."

For "a family close to suicide—they had two children, two bedrooms, and only one bathroom"—Stern restructured an apartment. A cunningly planned galley kitchen is separated from the dining room by a partition that recalls an Edwardian china closet. Its construction is startling but practical: Its "windows" open so that dishes can be taken out from both sides. "Columns are the most visible manifestation of any architectural period," Stern explained. "But postmodernism is not just a way of having fun with columns." In fact Stern's columns are thoughtful. In the hall and doorway of the living room, plain columns set up a rhythmic pattern; in the master bedroom, the outline of a column becomes the opening between the bedroom and the small work area; and in the children's rooms, truncated columns are part of the units that hold books and toys.

Columns, pediments, and curved cabinet, far left, were added to a postmodern apartment by Robert A.M. Stern. Columns were also used to form a child's bookcase, left above. In the master bedroom, left, a cutout wall hides the desk area.

Photographs by The New York Times/Gene Maggio

Sometimes, however, postmodernism's references to architectural history tend to be the architect's rather than the client's. "We never knew we were postmodern," shrugged Beverly Hill and her husband, Parviz Eftekhari, who asked Wayne Berg to redesign their apartment. The architect Berg came up with the idea of taking fragments from an imaginary villa and putting them inside the high rise. But first he painted the entire space pink. "White already has a meaning in modern architecture—pink gives a surreal, neutral quality." Two cardboard columns with palm tree tops "indicate that the room is outdoors," and part of one wall looks as if it's eroding. A wall painted in terra cotta suggests a villa exterior, while a colonnade and the bedroom storage wall are compact recollections of Renaissance grandeur. "I wanted to miniaturize the idea of a house exterior," Berg said.

In a city apartment, Wayne Berg used palm tree–topped columns to create a dramatic entranceway, left. In the theatrical living room, above, there are crumbling walls and cutout architectural elements.

David Brittain

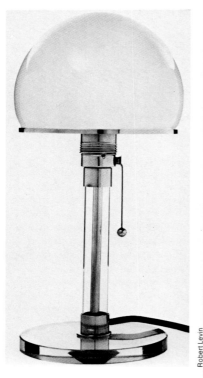

Reproductions of Eileen Gray Transat chair, René Herbst side chairs, and Fortuny lamp in a room by Andrée Putman, far right. Gray's Lota sofa, top, is at Beylerian, and her Satellite mirror, above, at Furniture of the Twentieth Century. Wilhelm Wagenfeld lamp, right, is at Lighting Associates.

Robert Levin

Reviving modern classic designs

The enduring mystique of the work created in the period of the Bauhaus—the influential and innovative German architectural school of the 1920s—is an inescapable facet of modern design history. The works of this era form the basis for furniture reproductions that are regarded as modern classics, and they encompass pieces by lesser-known architects of the period, including Eileen Gray, Robert Mallet-Stevens, and René Herbst.

Many of their furniture designs were never mass-produced and are being rediscovered today. Gray, the Irish-born designer who lived most of her life in Paris until her death there in 1976 at the age of ninety-seven, experimented with industrial materials. Her use of celluloid, perforated metal mesh, industrial felt, and corrugated materials resulted in prophetic examples of current high-tech designs. Her clinical-looking mirrors were also uncannily ahead of the times, as were her pivoting-drawer storage elements, a luxuriously proportioned sofa, and upholstered lounge chairs.

Lamps are also a fertile area for reproductions. Ecart International's Fortuny lamp, available through Furniture of the Twentieth Century, is a dramatic fixture; and Lighting Associates is importing several lamp designs of the 20s and 30s, reproduced in Germany by Tecnolumen. One of the most striking is a 1924 design by Wilhelm Wagenfeld of which only fifty examples were produced in 1930.

Between furniture and art

"The barriers between art and furniture keep on dissolving," said Marian Goodman of Multiples Gallery, one of several where furniture designed and made by artists is shown. In stores as well as galleries, sofas have signatures, lamps are numbered, tables are part of an edition. Instead of a manufacturer's name, it may be an artist's that is attached—a fact that is not surprising, considering the unusual look of the piece and its elevated price tag.

"An artist may have none of the practical points of view in mind," said Christopher Sproat, an artist inspired by Charles Rennie Mackintosh and Josef Hoffmann, whose chairs are elongated. Others, like Larry Bell, become obsessed with function. "Furniture is worthless unless it's comfortable," he said of his Carpathian burl elm chairs and sofa.

"The one-of-a-kind aspect is what makes it expensive, not what makes it art," said Max Protetch, whose gallery has exhibited furniture by Richard Meier and Scott Burton. Burton's attitude toward furniture as art is pragmatic. "The pink light from below the table's surface will make people look wonderful," he said of his dining table for eight.

"My furniture is both furniture and celebrations of furniture, and some is indistinguishable from conventional furniture," said Richard Artschwager, whose pieces in plastic laminate and wood at the Castelli Gallery range from $9,000 to $20,000. Kim MacConnel's painted patterned sofas, chairs, and lamps, shown at the Holly Solomon Gallery, start at about $2,000 for a coffee table or lamp. Jane Kaufman's screens and curtains, often with beads and pearls, range from $7,000 to $16,000. "People tend to respect the works as both art and furniture," said Barbara Toll, an art dealer whose own loft is filled with artists' pieces. "I would never expect them to put drinks down on a piece of sculpture."

In Holly and Horace Solomon's apartment, a sofa by Kim MacConnel stands in front of a fabric painting by Robert Kuschner.

Robert Levin

1

2

4

5

3

6

All across the country there are a number of surprises to be found—especially if one is on the lookout for unusual houses. So, when James J.C. Andrews, a manager for rock-and-roll groups and a free-lance photographer, was on the road, he began taking pictures of what he called "the more unusual buildings" that he saw along the way. He is not, of course, the only buff of such architectural oddities, but his interest has turned into a full-time occupation. Although Andrews rarely peeked inside the structures, he has during his travels spent the night in a cement tepee and is still looking for a medieval helmet-shaped home in Vermont.

After seeing the Big Duck building in Riverhead, Long Island, Andrews put an advertisement in a preservation magazine asking for information on similar buildings. "The response was overwhelming," he said. This led him to, among other places, the Shoe House in Hallam, Pennsylvania. Built in 1948 by a shoemaker, it measures twenty-five feet high and forty feet long. "The living room is in the toe, the master bedroom and bath are in the instep," he said. The windows are made of stained glass with shoe motifs; the mailbox and the doghouse are also shoe-shaped. He found the Santa Maria House in Absecon, New Jersey, a replica of one of Christopher Columbus's ships. "She loves her house," Andrews said of the occupant. The interior, which has a mast going through the roof and a kitchen in the stern, is "sort of like loft living," he explained. In Lexington, Virginia, a canoe rental and tour guide office operates out of a coffeepot, and the owner lives in an apartment upstairs. But one of Andrews' favorites is a 1930s motel/apartment complex—a series of tepees in Tempe, Arizona. "Instead of a round bed, I found a round room and knotty pine paneling, as well as cast-iron twig furniture," he said.

On the Mother Goose trail

1. Tureenlike Mother Goose House in Hazard, Kentucky, is from 1940.

2. Coffeepot, now a canoe renting office, is in Lexington, Virginia.

3. Hallam, Pennsylvania, Shoe House was home to a shoemaker's family.

4. Santa Maria House, in Absecon, New Jersey, has a mast through the living room.

5. Orange building is a car rental office.

6. Cement tepee in Tempe, Arizona, has awning-topped windows.

48

54

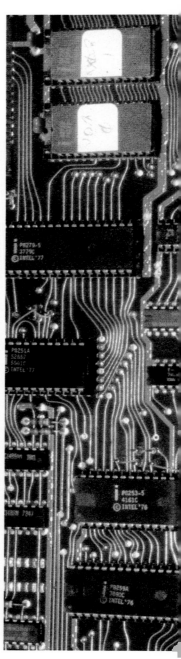

58

Lifestyles

The word lifestyle has lately acquired some special connotations in the world of home furnishings, coming to represent a way of life that is young, freewheeling, maintenance-free, and often budget-conscious.

But this type of lifestyle, obviously, is but one choice. There are many other approaches to adapting one's living environment to one's personal taste and requirements, and many factors determine the final look of an interior. Design and decorating remain intensely personal pursuits.

There are those who have the energy and ability to make decisions and have them carried out all on their own. But many others need a little professional help—especially if the space is tight and the budget limited. The demands of changing family arrangements call for different design requirements, and technological developments provide different design solutions.

This chapter presents a diversity of living experiences and attitudes, from the simple to the sophisticated, from a working country farm to a completely computerized city apartment. It touches also on some particular situations—a suburban couple who move to the city after their children are grown, but still want to provide a place where the family can gather; recently divorced fathers who are adapting to a new single lifestyle, but still want to make their children feel welcome on weekends. They are situations that may seem, at first, unique, but they are becoming increasingly pertinent.

80

When instinct is the guide

In the neatly cluttered kitchen, right, baskets are hung from hooks, and spices and grains are stored in labeled glass bottles. Antique lace was used to trim the canopy of the bed in "the little white room," far right.

The chair in the living room has been in her family for ten generations and was the only piece of furniture she brought from France. The doorstop is a large plastic bag filled with multicolored feathers. She found the wicker sofa in an abandoned house on Staten Island and bought the Art Deco ashtray for $20 from a dentist, who had it in his waiting room. The Edward Ruscha drawing "Oro Puro" was a trade from the artist in exchange for gold coins. The focal point of the living room is a huge flower painting by Andy Warhol, "when he was totally unknown, years ago. I thought he had a lot of talent," said Isabelle Collin Dufresne, an actress, singer, composer, and artist, who lives in a small duplex penthouse in Manhattan. "I designed the whole living room around it."

The apartment, with its wraparound terrace, sixteen-foot ceiling in the living room, and windows that frame multiple views, has the enviable quality of feeling like a private little house on top of the city. It has a relaxed charm and improvised feeling that is due to the intensely personal way in which Dufresne has decorated it. Every piece of furniture, every object, every plant has its particular and studied place.

"I never went to school to learn how to do it, but I really feel that I'm a born decorator," said Dufresne. She is also known as Ultra Violet, one of the members of Warhol's "Underground" entourage of the late 1960s. "It was a crazy period," she said. "And a lot of people from that time are just plain dead. I was in it for the artistic experience and was always concerned about my health. It was that feeling that kept me going."

These days, her life seems to be more sedate. She is, foremost, house-proud, reveling in arranging, rearranging, moving, adapting, sewing, inventing, and positioning the various art, mementos, and other objects that pleasantly clutter

up her apartment. Her talent lies not only in making the most of ordinary things—hanging a colorful array of hats, coats, and jackets on racks on the stairs, or draping a large piece of fabric over the piano—but also in constantly rethinking decorating details that might seem inconsequential to others. "I found that fabric in an attic and thought it was exquisite," she said. "I spent evenings repairing it."

Off the living room is what she calls "the little white room," a guest room with a bed built in above wooden cabinets. "Whatever I find that's white belongs in that room," she said. Wide eighteenth-century lace, a gift from her sister, hangs as the edging on the white gauze canopied bed. Plain white porcelain objects are displayed in a corner— an old tiled bathroom brush holder, a few pitchers, a foie gras tureen.

"I rarely buy anything," she said. "Friends gave me things, I found some, I bartered for others. I come across things all the time. And I recycle everything." She moved into the apartment in 1972 and little by little started refurbishing. A piece of brocade fabric was hung on curtain hooks attached to a molding in the bedroom. A pair of hospital beds, found at the Salvation Army, were attached and sprayed with gold paint for her top-floor bedroom. Invited to dinner aboard the Art Deco-style cruise ship *Caribia*, she managed to buy two chandeliers— one is hung in the living room, the other became a coffee table.

In the tiny kitchen, wood-fronted cabinets line the walls, and spices and grains are stored in glass bottles, all meticulously labeled. Every implement, pan, and dish looks as if it has been placed purposefully. "The most important thing in a kitchen is that there should be good storage for food," Dufresne emphasized. "Having food in the house is better than having money in the bank. It's a tremendous feeling of security."

In the bedroom, an old Louis Vuitton trunk holds accessories, far left. Isabelle Collin Dufresne and her dog, Hello, left. In the living room, below, the table is an Art Deco chandelier turned upside down and the painting is by Andy Warhol.

Moving a family to the city

Like many suburban couples before them, Fred and Flora March thought about moving to Manhattan when their three sons, headed for college or for jobs, were about to leave the large suburban home they had lived in for fifteen years. "The city is a focal point for all our sons and their friends," said the father, explaining why they were willing to give up a pool and a lawn but wanted to keep the ability to accommodate their three sons or other overnight guests.

They bought a two-bedroom cooperative apartment with an excellent view and asked Dexter Design to convert the space. "Not cute and not fussy, a functional place where everything would be hidden away," is how Barbara Schwartz interpreted the assignment. "Not drop-dead, but elegant and no mess," was the goal for her partner, Barbara Ross.

They started by removing the wall between the second bedroom and the living room. The new, enlarged den/living/dining expanse provided the apartment with its dramatic focus. The designers then had to put back into the room the elements that would make it function as a mini-dormitory. Two Murphy beds were concealed behind doors, and an under-the-window sofa doubles as a single bed. "It isn't a convertible," said Ross. "But there is storage underneath it for someone's valise or dirty laundry." The room, which retained its own bathroom and closet, can be divided with a hinged floor-to-ceiling folding door panel system. The panels—painted as a folding mural—allow the smaller space to be closed off for privacy.

Materials for the apartment were chosen for easy maintenance. The walls were painted gray, as was the cabinetry, and the low lounge furniture was upholstered in black leather. The floors were covered in gray tile "so that it would be easy to

Finding foldaway beds

The Murphy Door Bed Company Inc., at 40 East 34th Street, New York, N.Y. 10016; 212-682-8936, is the only manufacturer of the original Murphy bed. The company manufactures the mechanism for the beds, then distributes it around the country. Some outlets are:

• Lew Raynes Inc., 40 East 34th Street, New York, N.Y. 10016; 212-532-7190. Custom-made cabinets in wood and plastic laminate to fit any space.

• Manhattan Cabinetry Inc., 1612 First Avenue, New York, N.Y. 10021; 212-628-2904. All varieties of custom-made cabinets.

• Murphy Bed Sales Company, 1513 Gardiner, Los Angeles, Calif. 90046; 213-247-8039.

• Colorado Building Specialties Inc., 11000 East 40th Street, Denver, Colo. 80239; 303-371-5750.

• Modern Wall Systems Inc., 20 East Camel Back Road, Phoenix, Ariz. 85012; 602-248-9155.

• Murphy Beds, Etcetera, 3949 North Federal Highway, Ft. Lauderdale, Fla. 33308; 305-566-1110.

clean, impossible to ruin, and so the furniture could be moved." Two tables, one under the window, the other closer to the foyer, can be put together for sit-down dinner parties.

Recessed lighting could not be put in the concrete ceiling, so the living room and foyer ceiling was dropped. This created a reveal between the walls and the ceiling edge, where a series of inexpensive incandescent tube lights was installed in a rythmic pattern.

For other ways to achieve flexible sleeping accommodations see pages 64 to 69, 106 to 107, and 140 to 143.

Fred and Flora March, opposite left, in the living/ dining room of their Manhattan co-op. The folding door system allows the adjacent den to be used as a second bedroom. Jerry March unfolds one of the two Murphy beds, left.

Photographs by Robert Levin

Modern living down on the farm

It isn't an ordinary farmhouse, and it certainly can't be called a converted barn. In the barn/farmhouse created by Paul Segal Associates Architects, the New York architectural firm, there is more to country living than simply being down on the farm. "How often does one get to design something for people, plants, animals, and machines?" said Paul Segal, a Brooklyn-reared architect who by his own admission is unfamiliar with barnyard antics.

The animals in need of accommodations included a goose, four cows, five calves, two horses, a rooster and his harem of hens, and two dogs. And then there was Brent Lamour and his family who needed a place to call home.

The complex, which has about 4,600 square feet of interior space, cost less than $150,000. Although the barn/house is a year-round residence for the Lamours, city people who escape to the country on the weekend might enjoy a similar environment and see the project as an alternative to a traditional rural renovation.

The undertaking began when the owner of the property, in Westchester County, New York, called the architect when the barn burned down. Instead of simply replacing the barn, Segal and James Biber, the project designer, designed a complex and innovative structure. The 6,000-square-foot complex includes a small, skylighted, uninsulated barn; a greenhouse atop a hay storage space; a garage with

corrugated fiberglass doors; and the living space.

The original barn, which once housed circus elephants, had been an area landmark, situated on top of a hill in full view of the road. "We kept the new barn/house low, on a smaller scale, and gave it a sloped roof to make it more sympathetic to the types of forms that are indigenous to the area," Segal said. Wood was used throughout, with a post and beam construction and stained cedar siding for the walls.

"We wanted the means and materials of construction to be in the barn/country vernacular," explained Biber, who specified barn hardware for the sliding doors to the stable and bedrooms. "We call this barn-tech," Segal joked. Between the barn and the living space there is a 900-square-foot courtyard. "I used the European precedent of the farm," said Biber. "I thought of Swiss farms, where the buildings wrap around a courtyard,

Cows nuzzle each other by the south side of the farm complex, near the barn and greenhouse, far left. The architects specified barn hardware for the sliding doors to the stable, above.

and of Palladian villas." The cobblestones were recycled from the West Side Highway, spotted here and there with the yellow paint that once lined the center of the road.

Inside the main house, the living area includes a living room, large kitchen, and three small bedrooms. The western exposure of the house is its most closed facade, a wall of cedar punctuated with solid glass-brick windows. "The house was meant to turn its back on the afternoon summer sun," said Segal, who explained that efficient heat distribution had been a requisite.

"The living area is divided into two kinds of spaces," Biber pointed out. "One public, one private. One open, one closed. One day, one night." So while the bedrooms are Spartan and have windows that face east, the living room has an undulating window wall. "The idea was to make it look as if it was eroding, to create the image of this part of the house as a piece of something larger," he said.

"It's a self-ventilating house," Segal noted, referring to the louvered doors interspersed through the window wall. "This was not an original idea," he added. "I saw it done on Le Corbusier's Carpenter Arts Center in Cambridge." In the living room, across from the kitchen, there is a stepped-up ceramic-tiled hearth. And on it, instead of a fireplace, is a wood-burning stove. The all-white, open kitchen, which connects the living room to the bedroom corridor, is another pivot point, designed for Mrs. Lamour's cooking and canning. "After all," Biber said, "this is a working farm.

"Every part of this house is designed to be walked through," he continued. "All day long, people are going down to the garage, up to the greenhouse, through the walkways. It's a big circulation machine."

For another project by Paul Segal Associates Architects, see pages 92 to 97.

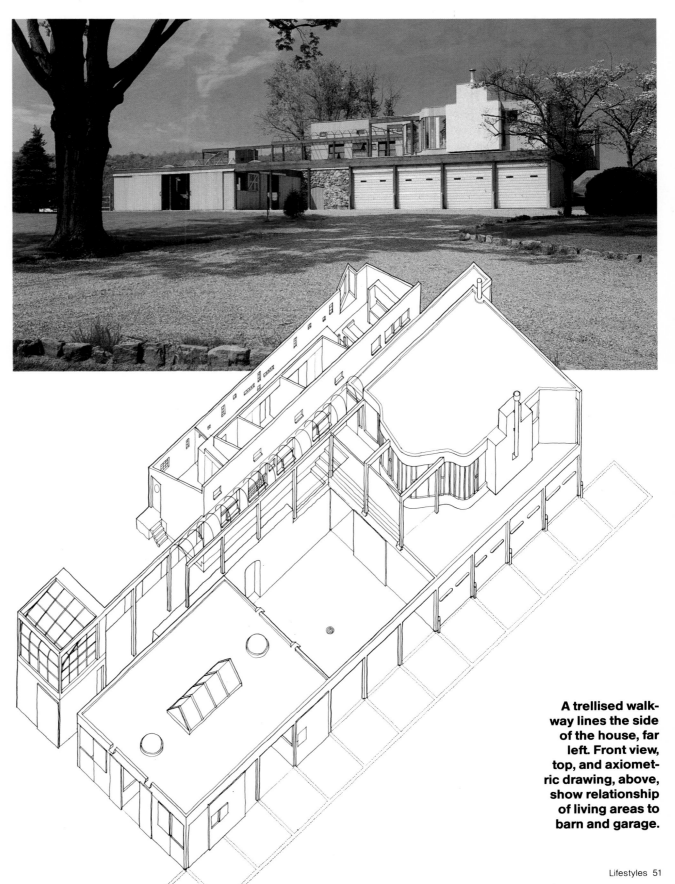

A trellised walkway lines the side of the house, far left. Front view, top, and axiometric drawing, above, show relationship of living areas to barn and garage.

Photographs by Norman McGrath

A wood-burning stove, factory dock lights, and an undulating window are features of the living/dining area, above. Small windows and sliding barn doors punctuate the hall, right. An all-white kitchen, far right, is at the center of the house.

Design demands of single men

The New York Times/Gene Maggio

Michael Ulick, above, moved from a studio to a loft and had Siris/Coombs Architects design the space. The long gallery area was delineated with wood cabinets and separated from the bedroom with blinds, right.

Bachelors have been thought of in two ways: the sophisticated bon vivant with the perfectly appointed penthouse, and the solitary single man in makeshift quarters who never gets around to having the sofa reupholstered. But a new type of bachelor has emerged—one for whom ambitious design decisions are a priority.

Michael Ulick, for example, a forty-one-year-old film producer and director of television commercials, hired Siris/Coombs Architects to design his 2,500-square-foot loft. "Everything had to be designed around his possessions," said Jane Siris, who undertook the project with her husband, Peter Coombs. These included an extensive library, as well as paintings, pieces of sculpture, antique toys, Navajo rugs, and a collection of photographs and prints.

A graceful row of free-standing cast-iron Corinthian columns was chosen as the boundary of a long gallery-type space, and custom-made cabinets by Peter Var of AVL Construction became important design elements. The cost of cabinetry and woodworking came to about $45,000. The perfectly detailed oak cabinets double as low dividing walls. Ulick's antique toy truck collection was positioned in cubicles along one side in a long bookcase/cabinet; smaller objects as well as a stereo system were placed in another cabinet that doubles as the back of the sofa.

The bedroom accommodates two of his larger possessions—a Claes Oldenburg sculptured car relief and an antique rolltop desk. The overall design was planned so that the bedroom, work area, and living room would revolve around a central focus that the architects called "the open courtyard of the dining room." There are no shades or coverings on the windows of the main living space; blinds were used above the cabinetry to close off the bedroom. The wood used,

The kitchen, left, has a roomy preparation counter and industrial lighting; the dining area, furnished with antiques, below, is in the "courtyard" of the loft.

the choice of industrial glass light fixtures, and the wood dining table all contribute to a feeling that recalls a cozy country house more than a slick city loft. "The idea was not to make it look too new," Coombs said.

Just the opposite was the goal in John Emmerling's apartment. "It was a chic little Manhattan divorce," said the forty-two-year-old advertising executive. "I kept the apartment, she kept the furniture, and we're sharing joint custody of the designer." The designers, John Stedila and Tim Button of Stedila Design, had done Emmerling's office four years ago. "I began to enjoy that modern environment," Emmerling said. "And, after living with American country antiques, I needed a change and got them back."

Designer and client started by concentrating on the apartment's traditionally proportioned living room. Emmerling wanted it to function as a dining room as well, and perhaps provide for some sleeping accommodations. He spent about $27,000 on the living room and foyer, including all the construction, art, and furnishings. A double sofa, one side of which is used as banquette seating for the dining table, converts to a queen-size bed. A series of long, low, shiny Formica counters both divide the room and act as backs to the low seating. A marble table near the windows is intended for dining. "The room was designed to have dinner for four or a party for thirty or forty," Stedila said. "What we didn't need was a lot of chairs around a table."

In Michael Ulick's spacious bathroom, the shower is installed behind a curved glass block wall, left.

Roger Bester

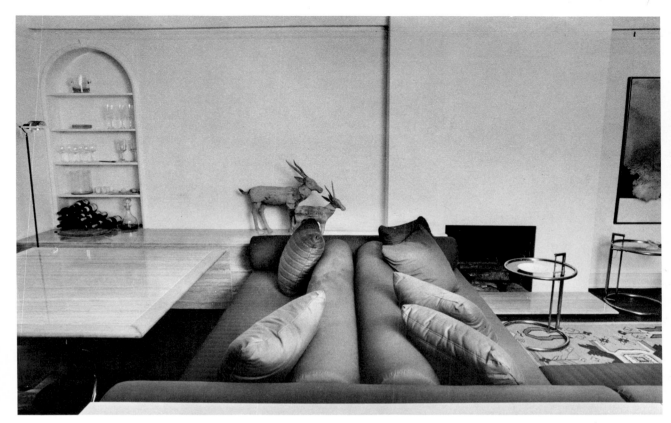

John Emmerling,
above, had his
living room redone
by Stedila Design
to function for
small dinners or
parties. When used
as a guest room,
the sofa converts
to a bed, left top
and bottom.

Photographs by Robert Levin

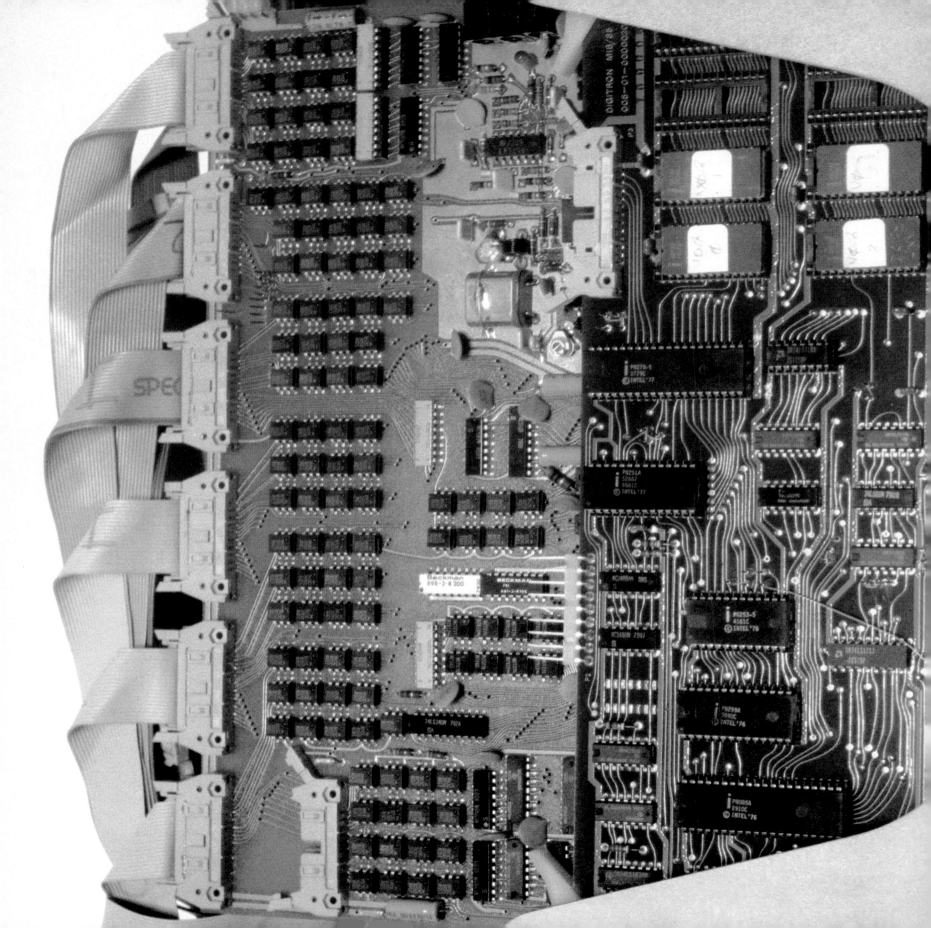

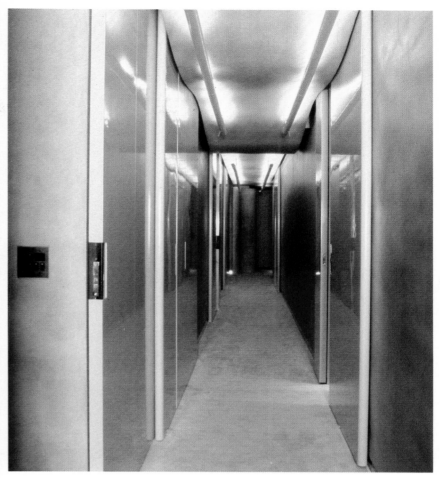

Lights go on, doors open, as if by magic. "It's all sensored," said Brian Thompson, a lighting wizard who specializes in a growing area in home design—the computerized environment. In a duplex, he installed a complex lighting system, including cold cathode, recessed low voltage, and neon. "I call it addressable control," said Thompson. "The light sensors allow for the right amount of light in certain rooms at different times. The effects change as people move about the space." Under the carpeting there are sensors that move the light ahead as one walks down the hallway, and the lighting dims and changes color as the evening progresses—all programmed in advance to operate on push-buttons. "You couldn't live here if you had to think about it every minute," said Thompson.

Lighting for mood and hue

The special lighting effects planned by Brian Thompson for an apartment include under-the-carpet sensors for a hallway, above. Control circuit board is at left.

The lighting in the living room, far right and top, changes during the day and can be adjusted to create different moods and hues, above.

Custom electronics

• Audio Command Systems, 46 Merrick Road, Rockville Center, N.Y. 11570; 516-766-5055; 122 South Robertson Blvd., Suite 205, Los Angeles, Calif. 90048; 213-273-3352. Audio-video remote control systems.

• Boulton Stereo Systems, 380 Madison Avenue, New York, N.Y. 10017; 212-697-4900. Modular remote control units for stereo, tapes, and radio stations.

• Piping Audio, Inc., Cado/Royal System, Inc., 979 Third Avenue, New York, N.Y. 10022; 212-758-1255. Wireless remote control units.

• Retina, 251 Park Avenue South, New York, N.Y. 10010; 212-475-0900. Custom lighting and sound controls.

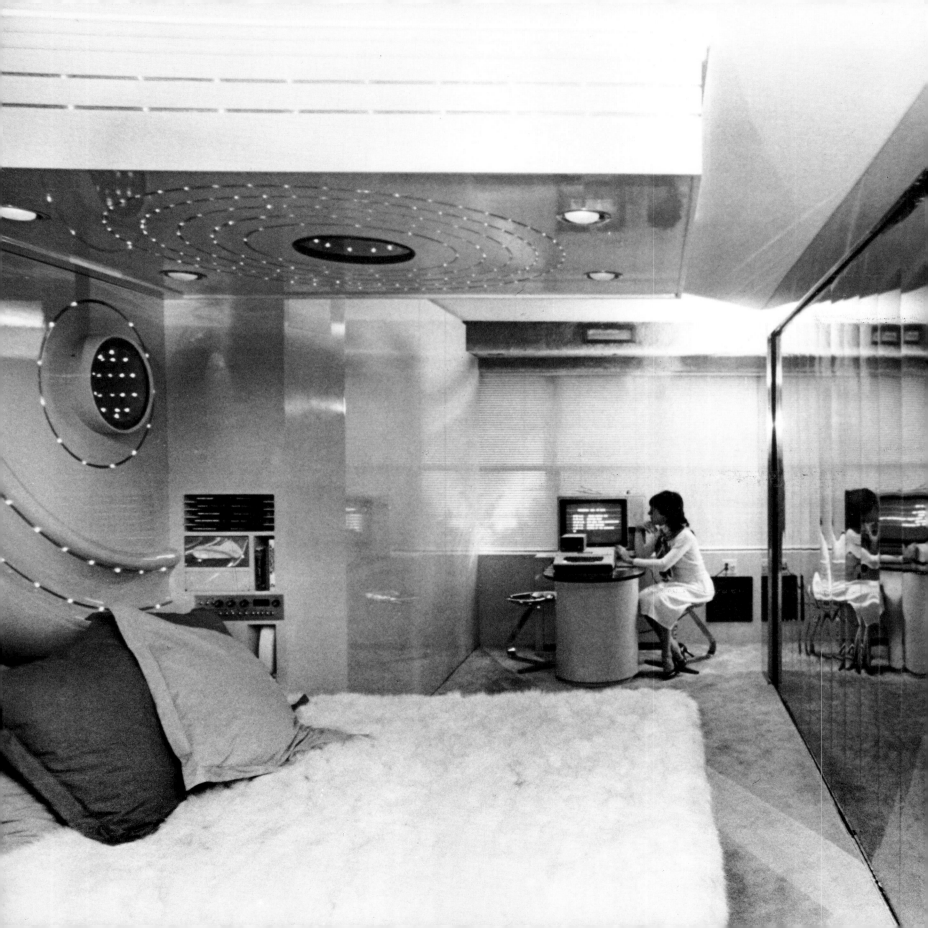

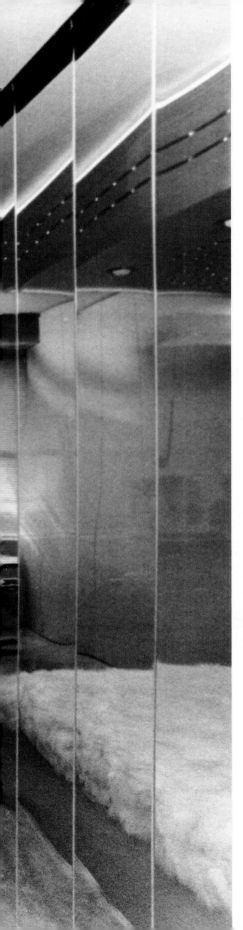

Jane Victor's apartment might be mistaken for a parody of the over-designed interior—there are flashing lights, moving partitions, sculptured surfaces, and control panels that would look more at home in a 747 cockpit than by the bed. Victor is an interior designer with a keen interest in residential space-saving ideas made possible by the latest electronic systems. Although small units for controlling temperature, lighting, and security have been inconspicuously integrated into numerous residences and many people have computers at home, the understated approach did not appeal to her.

With her associate, Rudy Yanes, she decided to use as a laboratory the compact Greenwich Village apartment that she shares with her husband. Lighting, storage, security, and sound were the functions that the two designers set out to control electronically, using technology manufactured by Retail Data Service.

Now the bedroom, dominated by a neon-lighted canopy bed, is a shiny swirl of lights, and the living room is an expanse of mirrored walls that reflect, somewhat disorientingly, mirrored beams that crisscross the ceiling. These beams were designed by Victor to disguise the electric wiring required by the temperature-controlled bar for wine storage, the digital clocks for time and temperature, the television on its swing-out shelf, and the dimmer-controlled lighting that allows for varying the room's visual effect.

In the small kitchen, appliances are programmed to go on and off automatically. The electronic security system would notify the building concierge, the designer's office, and the police if anyone were to enter the apartment.

It is in the master bedroom that Victor displays her full range of electronic commands. A home computer, for example, advises her that her coffee is being made, what

the temperature of her bath is, and what appointments she has made for the day. "Our lives are very cluttered and we must free ourselves from mundane activities," said Victor, pointing out the automation possibilities she has devised in the room. On either side of the bed and by the door of the bedroom, there are control panels for the sound system, the different kinds of lighting, and a digital clock radio. A separate panel, by the window, controls the security system. At her bedside is a book; its title is, appropriately, *Basic Electricity.*

The room is a long and narrow space, so she decided against doors on all the closets. On one side, behind conventional doors, are her husband's clothes. But on the other side, behind a shiny paneled wall, she experimented with electronic commands. At the touch of a switch, the multiple panels open up; with a faint whirring sound they disappear behind the closet to reveal a stereo system and compartments for handbags, shoes, and clothing.

Victor's elaborate system of electronic gadgetry was expensive to install, not only for wiring but also for the custom cabinetry required. It would cost about $75,000 to duplicate. But the preprogrammed lighting, for example, which proved energy efficient, can be achieved with small, inexpensive units. Home computers have also become practical additions to the home.

There is no manual backup for Victor's system, so in the case of an electrical failure, she would have trouble getting to her handbags or sweaters. But she has prepared for even that possibility. "I have an already-packed overnight bag tucked away on the other side of the bed," she confided.

For other applications of home computer and remote control systems, see pages 58 to 61 and look in the catalog under "Lighting."

Lights, sound, and action

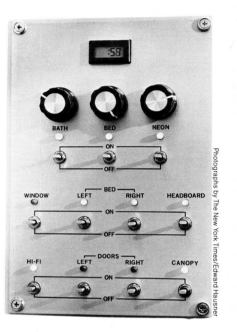

Photographs by The New York Times/Edward Hausner

Designer Jane Victor at the computer in her bedroom, left. The lights, sound, and motorized closet doors on a track are controlled electronically from a panel, above.

Life with weekend fathers

Arnold Kaplan, shown above with his daughter, Elan, turned a closet into a miniroom for her weekend visits. Elan and friend, Alexis Katz, in the space where she keeps toys, clothes, and books, right.

When Jack Nessel, opposite left, renovated a small duplex, he set aside a room for daughter Jennifer, far right.

Arnold Kaplan consulted with Elan on every piece of furniture. Jack Nessel renovated a diminutive duplex with Jennifer in mind. C. Ray Smith worked out an ingenious storage solution for Nino's toys and paraphernalia.

They're not architects or designers working with their clients, but weekend fathers, separated or divorced, and they have come up with some of the most versatile space planning in the city. While setting up housekeeping on their own, these fathers have created part-time homes for their children.

Kaplan, who says he didn't have "a piece of furniture to my name" when he moved to the one-bedroom apartment, went shopping "for everything" when his daughter, Elan, was seven and a half years old. "At the time, we both needed encouragement and support, and wanted to do things together, so decorating the apartment became an adventure," Kaplan said. "But immediate delivery was the primary thing to be considered."

Elan accompanied her father to a neighborhood furniture store, where she jumped on the floor-sample sofas. She declared them to be "too hard or too mushy" before deciding on the modular unit for the living room, which she now sleeps on when visiting. She also selected the shiny black plastic Italian-designed table and chairs, and many of the accessories.

In Kaplan's apartment, there are toys on the bookcase, a doll in the

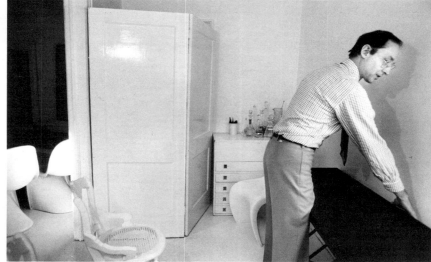

C. Ray Smith's small but elegant dining room, top left, becomes a playroom and bedroom when Nino comes to stay. The table is moved aside, the screen un-folded, and a bed assembled, above. Nino at bedtime, right.

Photographs by Raeanne Giovanni

fruit bowl, and Elan's prized Olivia Newton-John record stored with her father's record collection. "I didn't want to separate her things too much from mine," he explained. There just wasn't enough space for Elan to have her own room, and the solution was to give Elan her own walk-in closet. Now, Wonder Woman guards the door, a gaggle of plastic geese sits nearby, a bike is parked by the side, and a sign proclaims, "This is the wonderful world of Elan." Inside, she has her own neat storage system for her "weekend" belongings and plenty of wall space for pinning up paintings and cards.

"I didn't do anything with this place when I was just renting," said Nessel of his tiny West Side co-op. "But once I was able to buy it, I decided to fix it up so that Jennifer could have her own room."

He asked an architect, Steve Robinson, to plan the duplex space, now pristine in gray, black, and white—gray carpeted platforms, black upholstery, folding chairs, Italian lamps, and plain white walls. But his teenage daughter's room is still rather bare. A patchwork quilt covers her bed, and she's thinking about an antique brass headboard, "to go against the grain," said the teen-

ager mischievously.

When Sinclair Scott Smith, known as Nino, was five years old and came to stay overnight, Smith converted his elegant dining room into the child's playroom/bedroom. "The table folds up and gets moved to the side to be used as a console," explained Smith. A two-panel red-backed screen is opened up, revealing Nino's artwork. Toys stored in baskets are brought out, and at bed-time Nino helps his father assemble a tubular steel bed. "In order to keep everything white and for these colored elements to appear, they must be put away at other times," said the fastidious father,

emphasizing that the space must function in both its roles.

How does he feel about a small boy armed with a box of crayons running around the all-white apartment? "It's wonderful," he said. "The floor is covered in vinyl, the chairs are plastic. Thanks to plastics—and lighter fluid—we can all have white apartments."

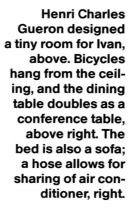

Henri Charles Gueron designed a tiny room for Ivan, above. Bicycles hang from the ceiling, and the dining table doubles as a conference table, above right. The bed is also a sofa; a hose allows for sharing of air conditioner, right.

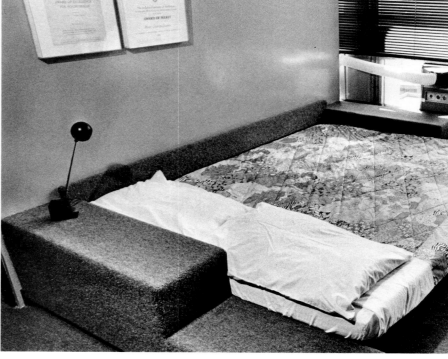

Like many divorced fathers, Henri Charles Gueron always wanted his son, Ivan, to feel at home on weekends in his studio apartment. But when Ivan moved in full time, the father quickly realized that "there was just a limited amount of things you can do to fit two people and their belongings into an approximately 16 1/2-foot-square studio, with a foyer, a dining alcove, a kitchen, and one bathroom."

Gueron, an architect, wanted a separate, private space for Ivan. Sleeping on the sofa might be okay for weekends, but the need for privacy required another approach. So he created a room within a room, ingeniously laid out to accommodate the twelve-year-old's needs. While the floor is the same height as the rest of the apartment, a seventeen-inch-high lift-up platform is a base for the living area, and there is a loft bed five feet off the floor.

Gueron also provided space for a chair that folds out for his son's overnight guests, a work surface and desk chair underneath the bed, and storage inside the platform. Ventilation of the new room was accomplished by a fan above the door and by routing a flexible hose from the single air conditioner into' Ivan's room. The dividing wall includes four inches of fiberglass batt insulation. Father and son each have his own stereo and television; the shared telephone has an extra long cord.

Gueron estimated that he spent about $1,500 on construction for the new room. Although small, it seems adequate for the present. "Everything is fitted to within an inch," said Gueron. But Ivan, who is five feet two inches tall and growing, has pointed up the temporary nature of the arrangement. His father sighed, "When he's taller we'll have to think seriously about moving."

For other solutions to tiny spaces, see pages 108 to 113, 116 to 119, and 122 to 123.

A studio for dad and son

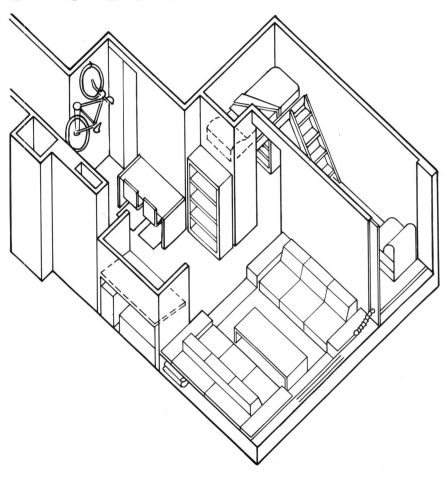

The new bohemia in design

Photographs by Gilles de Chabaneix

Maurizio Benadon and Bénédicte Siroux, above. In their loft, left, the casually slip-covered sofa contrasts with sophisticated furnishings— including an Antoní Gaudi chair and an Eileen Gray rug.

When Maurizio Benadon, a real estate developer from Lugano, Switzerland, who is converting the Hellmuth building, a loft residence in Chelsea, and Bénédicte Siroux, a former Paris model, came to New York, they moved into an empty seventy-two-by-thirty-five-foot loft space. "This was to be a temporary place to live, so nothing was fixed and everything was planned so that we could move out easily," explained Siroux, who is a partner in a furniture importing company. "We had nothing but a few paintings by friends and had to start from absolute zero."

The couple's philosophy is typical of a kind of antiestablishment decorating: a new bohemianism that is simple, unselfconscious, mutable, and flexible. This is a design esthetic where emphasis is placed on the visual rather than the functional. There are no built-ins and no interior walls in their home, the furniture looks haphazardly placed, and there is a striking contrast of objects. Light streams through huge windows, a vase is placed on the floor, a piece of sculpture is highlighted on the wall, and the loft has a romantic aura that recalls the studios occupied by the bohemian artists and writers in Paris in the beginning of this century.

It is a casual but carefully orchestrated approach in which the occupants' personal values and tastes can dominate. "We've tried to improvise and adapt to America without forgetting our European background," said Siroux. But where the bohemianism of the past stemmed from poverty, New York's current crop of bohemians have both money and options. "We have priorities that are not only based on a matter of budget," said Benadon.

The raw loft space featured a tangle of pipes in a corner, rough walls, an unfinished wood floor, and a wavy cement ceiling. "All part of the charm," said Benadon. "We could have made it perfect by

Photographs by Gilles de Chabaneix

The bed is behind bookcases and the television set atop a cable spool, above.

72

The double sofa is
a 1950s find. A
wood palette
serves as a coffee
table, above.

Reproductions of
René Herbst
chairs surround a
table by Andrée
Putman.

smoothing out the walls or putting in a dropped ceiling, for example, but that would have ruined it," he said. "Europeans fall in love with lofts because of their scale," he added. "This is a space of palatial proportions and for us that's the ultimate luxury. We tried to preserve what this represented for us."

Sheer curtains were hung from pipes that happened to be in front of the windows; the kitchen was partially hidden behind a thin wall. The bed has been demurely placed behind two painted bookshelves, and one of the sofas is slipcovered in white cotton fabric. At the bottom of the bed is what Benadon called "an important Caucasian rug"; a television set sits atop a cable spool, which was found in the street. But there are also more sophisticated touches—reproductions of rugs by Eileen Gray and chairs by Antoní Gaudi and René Herbst.

Like others who have a similar attitude to their surroundings, the couple say that they care primarily about the way things look to them. "That's why we'll buy a turquoise 1950s sofa rather than put in kitchen cabinets," said Siroux, "and we would rather sit on a packing case with real silverware than at a beautiful table with plastic knives and forks. When something is not finished, it's alive," Siroux explained. "When it's done, it's like death. That gives me a feeling of real anxiety."

Gerald Incandela, a Tunisian-born photographer, also lives in a commercial building that has been converted to residential use. He found the small apartment when he arrived in New York a few years ago.

Incandela is settled in his apartment, but the interior has kept its temporary look, one that is tinged with an air of surrealism. The chairs are covered in sheets; the sofa, upholstered in terry cloth, is nestled in a jungle of papyrus plants; sheets

Photographer and artist Gerald Incandela, above, furnished his apartment, right, with a metal chair, a terry-cloth upholstered sofa, a lounge chair covered with a sheet, and a forest of papyrus plants.

Bill Logan and Gill Anderson, above, design things when they need them. The guest room, right, is behind a screen-like partition, with an inset window.

of white paper hang from the ceiling and are also used for lampshades; a solitary metal chair stands in the middle of the room. A bust of Napoleon looks out the window. "I found it in a dark library, and wanted to give him a break," he explained. "That's why I have him looking out the window."

Now, some of the plants are turning brown and one of the tables is rusty. "I like that feeling of abandon," he said. "It's a little like a country house that's been closed up, where there is a lot of white and some of it a little dirty."

Gill Anderson, an architectural designer, was about to give birth to her first child, and her mother was due to arrive from England any day. So a guest room was essential for the loft she shares with her husband, Bill Logan, an architect and furniture designer.

Her husband constructed one in a day. "A bit of a joke," he admitted. The partitioned-off area was set up in a matter of hours, by anchoring plywood panels with tension wire to the ceiling of the loft. "It has no acoustic insulation," he added. "I doubt my mother-in-law will want to stay too long. But it does feel like a room—even if it's only a screen."

Both Logan and Anderson are from the "if we need it we'll make it" school of design. A row of shelves, for example, was put together in a night out of metal studs and plywood. "I consider myself more of an inventor than a designer," said Logan. "Our design philosophy is related to stage design and making things work. I guess, like life, this loft is just one big chess game."

For other reproductions of architects' furniture, see pages 34 to 35, 204 to 205, and 222 to 225.

The living room, top, has a collection of old chairs and a table by Logan. Enclosed for privacy, the bedroom, center, has stenciled walls. The storage unit, above, is made from wood boxes and metal studs.

Perfect house plan

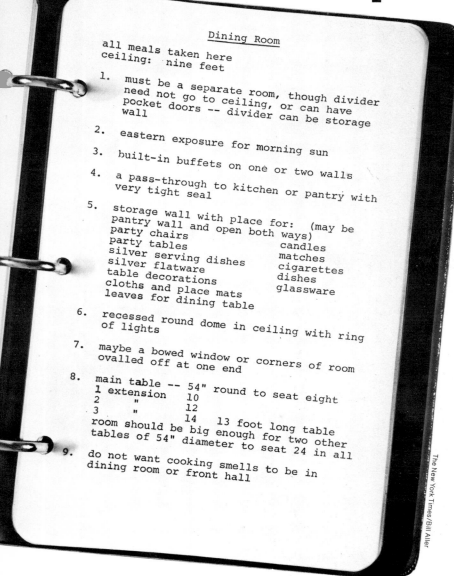

Dining Room

all meals taken here
ceiling: nine feet

1. must be a separate room, though divider need not go to ceiling, or can have pocket doors -- divider can be storage wall

2. eastern exposure for morning sun

3. built-in buffets on one or two walls

4. a pass-through to kitchen or pantry with very tight seal

5. storage wall with place for: (may be pantry wall and open both ways)
   party chairs
   party tables   candles
   silver serving dishes   matches
   silver flatware   cigarettes
   table decorations   dishes
   cloths and place mats   glassware
   leaves for dining table

6. recessed round dome in ceiling with ring of lights

7. maybe a bowed window or corners of room ovalled off at one end

8. main table -- 54" round to seat eight
   1 extension   10
   2   "   12
   3   "   14   13 foot long table
   room should be big enough for two other tables of 54" diameter to seat 24 in all

9. do not want cooking smells to be in dining room or front hall

If a prize were awarded for most organized house planning, Vivian Schulte would be a major contender. For twenty years, she and her husband, Arthur, now a retired investment banker, lived in an older home in upper Westchester. "I had a lot of time to make notes on the things that annoyed me," she said. That was how Vivian Schulte started planning her dream house.

Her exhaustive and unflagging approach began three years before construction started, as she started compiling a small black notebook that listed both the luxuries and fifty-three "practicalities" that she wanted included in the design.

Once she and her husband had settled on a site and agreed to a budget, Schulte started interviewing architects, keeping a record of her impressions: "Richard Meier: super, but fee too high, personal stamp very strong"; "Gwathmey & Siegel: too radical and dramatic"; "Yann Weymouth: recommended by I.M. Pei; very talented but not enough experience in residential work"; "Myron Goldfinger: too jazzy and theatrical." After twenty-three interviews, the couple settled on Victor and Viorica Belcic of Belcic & Jacobs. "I was her interpreter," said Belcic, a Rumanian-born architect. "She knew exactly what she wanted," he added, in what some might consider the ultimate understatement. Schulte specified every imaginable detail, including ceiling heights and room sizes, counter space and closets, electrical outlets and ventilation, bookcases, landscaping, exposures, placement of furniture, type of lighting, towel racks, and even telephone jacks.

She had carefully reflected on the couple's life-style, how they entertained, exercised, relaxed. She worked out circulation patterns, dividing the house into three areas: service, living, and sleeping. Before moving out of her old house, she sketched the outline of every piece of furniture to be used in the new

house and noted its measurements in her notebook. "Once it's in storage," she explained, "one forgets how big or small it is."

From the porte cochère ("to shelter guests on entering") and the open company coat closet ("there's no reason to conceal it") to the car stops in the garage ("so that you know when the automatic doors have been cleared") and a double, mirror-image bar to serve both living room and pool room ("nothing moves except the bartender"), every detail had been carefully entered in her notebook.

There was to be neither an attic nor a basement, because "it's cheaper to replace it than build a room to store it in"; no thresholds "so that there would be nothing to stumble over," nor wooden baseboards, "too hard to clean." But there are nonslip treads on the dramatic spiral staircase that links the hallway to the second floor, vertical silk-thread-covered blinds for the living room ("I'm very antidrapery"), and a screened-in informal eating area next to the dining room ("we don't like to eat on trays").

The dining room drawers were built to fit the couple's place mats, and a separate closet holds the dining table's extra leaves and folding party chairs. Round tablecloths are hung on a fabric display rack in the closet, so that they won't crease. The controls for the dining room hot tray are in the pantry, not the dining room, because "they're too ugly." And there is one large, empty closet. "That's for our future elevator, with wiring for a five-horsepower motor, when we can't make it up the stairs," she said.

In the bedroom, clothes are neatly hung on high rods, shoes on lower shelves. Shirts, scarves, and underclothes are in plastic see-through boxes. One side is for summer, another for winter. And in the center of the dressing room there is a large table for packing suitcases as Schulte spends part of each

winter in Florida.

But it was in the planning of the kitchen that Schulte, who was a food and home editor for fifteen years and holds a Ph.D. in foods and nutrition, excelled. She planned storage and circulation patterns with military precision; measured all her small appliances and had three separate electrical circuits installed for them; included file drawers, bulletin board, blackboard, and shelves for cookbooks and telephone books. She specified a special area near the back door for "unpacking boxes, with a sink with a high faucet for washing mops and filling tall vases, shelves for storing vases, and a special rack for drying mops."

In the indoor pool next to the living room, Vivian Schulte swims every morning. Even then she keeps her eyes open. "When I swim, I'm eye level with the garden outside," she said. "That's when I see if there are any weeds."

For another organized perfectionist's design scheme see pages 84 to 87.

Vivian Schulte, above, in the indoor pool. She and her husband planned the house with Belcic & Jacobs, architects. Before construction, she kept a notebook, a page of which is at far left. Specifications for the dining room, left, included table size and storage.

When the architect is the catalyst

When Sandy Hill and Bob Pittman were married, they decided to start off their new life together by moving into a new home. "We had equally nice apartments," she said. "But we felt like visitors in each other's homes." Their search led them to a sky-lit Manhattan loft large enough to accommodate the possessions of both, but not so big as to be overwhelming.

But there was the question of their diverging tastes. She liked a more old-fashioned style: traditional furniture, antique silver, pastel fabrics. He was the modernist, preferring hard-edged pieces and a cooler, more industrial esthetic. They adopted the code name of "Dream House" for their loft and hired Richard Oliver, a young architect associated with the postmodernist movement. "The solution for the Pittmans was not to separate their preferences, but to fuse them together," said Oliver. "It's certainly not a modern scheme in that many traditional images are combined. This loft is about elements that speak to things in each of them."

Oliver's plan was unusual. Instead of centralizing the living room area in the 1,700-square-foot loft, he decided to group the bathroom and the kitchen under the skylight, so that both areas could take advantage of the daylight. "The time of doing lofts as lofts is over, we wanted more of a sense of definition," he said, pointing out such "houselike" elements as the spacious entry hall, the old-fashioned pantry, walk-in closets, the separate bedroom, and big bathroom and kitchen. But, except for the bathroom, there are no doors.

Oliver also put up rather strange-looking interior walls; they are cut open, jut out, or snake into the main living space. "It's a lot of stagecraft, and a way of setting up a false perspective," he said. The walls and columns are endowed with exaggerated moldings. "They're not

Bob Pittman, left, leaned toward the high-tech esthetic. Industrial factory lights hang in his open kitchen, above.

Architect Richard Oliver, left, combined the couple's tastes and gave the loft a post-modern look. The stair, above, leads to tiny guest room.

Sandy Hill, left, wanted to keep a more countrylike feeling. The antique table and pine chairs, above, are in the dining area.

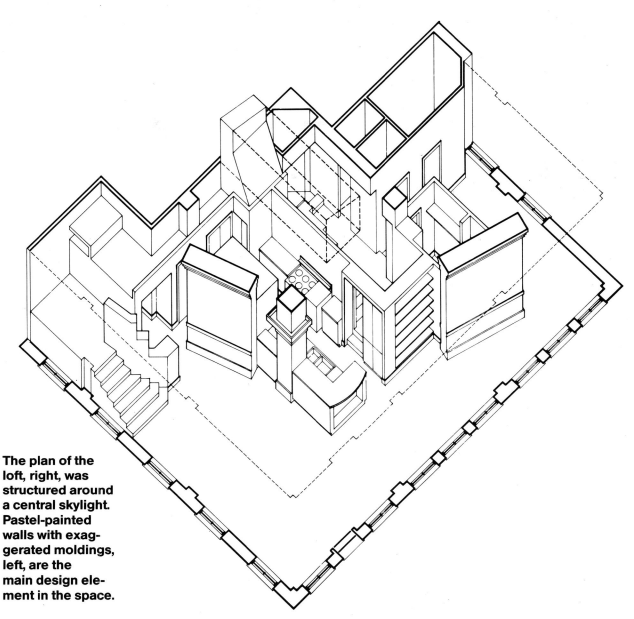

The plan of the loft, right, was structured around a central skylight. Pastel-painted walls with exaggerated moldings, left, are the main design element in the space.

reproductions," he said of the base, chair rail, and crown moldings, "and are not intended as an ironic comment on moldings. They're meant to evoke traditional feelings about such forms, but in a nontraditional way."

Then there were the design extras that appealed to both the Pittmans, including a tiny guest room/den that is situated up a wide flight of stairs. "A touch of Hollywood, because they're overscaled for the space they lead to," said Oliver of a small flight tucked away

at the foot of the bed, leading to the entrance. "My version of Victorian sneak stairs."

The choice and placement of the furniture tend to reflect Sandy Hill's taste for the traditional. There is a comfortable sofa in the living room area, and an antique side table next to it. The glass-topped coffee table in front of the sofa is her husband's choice. The dining room table and chairs are of pine, and her family antiques are scattered throughout the loft.

"We discussed the colors at

length," Pittman said of the predominantly pastel interior. And because they couldn't decide on one color for the space, they came up with twenty they "couldn't live without." These include about four shades of gray, mauve, a color called macaroon bisque, and lots of pinks, including raspberry. "We painted it all ourselves," Hill added, proudly. "We really both believe that that's part of the loft spirit."

For other postmodern schemes see pages 30 to 33.

Architect Parker Zaner Bloser in the well-organized workroom of his Tribeca loft, above.

The train compartmentlike bedroom has foot lockers and vertical storage shelves, above right.

The meticulously built bookcase incorporates stereo speakers in gridlike unit, above far right.

Doing it all by oneself

Until four years ago, Parker Zaner Bloser had never built anything larger than an architectural model. But he needed a place to live and decided to do it all himself. "I had literally never wielded a hammer," said Bloser, recalling how on his first day of renovation he went out to buy "the best hammer and saw I could find."

Two years later, his 2,500-square-foot space was a monument to the perseverance of a methodical perfectionist. It could also be an inspiration to all the do-it-yourselfers who, with the best intentions, never get around to finishing a project. "I'm very Teutonic," he admitted. "If I start reading a book, for example, I finish it. Even if I hate it, I finish it." Did he grow to hate the project? "It was therapeutic for a year," he said. "After that, it was tiresome." But it did get finished.

Bloser bought the first loft he ever looked at and then moved in immediately. It was, he recalled, "a mess—great holes in the floor, windows front and back but not on the

sides, and a floor that was three inches higher on one side." He started by drawing the walls on the floor with chalk. "Then, I simply built them all askew so that they would make up for the uneven floor and look neat and right-angled," said the Harvard-educated architect, who admitted that he really knew very little about construction. "I read about it," he said.

As a client, he demanded a placid environment and built-ins for everything. "I would never acquire anything I didn't have a place for," he said. "If I thought something was beautiful enough to own, I would probably put it in storage." He started with the cube bookcase that incorporates the aquarium. Like the stereo—and even the bedrooms— the aquarium is set into a structure. It is lighted, also like the stereo, from the inside.

The two boxlike bedrooms are tiny. "I conceive of a bedroom as a place to go to sleep," explained Bloser, who incorporated foot lockers into each room and closets on

both sides of the beds. "I've always loved traveling on trains."

There are squares everywhere. The living room is built on a square, the windows were all supposed to be square (two couldn't be), and the architectural model in the living room is "pseudo-Palladian," with the obligatory square floor plan. There are more squares in the bathroom, where glass bricks enclose the shower. The bathroom, however, contrasts with the rest of the space, for it is large and luxurious. The big half moon shape is exactly in the center of the space, and Bloser set in the mirrors along the wall, again to echo what he thinks of as train interiors.

A plumber was hired, as were an electrician and a contractor to put in the floor tile. But most of the wiring, all the wall tile, the painting, and the construction were done by Bloser, working alone. "Sometimes I would work day and night," he said. "Other times, I would declare a holiday." Working on his own and for himself, he could specify the materials he wanted and he bought expensive tools and "the best paint." Instead of metal studs, he put in wood ones. Instead of fluorescent bulbs, he used incandescent tubes for all the indirect lighting. He insisted on invisible hinges throughout and regrets his choice of hollow core doors. "Next time they'll be of solid

wood," he said.

"I have no idea," he said when asked to estimate the cost of materials, and finally decided that $15,000 was the minimum he had spent. "Every time I went to the lumberyard, I thought, 'Thank God that this is the last time.' Then there were forty more trips."

Would he do it again? "Absolutely not," said Bloser, who lived in a construction site for months at a time and felt a sense of relief when the renovation was over. "I'm blissful," he said. "It's so nice to have some extra time."

For another perfectionist's plan, see pages 78 to 79.

Cube-shaped bookcase, above left, was the first project to be done in the loft renovation.

The architect made the painted screen and the low tables in the spacious living room, above.

Rooms that echo the past

Robert Levin

Most decorating projects are, for clients and designers alike, flights of fancy. They are re-creations of imagined rooms, wished-for ambiances, longed-for spaces. But some projects become even more personal and subjective endeavors, when what is being re-created is a place that was experienced by the client in the past and is still important to him in the present. These are specifically remembered rooms—rooms with a special meaning for their occupants, rooms that they did not want to live without.

George Lang, a restaurant consultant and designer, calls it his "little room." And that's exactly what

it is: a neat, small study on the second floor of his duplex apartment. There is a red rose in a crystal vase on the table, yellow-and-white-striped wallpaper, and embroidered ribbons hung over a picture frame.

It is a re-creation of a room from Lang's childhood. "That's where I go to bring back deep-printed images that would otherwise only return to me in my sleep," said Lang, who reconstructed the room from the one he remembered in Szekesfehervar, Hungary, forty-five miles from Budapest. He decorated the room from memory, recalling the wallpaper as well as the moss-

green, striped fabric on the chairs, with its pale, flowery design. "I used instinct to approximate the past," said Lang. "But I was careful not to re-create the past literally. The room has the spirit of my childhood, with certain elements carefully reproduced, but not all."

The double wood wall molding, the small fruitwood table, the profusion of small pictures, and the junk shop radio are carefully duplicated, but there is no rose garden outside and Lang has to make up for that with hanging plants. "You don't have the feeling you're in a staged museum room," he said. "And it's not Disneyland. It's just an overall

Robert Levin

memory that envelops you when you enter."

Three years ago, Michael Wager, an actor, moved out of his traditional apartment and into a loft. Although the 6,000-square-foot space boasted a corner view, "I knew I would regret leaving my turn-of-the-century-style bedroom," he said, recalling his apartment in Manhattan's landmark Dakota building. But Peter Stamberg, a designer who was helping him with the move, suggested: "Don't regret it, just redo it."

The bedroom re-creation started with the wallpaper—a beige background, brown-scrolled William

Morris paper that has covered the walls of two of the actor's past bedrooms. Despite the size of the loft, the bedroom was built to be the same small size as its antecedent and tucked away in a far corner, away from the magnificent windows. "I can't bear the light," he said. There are the same silk drapes and rug, and Wager's elaborate brass bed was moved in, as was his quilt-covered night table, which holds familiar photographs. The air-conditioning grilles are in the same place, the same artwork is hung on the walls, and on the bed are ten-year-old Porthault sheets and pillow covers.

"He's French and he wanted a little toy, to feel as if he were back in a Paris sidewalk café," said Alan Magioncalda, who with his partner, Ted Heaney, created a nostalgic bistro for a client's dining room. The dining room is set inside a raised boxlike room one step up from a lavishly carpeted living room. A carpenter was hired to build the mahogany paneling and the banquettes. But when the designers suggested that brass rails should be put above the banquettes—like those used in real Parisian bistros to hold coats—the client balked. "There's no reason to be that authentic," he said.

George Lang recreated his childhood room in Hungary as a study, opposite top. Costumed actor Michael Wager rehearses in his loft bedroom, above. Alan Magioncalda and Ted Heaney designed the bistro-like dining room, far left.

Space

144

At the crux of most modern design projects are the problems inherent in the division of space. Single-family houses are becoming a luxury of the past, and apartments in most major cities are getting smaller and less adaptable. The loft revolution has underlined the point that, even in larger and more economical spaces, one must plan and organize an environment if it is to be efficient and pleasant to live in on a daily basis.

Considerations about space have also led to a changing role for the interior designer and architect. They do not simply provide a cosmetic function, but undertake an organizational job that relies on particular professional and imaginative skills. Given the rising costs of any interior renovation project, the designer must constantly be conscious of the financial impact of the plans and their execution.

Both large and small spaces have their particular problems—from too little room to accommodate one's possessions to so much open space that privacy is lacking. Whether one lives in a 600-square-foot apartment or a 3,000-square-foot loft, storage is always a factor, as is the quality and quantity of light in an interior.

Modern design is often a design of adaptation—being able to convert a dining room into a bedroom with little effort, being willing to change a traditional layout into a more convenient one, and being able to look at the division of space with an open mind.

Paul Segal Associates Architects planned a dramatic, translucent, fiberglass-walled conservatory attached to a Long Island house. The interior space features diffused light, large glass windows, and a bluestone-slab floor.

A space for all seasons

The trio of houses hidden among the brush-oak trees on a winding country road is intriguing. At first, their angularity and emphatic new-ness are just what one expects from Long Island vacation houses. But each incorporates a surprising and dramatic element—a white corrugated, shedlike structure that contributes to the modern profile. They are the result of a two-year project by Paul Segal Associates Architects, a Manhattan-based company that served as designer, contractor, and builder.

"They're a little outside of the normal realm of living spaces," admitted James Biber, the project architect and builder. Each of the heated houses has an enclosed, unheated space that measures 32 feet square and is 24 feet high. It is a dramatic kind of room that the architects dubbed a "conservatory" —a space not unlike a country barn or an industrial shed, and a close relation of the screened porch.

The way the conservatories relate to the houses is different in each case: One house wraps around the room; in another, the conservatory is attached to the living room; in the third, it is connected to the back of the house. In all, however, the conservatories are adjacent to the kitchen, dining, and living areas. Sliding glass doors off the living room separate the house from the conservatory, whose large windows frame exterior views and provide ventilation. The houses measure from 1,650 square feet to 1,800 square feet without the conservatories and are situated on two to two and a half acres of land.

"The things that make a nice win-

The conservatory
has a shedlike
exterior, left.
Glass window and
door openings
provide extra ven-
tilation. The plan,
right, shows how
the conservatory
is adjacent to the
house's living
room area.

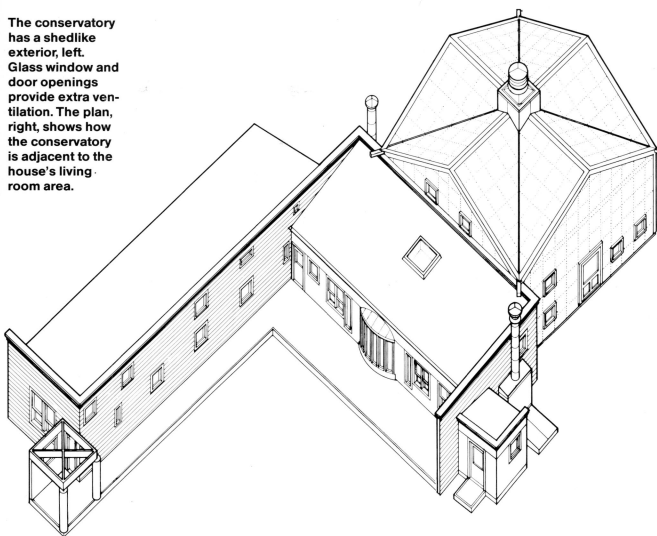

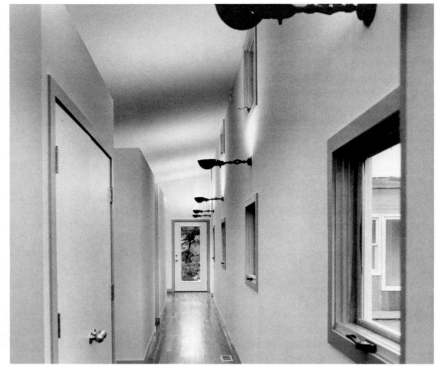

Access to the living room from the conservatory is through sliding glass doors, above left. A striking vista is provided by the placement of the bedrooms along a long corridor, above right. An open pass-through separates the kitchen from the dining area, far right.

ter house are not necessarily the things that make a nice summer house," Segal noted. So the architects designed houses that have distinct winter and summer spaces. "The winter space is cosy, enclosed, and energy-efficient," Segal said. "The summer space is expansive, light, and breezy." Biber saw it as a summer living room, studio, greenhouse, or gym.

When designing the summer space, Biber thought of European shopping galleries and arcades with their special quality of diffused light. "Stunning inside, even on a cloudy day," he recalled. To capture that, the architects used translucent corrugated fiberglass. The architects specified four-by-four-inch cedar framing, heavy-duty fire-resistant corrugated fiberglass wall panels, and natural bluestone slabs for the floor. The slabs are set directly into the sand floor without grout so that each can be lifted up individually—to plant a tree, or install a hot tub, for example. Steel columns, twenty-two feet high, support the roof.

The imaginative design of the interior of the houses attached to the conservatories was meant to make the most of their relatively small size. The living rooms are about twelve feet wide, the master bedrooms are twelve by fifteen feet on the average, and the other bedrooms are about ten feet square. Each of the conservatories is equipped with a ventilator at the top, but air conditioning was not included. "The key to not needing it is good ventilation," said Biber, who pointed out the houses' big and small, square and rectangular windows. There are also clerestory windows, windows at eye level, and windows to look out of while doing the dishes or sitting in the bathtub. But all in all, the conservatories remain the design stars. And, if given the choice, Biber would opt for that design element above all. "I go for the single spectacular space," the architect admitted.

For another project by Paul Segal Associates Architects, see pages 48 to 53.

David Kelley

Translucent corrugated

For the conservatory, heavy-duty fire-resistant corrugated fiberglass was attached to four-by-four-inch cedar framing. Twenty-two-foot-high steel columns support the roof. The fiberglass does not degrade under ultraviolet rays. Although the translucent material is available at many lumberyards, information can be obtained from the H.H. Robertson Company, Resolite division, P.O. Box 338, Zelienople, Pa., 16063; 412-452-6800.

Axial plan: focus on view

In renovation projects, the dilemma is fairly common: How can designers integrate the available range of modern technologies into an interior that has a more traditional look—and come up with a floor plan that takes advantage of the space's best features? The spectacular views from a Greenwich Village penthouse prompted Shelton, Stortz, Mindel & Associates to resolve the dilemma by organizing the spaces on a series of diagonal axes and by building a number of bays to incorporate a sophisticated lighting system.

A bay was constructed around each of the newly installed windows —and while each bay incorporated all the necessary engineering functions, it also acted as a frame for both the exterior views and interior vistas. "The bay system gave us a lot of mileage," said Peter Shelton, one of the architects.

"It allowed us to take care of lighting, air conditioning, electrical wiring, and sound speakers, as well as provide each window with a banquette," added Lee Mindel, another partner.

Since the windows themselves became the focal points of the apartment, special emphasis had to be placed on the lighting. Too many reflections would detract from the views, so the architects designed a threefold lighting system. "Two of the systems were developed so that one could see out at night with few reflections and a third was for extra bright light," said Bob Stortz, the third partner. Neither the floor lamps nor the pin spots concealed in a slot above the windows reflect in the glass.

The comfortable and pleasantly old-fashioned furnishings (an Indian dhurri rug and plump sofas) as well as the choice of materials (bleached ash wood, green marble, and white porcelain tile) counterbalance the dramatic floor plan and tone down the emphatically modern interior scheme.

A series of crisply defined window bays is the primary design element in the living room of this duplex apartment that offered a kaleidoscope of magnificent views, right.

Photographs by Bo Parker

The plan, on a
series of axes,
organizes both
interior and exte-
rior vistas. The
opening in the
cabinet, above,
allows a view into
the foyer. Custom
lighting highlights
individual objects
and minimizes
reflections at
night, right.

Elements
to shape
a space

Photographs by Robert Levin

Raul Rosas devised a system of doors between a loft bedroom and living area, right. Mirrored on one side, the doors create visual effects when pivoted differently, above.

There are times when one needs to adapt a living space—by opening up a large area or, conversely, by closing off a portion to insure privacy. Designers and architects have responded with strategies that revolve around the innovative use of doors, partitions, and walls.

The renovation of a loft belonging to Jack Brusca, a painter and jewelry designer, is a case in point. Despite its single row of windows with a southern exposure, little daylight reached the kitchen, one hundred feet away. Raul Rosas, the architect in charge, also needed to find a way to separate the bedroom from the open living area. His inge-nious remedy to both problems was a pair of seven-foot-square pivoting doors that abut one of the loft's structural columns.

"We wanted to get away from the idea of enclosed, separate rooms," Rosas said. For reasons of budget and engineering, he used hollow core doors, two for each panel. Joined at the top and bottom, a steel rod runs the full height of the panels, allowing the doors to pivot 360 degrees. "The doors don't go all the way up to the ceiling," Brusca observed, "because there's no need to separate the two areas acoustically. The doors permit me to close off the bedroom while maintaining the feeling of open space." But the most dramatic element in the installation is that the pivoting doors are painted on one side, mirrored on the other. "That's how I control the light," said Rosas. "The sun that comes in through the windows is refracted off the mirrors and into the kitchen."

Another clever method of creating flexible space involved the designer Kevin Walz, who by his own admission "always has to move something." When he was asked to redesign a corporate apartment for Della Femina, Travisano & Partners, an advertising agency, the client did not want any construction work done because it was a rental. The firm wanted to use its two-bedroom apartment as lodging for clients and for business meetings.

Walz devised a series of movable, lightweight, curved walls that can be used to make the main L-shaped space appear more interesting; the walls can also separate the dining from the living area, and camouflage a bar, stereo, and record storage area in the foyer. The four-and-a-half-inch-thick walls, one fifty-four inches high, the other seventy-two inches high, are made from quarter-inch plywood over two-by-four-inch studs. The smaller of the two units weighs about sixty

pounds, the larger about one hundred pounds.

"They're not the kind of thing you would move every three minutes," admitted Walz. Neither is the thirteen-foot-long sliding door that he installed in another apartment between the living room and den. "It weighs a lot but slides easily," he said. The client had requested a way to create a more private area off the living room. The sliding partition which runs along a ceiling-hung track is made up of five chipboard panels riveted together. Summarizing his changeable design element, Walz called it "permanent flexibility."

Kevin Walz had riveted panels of chipboard hung on a ceiling track, left. Lightweight curved walls were his solution for a rental apartment, creating a private dining area, opposite. They can be moved aside, below.

Dining room to bedroom

In a Brooklyn apartment designed by Patchel, Byron and Associates, the dining room, right, doubles as a second bedroom, above, when the table is moved over and the bed drops down from inside the closet.

Too dark, too small, too high. When apartments are hard to find, people tend to settle rather than choose, and then it's the interior designer, wielding his T-square, graph paper, and measuring tape, who is called upon to solve the seemingly insoluble.

Out of adversity, there is often ingenuity. Because the solutions are not necessarily earthshaking, but rather represent the bread and butter of their trade, designers tend to be modest about these projects. "We only did what the client asked for," said Estelle Patchel, who with her partner, Michael Byron, renovated a small one-bedroom apartment. "He wanted a place where he could put up overnight guests," she said. "We discussed it and decided to create a room within a room."

"There was a lot of demolition involved," Byron said. To make the dining room double as the second bedroom, closets were knocked out so that the room could be approached from the adjacent living room as a totally separate space. Plain-fronted cabinets line one wall; behind one set of doors is storage, behind the other is a Murphy bed. Instead of solid partitions for the other walls, the designers opted for vertical blinds. "They're our replacement for Japanese shoji screens," Bryon said. The blinds are left open when the room is used for eating, closed for added privacy when it is used for sleeping.

The dining room furnishings were kept sparse—a high-gloss plastic laminate top placed on two restaurant bases, with leather chairs around it. "The table is moved to the side," Patchel said, "and the cabinet doors are opened for the bed to be let down." Including the designers' fee, the bed, furniture, vertical blinds, construction, and carpeting, the cost of the renovation was about $9,500.

For another Murphy bed solution, see pages 46 to 47.

Photographs by Robert Levin

Drama on a small stage

The challenge of the small apartment interested Joseph Paul D'Urso, a minimalist designer who had explored extravagantly proportioned rooms in his usually larger-scale projects. The tiny duplex offered only a two-room apartment and a separate storage room above it, but D'Urso believes the result is one of the "most inventive things I've ever done." The finished space is a complex, Chinese puzzle type of interior—with a soaring stair, romantic overtones, and a sense of being in a mysterious interior.

The clients planned to use the apartment only as a pied-à-terre, therefore some of the usual concerns, such as storage, were not of primary importance. They wanted a visually exciting apartment that would act as a backdrop for their chair and modern art collections.

The designer had a section of the ceiling removed and a steep diagonal stair installed between the building's beams. Instead of filling in between each riser, the underside of each tread and riser was Sheetrocked separately. Painted white, the stair—particularly when viewed from below—creates a strong sculptural element and is a focal point of the apartment.

In the bedroom, by placing the bed on a raised platform above the opening for the stair, D'Urso was able to take advantage of the view of Central Park and the Manhattan skyline, at the same time achieving the diversity he wanted. While the window on the lower floor had a northern exposure, the windows on the upper level faced east and west. By opening the ceiling, D'Urso observed, "what is a window for the bedroom, is a skylight for the living room, and a room that had one exposure now has three."

For reasons of economy, the plumbing connections were not moved, which is why the bathroom is near the living and dining areas, on the floor beneath the bedroom. "I felt that I should be answering

Designer Joseph Paul D'Urso brought drama to a tiny living area by turning a steep staircase into a sculptural event, far left. The bathroom sink, left, remains exposed to the living area.

A section of living room ceiling was opened up to allow light from the upper level to filter down and mix with light from the window at right, which became a focal point of the space.

questions like 'what kind of privacy does one actually need to wash one's hands, to brush one's teeth?'" D'Urso said. He enclosed the shower behind a low wall, kept the toilet completely private, and situated the sink next to, and open to, the living room. "It's presented as a piece of sculpture," he said.

The living area focuses on the tall window—the only one whose original molding was retained—and contains a sixteen-foot raised banquette with leather pillows.

While the former tenant fought the idiosyncratic nature of the rooms by filling in all the niches, D'Urso made the most of the way the walls at the top of the building leaned in, and gave the apartment a visual dynamism based on dramatic diagonals. The small duplex is an example of an intricately condensed design that succeeds in creating smooth transitions between the different areas. "It's all about maneuvering," he explained. "In a small space like this, you can't just cut into it. This was like delicate surgery. Because of the fact that space is becoming more valuable all the time," he added, "I see this as the way many such small places will have to be perceived— more compressed and vertical, with little tentacles reaching out for light."

For other designs for small spaces see pages 120 to 121 and 122 to 123.

Photographs by Rick Barnes

MADE
IN
U.S.A.

A sixteen-foot-long leather-pillowed banquette, above, is the main seating. The space's architecture dictated the shape of the diagonal black closet door, right. The bed was raised to capture a skyline view, far right.

Visually scaling a high wall

While many people despair when faced with the meager eight-foot room height that a new building so often provides, living under a twenty-foot ceiling can prove to be equally cumbersome. Too big is as problematical as the albeit more common complaint, too small.

"The scale was enormous and quite a problem," said Juan Montoya, who designed a prototype apartment for a renovated factory in Manhattan's West Village. The space featured striking views of the Hudson River, an overhanging balcony, and an angled skylight window in one wall. But the bare walls were "too high, too overpowering," he said.

Using nine separate pieces of canvas, the designer created an enormous 12-foot-square hanging that is delineated with adhesive tape into 2-foot-square grids. The upper left square sports a black triangle. "To create the effect of the forty-five-degree angle window," said Montoya. "The huge grid brings down the tremendous height of the room, and relieves it," he explained, adding that the only cost for this do-it-yourself project was the material.

For another scaling design solution see pages 220 to 221.

Robert Levin

114

Making the wall graphic

To create the thirty-six module, 12-foot-square wall piece, designer Juan Montoya stretched, primed, and painted two-by-two-foot pieces of canvas. One corner of the upper-left-hand square was painted black to break up the pattern. Each of the thirty-six canvas squares was hung on the wall. One-eighth of an inch wide graphics tape was used to edge the panels, creating the grid-like effect. Materials for the piece are available at Pearl Paint Company, 308 Canal Street, New York, N.Y. 10013; 212-431-7932.

Designer Juan Montoya stands in front of the thirty-six unit, 12-foot-square canvas wall graphic he devised to give scale to the 20-foot-high loft wall.

Shaping the small space

BED AREA

KITCHEN

BATH

In a brownstone
studio, right,
designer Douglas
Frank reorganized
the space with
full and partial-
height walls.
The bedroom is
behind the angled
wall at right.

KITCHEN

BED AREA

DRESSING AREA

BATH

In Renée Guest's studio, the designer placed the bed in an alcove and separated it from the main living area with a wall of vertical blinds. Plan, above, shows separated living functions.

In the days before apartment shortages, studios were residential stepchildren. But today a tiny apartment may be valued for its advantageous location or because these small spaces can be economical. The occupants, instead of simply making do with the ubiquitous convertible sofa, are investing in their studios and asking designers and architects to rethink the spaces completely. One designer who completed two such projects is Doug Frank, who heads his own New York company, Frank Design.

Although his style is in the minimalist tradition, Frank points up a change in approach being taken in the design of small spaces. It involves putting in architectural elements—partial-height and full-height walls, built-in storage and seating, some platforms—instead of taking down walls to open up a room. It is an approach that might be called postminimalist; it makes a space look as if it had been stripped bare while actually adding many structural elements. "Building in a small space has to do with creating an illusion that there's more rather than less space, more going on than actually is," explained Frank. "And, more importantly, that there's somewhere to go to."

In a brownstone studio he planned for Michael Gustafson, an art student, Frank restructured the fifteen-by-twenty-foot room to take advantage of its existing features—"pretty good proportions, high ceilings, and a dramatic bay window"—and came up with an innovative and unusual layout.

A platform was built to lead up to and offset the bay window. "The floor of the platform," Frank said, "creates a vantage point for the studio"—and is just the right spot from which to view the sinuous lavender blue wall that acts as a baffle for the dressing room and is the apartment's major architectural focus. A small area near the bay window was chosen for the bedroom. Al-though the walls are six and a half feet high from the main floor, they are only four feet high from the bedroom's platform floor—"so you can look out and not feel confined," he said.

On one of the main side walls, a column was filled out to create a mirrored niche for the banquette. "A way of putting in elements that look as if they are part of the original architecture," Frank said. A twenty-six-inch-high table functions both for dining and as a coffee table by the banquette. The bathroom was retiled and refixtured, and the kitchen equipped with new hardware, appliances, and counter tops. Including furniture, the renovation cost under $18,000.

Some of the same design tricks were applied to another studio, whose occupant, Renée Guest, is a women's clothing retailer. "She had a lot of clothes," Frank observed, explaining how he created four large closets and a dressing table area connected to the bathroom. He placed the bed in an alcove, separating it from the living/dining area by a wall of vertical blinds. A small entrance foyer "acts as a baffle so you don't walk directly into the main space," he said. "You have the illusion that there's another place beyond." The renovation of this approximately eighteen-by-twenty-two-foot studio cost about $15,000.

In neither residence is there a sofa bed to be seen. "I feel very strongly about that," Frank said. "Beds in living rooms never really work. You should have an honest-to-goodness bed to sleep on."

For other designs of small spaces, see pages 108 to 113 and 122 to 123.

Photographs by Robert Levin

Making more of an L-shaped studio

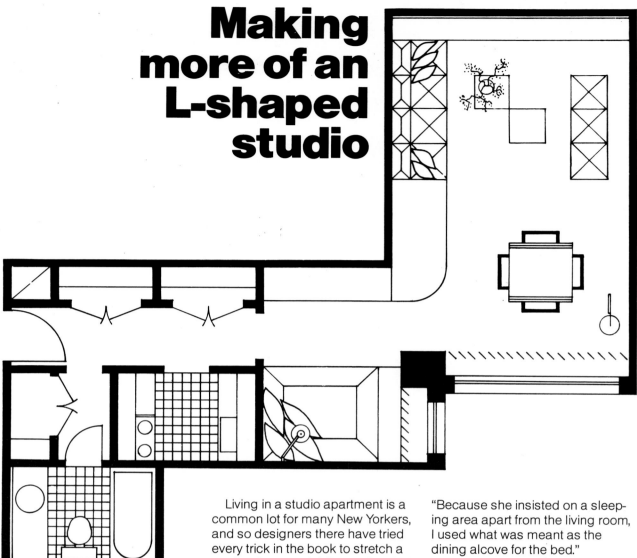

Birch Coffey diversified a typical L-shaped studio, whose plan is shown above, by placing the bed area near the kitchen and making optimum use of the living area for seating and storage, far right.

Living in a studio apartment is a common lot for many New Yorkers, and so designers there have tried every trick in the book to stretch a confined space. Adding to the challenge is the fact that many of the clients are renters who do not want to spend a lot of time or money on their small apartments. But Iris Soodak, an administrator in the city government, was an exception.

When she moved to a conveniently located L-shaped studio a few years ago, she brought "the accumulation of many former apartments." Looking at the result, she knew she needed help. "It just didn't work," she recalled with a sigh. "A studio needs unification."

"I basically wanted to separate living and sleeping functions," said Birch Coffey, the designer she hired.

"Because she insisted on a sleeping area apart from the living room, I used what was meant as the dining alcove for the bed."

That, of course, has been done before. But what was unusual here was the way the designer handled the storage in the studio. A custom unit was designed that starts in the bedroom area and winds into the living room space. Soodak spent under $15,000 on the total renovation of the studio, including all the built-ins and furniture. "I used the same materials throughout," Coffey said. "Visually it looks like one room that's bigger than it actually is, yet the areas are separate."

For other solutions to studio spaces, see pages 68 to 69 and 116 to 119.

Robert Levin

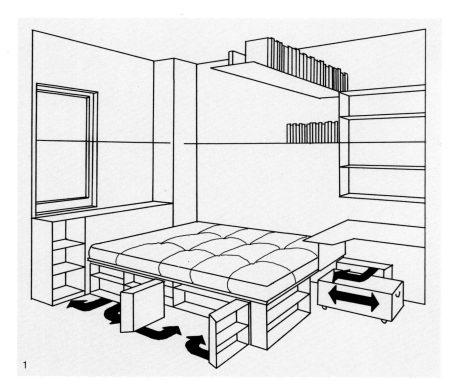

1

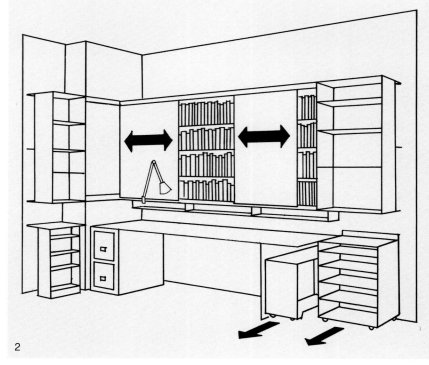

2

Coping with tiny places

In a skit about an astrophysicist, in which he was asked to name the greatest problem in space, Sid Caesar offered the reply, "closet space." If few people appreciated the comedian's farsighted assessment back in the 1950s, today it seems increasingly apropos. The old design solutions—the Murphy bed, the racks of wire shelving, the mirrored wall—may no longer be enough to solve today's more drastic space crunch.

These days, many of the people who work at home in small one-bedroom or studio apartments need space to conduct a business meeting and to receive potential clients. And there is little doubt that sitting on the bed is not an appropriate solution. The scarcity and expense of urban apartments have made personal inventiveness and design ingenuity a necessity.

"One day, we just realized that our ideas were needed," said Jean Weiner, who with Paul Shafer is a partner in Cobuild Associates, a New York-based firm that specializes in custom designing small

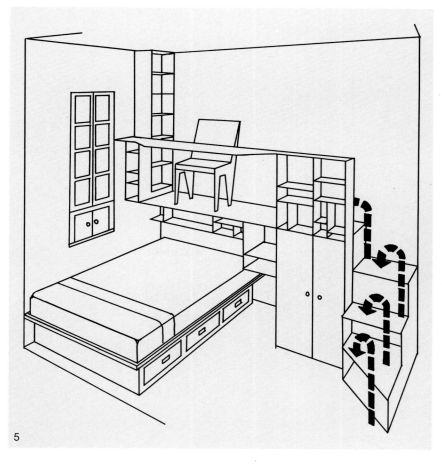

5

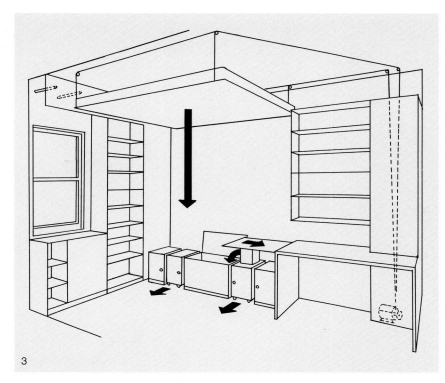

3

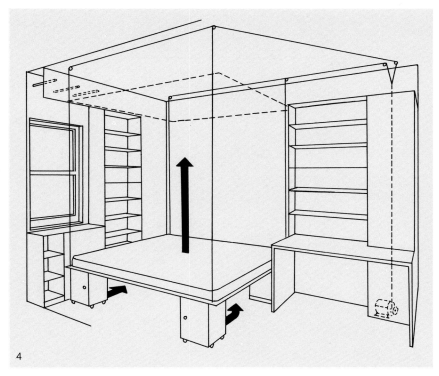

4

spaces. Although most of their projects are based on particular solutions to specific clients' needs, their rooms include ingenious ideas for many people who must live and work in restricted spaces. Beds on pulleys, storage boxes on casters, sliding panels over bookshelves, and under-the-bed storage are only some of the trademarks of what might be called the company's Rube Goldbergian school of design, which leans more toward the functional than the esthetically striking.

For a client who owned what Cobuild thought was an "immense amount of books" that had to be kept handy in a seven-by-twelve-and-a-half-foot room where she could write and sleep when her children visited on weekends, the designers came up with pull-out bookshelves on hinges, boxes and bookshelves that fit under the bed and can be pulled out when needed. The construction for this project cost $1,100.

When a free-lance illustrator and writer needed space to put up her drawings without sacrificing book-storage, the designers came up with two sliding bulletin boards that can butt up to each other for a large display area and can also slide apart for access to the books on the shelves. Oversize drawing pads and drawings are kept behind the bookshelves built with a false back. The ten-foot-long work area cost $1,200 to build.

Marc Jacobs, a private tutor, was another special case. Although Jacobs lived in a one-bedroom apartment, he wanted to do his tutoring in the six-foot-nine-inch by thirteen-foot bedroom, which has only a nine-foot-high ceiling, rather than in the living room. And although he required a queen-size bed, he didn't want the room to look like a bedroom. The designers suspended the bed near the ceiling on a system of pulleys, equipped with a one-third horsepower motor so that it can be lowered at night. Pull-out storage drawers, used as a desk during the day, roll out to become the base of the bed. The renovation of the room cost $1,200.

"In the up position, the bed is so close to the ceiling that it looks as if the ceiling is recessed," Shafer said. "And it never needs to be made."

For a teen-ager's six-foot-six-inch by eleven-foot room with a nine-foot-nine-inch ceiling, that was once a maid's room, the designers reversed the concept of the loft bed by building a loft desk over a floor-level bed. The project came to about $900. Access to the desk area is attained by walking up storage-unit steps.

Many of these design ideas are based on the Chinese puzzle approach: a masterly way of fitting together all the component parts. "Sometimes it takes a while to work it all out," said Weiner, who estimates that most projects take from two to four weeks to plan and build. But they are confident that their ideas will be needed for some time. "Tiny rooms are the wave of the future," Weiner promised.

For other solutions to converting rooms, see pages 68 to 69 and 106 to 107.

1. For extra storage in a seven-by-twelve-and-a-half-foot room, bookcases swing out from under the bed.

2. An illustrator's twelve-by-fourteen-foot work area has sliding bulletin boards.

3,4. In a six-foot-nine-inch by thirteen-foot bedroom and office, the bed is on a pulley. Boxes wheel out to support the bed.

5. In a converted six-and-a-half-by-eleven-foot maid's room, a loft desk is over the bed.

Opening up the attic for effect

Tom Fox and Joey Nahem renovated the second floor of a Brooklyn house, above. The attic window remained when the ceiling was broken through in the living room, right.

The young couple who asked Tom Fox and Joey Nahem of Fox-Nahem Design to renovate the two-family house had some practical needs, but also wanted a dramatic interior space.

"They both grew up in big, one-family houses," said Fox. "More than anything, they wanted spaciousness." Unfortunately, spaciousness was, more than anything, the missing element in the upper apartment of the conventional house. The modest exterior, with its tiny front lawn, two front doors, and small attic window, gives little indication of the value of property in this residential Brooklyn neighborhood.

The original idea was to renovate the interior of the house completely, turning it into a one-family home. But after considering the cost of such a project (the clients insisted that the budget stay under $75,000), it was decided to keep the first-floor apartment as a rental unit and convert only the top floor. "It was all boxy little rooms," Nahem said. "But because both of them were used to big, separate rooms, it was hard for the couple to accept the idea of open planning."

The breakthrough came when the designers suggested opening up the ceiling that separated the living room from a crawl-space attic. The new living room, designed to include a dining area, has a special quality. With its beveled-edge window, high ceiling, and an unusual bright red palette, the space is striking without appearing empty.

Another challenge was the apartment's lack of storage space. "The clients had a lot of possessions—four sets of dishes, lots of glass pieces—and the wife wanted it all to be available," said Nahem. The designers installed two floor-to-ceiling closets in the living room, but covered the shelving with full-height doors so that all the objects could be stored out of sight. "They don't look like closets, but more like a wall," said Fox.

The hot and cold of it

When breaking through an attic floor, two practical considerations are as important as the design factors: insulation and ventilation.

It is likely that the floor of the attic has been insulated so that expensively heated air does not escape from the living areas up into the cold and empty attic. That insulation will, of course, be removed during the project. But insulation should then be installed on the ceiling of the attic for the same reason—to keep the heat from escaping through the roof. Batts of insulation can be placed between the rafters before the Sheetrock forming the new room's ceiling is installed. The insulation's vapor barrier should be facing in, toward the heated part of the house. Many attics have louvers in the roof's peak to counter a buildup of moisture in the unheated space. When the attic is made part of the heated living space, these louvers will need to be removed. But attention to ventilation is still advised. A ceiling fan, for example, will help cool the room in summer and will also, in the winter, help warm the living space by recirculating the heated air that flows upward.

Photographs by Robert Levin

Floors were sanded and bleached, and the design of the main living space is based on a series of levels, which were planned to offer different seating options.

Traffic patterns through the apartment were carefully studied. A pivoting panel acts as a door to the living area; a curved wall leads into the bedroom. "It was needed there," Fox stressed. "We didn't put in walls just for effect."

The designers had most of the furniture custom-made, including a polished stainless steel dining table and coffee table. "The surfaces catch the light and are very reflective," Fox said. But the upholstered club chairs are chubby and inviting. "These act as softening factors," he explained.

It is a dramatic room, so much so that one tends to overlook some of the more subtle and practical design solutions. The windows, for example, were small, unattractive, and garlanded with bulky, unsightly radiators. The designers installed a carpeted ledge all the way around the room, so that the radiators did not need to be recessed into the wall. Instead of installing expensive new windows, they completely covered the existing window wall with vertical blinds.

Because the clients might eventually move, the designers had all the permanent elements, such as the kitchen cabinets and walls, painted in neutral colors. The stronger shades were reserved for upholstery and pillows. "You don't feel you're in Versailles or the south of France," admitted Nahem, "but no one believes it's Brooklyn."

A shiny table separates the kitchen from the dining area, far left. The pillowed banquette and club chairs provide seating in the living room, above.

A trio of homes from one loft

Many couples who design and build a place to live discover the tensions involved in renovating—their relationship may have come apart while their home was coming together. But Laura Bohn and Richard Fiore, close friends who had often worked together, were wiser. "We both wanted our own beds and our own front doors," said Bohn, an interior designer. They decided that buying a floor large enough to be converted into three separate, if not equal, apartments was the solution for their particular way of life. "We decided to pool our resources into this project," said Fiore, vice president of Abcon Industries, a concern that specializes in building rehabilitations.

Bohn and Fiore, who formed a legal partnership for the project, knew that their arrangement had special financial and design requirements. "It had to be big enough for our two apartments and for a rental apartment that would pay the mortgage," Bohn said. "We knew we had to have windows on all four sides, and that the space had to be a top floor" so that the conversion could provide each apartment with two fire exits—one to the roof, one to the interior fire stair. After a year, they found a full floor in a commercial building, about 3,300 square feet of space.

"I was the designer and Richard the builder," said Bohn, who took 1,200 square feet at the south end. She was responsible for the layout of all the interiors, but in her own apartment she was best able to exercise her design judgment. "It's carefully thought out so that nothing happens," she said. "I did work it out so that I could get the south end of the floor, because I'm the plant freak." Her apartment is straightforward but incorporates several interesting design ideas. Her closet is a seven-foot-high, nine-foot-wide freestanding sculptural cylinder, and in the bathroom is her pièce de résistance: the bathtub. It is a five-foot-wide, two-foot-deep galvanized metal horse trough, ordered for $100 from a farm catalogue and epoxy-painted. "All the architects I spoke to had a million reasons why I shouldn't use it," said the determined Bohn, who had the tub put in anyway. "It isn't cold, nor does it get pitted," she said. "And it doesn't take long to fill." But the installation did prove to be a problem—"this is definitely not something a novice should try," she admitted.

The third apartment was carved

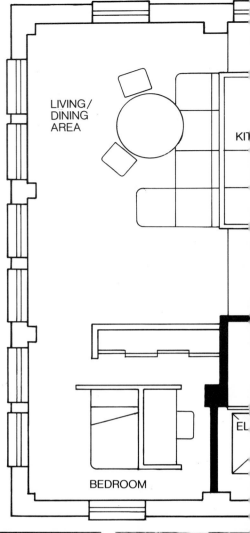

LIVING/
DINING
AREA

KIT

BEDROOM

EL

Plan of the 3,300-square-foot loft, top right, that was divided into three. Richard Fiore, right, got the largest space. Tenant Joseph Lembo's space, right center, pays for the mortgage. Laura Bohn, far right, opted for an open plan.

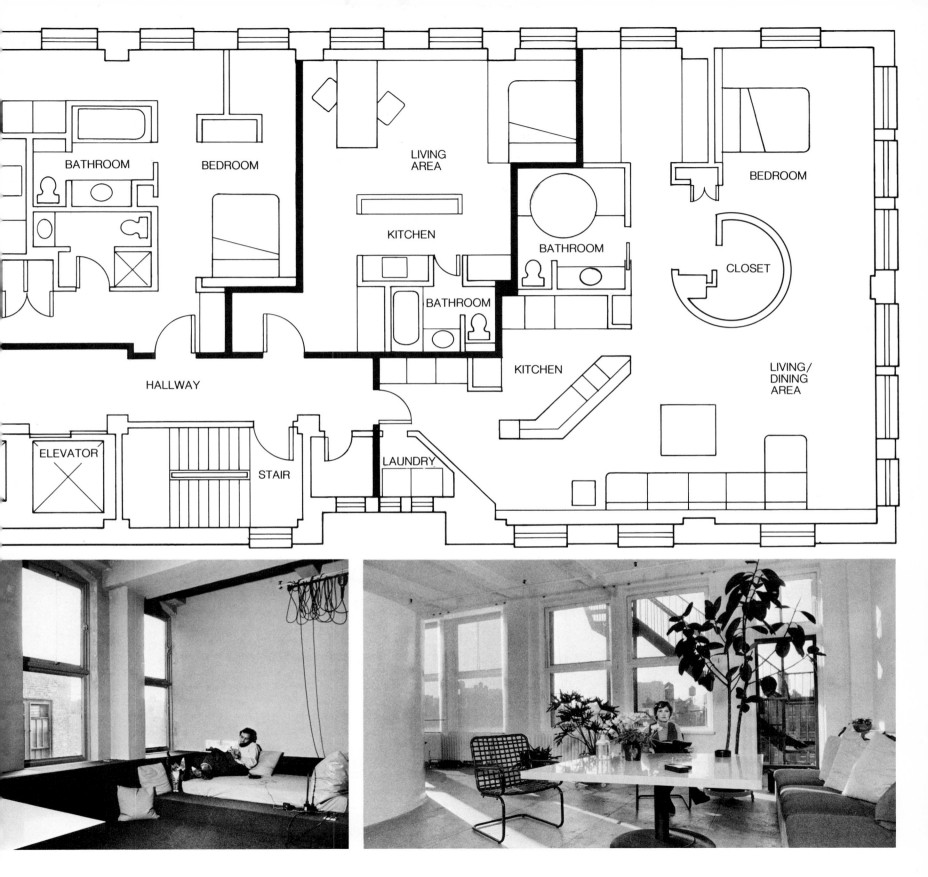

BATHROOM

BEDROOM

LIVING AREA

KITCHEN

BATHROOM

BEDROOM

CLOSET

BATHROOM

HALLWAY

KITCHEN

LIVING/ DINING AREA

ELEVATOR

STAIR

LAUNDRY

out between hers and Fiore's. In the planning stages they each kept expanding into that apartment until the studio space measured only about 400 square feet. That, however, was just what was wanted by Joseph Lembo, a designer. "It's small, but organized," Lembo said. "Within one space there's a lot of variety." He chose a simple, bare decorating scheme, emphasizing the color and texture of walls and floors. "We have only the outside hallway in common, so we all were able to retain our privacy," added Lembo. "Sometimes we even make dinner together, but eat separately. I couldn't imagine doing that in any other apartment building."

Fiore, who shares his apartment with his son, Fred, needed the most room, and Bohn designed a 1,500-square-foot, two-bedroom, two-bathroom scheme for him at the north end of the floor. He has quarry tile floors, a bathtub with a view of the Empire State Building, and a bed placed squarely beneath a huge skylight.

It was not all smooth going between designer and builder. "We were under a lot of pressure, of time and money—next time we'll have more fun," Fiore said of the fourteen-month project. "Now, I'm more tolerant of designers," he said.

Richard Fiore waters plants under the skylight in his bedroom, far left. Joseph Lembo's tiny space is minimally furnished, left center. Laura Bohn's bathroom has an epoxy-painted horse trough as an oversize tub, left.

A view of the dining area from the greenhouse level of Richard and Betsy Smith's loft, designed by architect Peter Townsend.

On the vertical: a three-level loft

Lofts are popular because they offer design elements that are always at a premium—space and light. But as more commercial buildings are developed, loft dwellers find that they have to settle for smaller and darker spaces, often places where the only windows are at either end. And architects and designers find they have to come up with innovative spatial solutions—in the case of long, narrow lofts where there is access to a skylight, for example, it is the vertical rather than the horizontal possibilities that can be emphasized.

"The most important thing in a loft is the placement of the windows," said Peter Townsend, an architect who recently completed a renovation for Betsy and Richard Smith and their two sons, Edward and Harry. The Smiths took over three floors in a commercial building; although the top floor was capped with a skylight, the other lofts were fairly dark because the building had only two windows at one end and three at the back of each floor.

The contractor who owned the five-story building and the architect decided to divide it into two duplex spaces and a ground-floor loft. The division of the building was a way to take advantage of the skylight and, according to the architect, "bring light into the center of the space." The Smiths took over the first, fourth, and fifth floors, retaining the roof rights and using the first floor as a painting studio for Smith. On the top floor, a greenhouse was added to and integrated into the skylight.

It was necessary to have a new stair installed to go from the fourth to the fifth floor. But, by adjusting the building's original public stair so that it took up less space, the architect was able to make room for a second staircase that would run from the fourth floor all the way up to the roof—a distance of thirty-four feet.

The design particularly pleased Smith, an English artist, who is used to working with dramatic spaces and is known primarily for his large ceiling-hung, kitelike sculptures. "I like the way light happens in this space and the way it is reflected on the different surfaces," he said. Living in a vertical rather than a horizontal two-floor space was also appealing to his wife, a landscape designer. "I'd had it with one-floor living—the dishwasher behind the bed and the kids skateboarding around," she said, recalling the loft that the family had occupied earlier. "This was my opportunity to have a room of my own."

With the exception of the exposed brick walls, every surface in the loft is new. The pine floors, Sheetrock walls, windows, mechanical ventilation, plumbing, heating, and all furnishings were included in the renovation. Construction costs came to about $35 a square foot.

The duplex loft was divided so that bedrooms, bathrooms, and family room were on the lower floor, and the living room, dining room, kitchen, and laundry room on the floor above. The family room/library on the fourth floor was carved out of extra space under the stair.

"You have to choose very carefully what you put near the windows," Townsend said. "In many lofts, the kitchen might be enclosed in the center of the space and has to be mechanically ventilated; here it was decided to put it on the main floor under the windows." The bathrooms, on the other hand, are all interior rooms and are equipped with fans. Clerestory windows in the walls allow the skylight to be taken advantage of. But, as in many design projects, that brings about further considerations. In this case, the architect is thinking about how the skylight will have to be cleaned. "We might just have to work out a rolling scaffold," he said.

A diagonal stair connects the loft's three floors and leads to the skylight-topped greenhouse, far left. The kitchen, dining area, and living area are at center, left top. The study on the lower floor also gets natural light, left bottom.

Photographs by Robert Levin

Spatial links: bridges or stairs

To some people, there's nothing to a space unless there's somewhere else to go—upstairs, downstairs, around, or under.

Spiral staircases, cantilevered stairs, and overhanging catwalks are not for families with small children, nor for those with vertigo. But for those who are willing to go to some effort to make the most of the spaces they are renovating, there are many possibilities. In the loft shown on the opposite page, two separate stairs were used to gain access to an "upstairs" bedroom; in the brownstone renovation, above, a bridge and a spiral stair

allowed for flexibility in what might otherwise have been a rather ordinary interior.

The 2,500-square-foot loft owned by James Armenakis and his wife, Diana, had a square shape with ten-foot ceilings, a small bathroom, what the owners called a "basic kitchen," and skylights. "We didn't want to feel we lived in a hall and wanted to separate the bedroom from the main living area," said Armenakis, who hired Frederick Lee, an architect, to undertake the redesign of the loft.

A raised floor area with a shed roof and four windows had good

views to the south, so it was chosen as "the ideal location for the bedroom," Lee said. "By elevating it, we created a separate, private area." That also created a situation in which the bedroom was upstairs, the bathroom downstairs. As the architect was soon to ask himself: "How do you get from the bedroom to the bathroom without the awkwardness of having to walk through the main living room area?"

Thomas Jefferson's house at Monticello, where independent passages allowed for separate routes for familial and service activities, gave the architect the idea of hav-

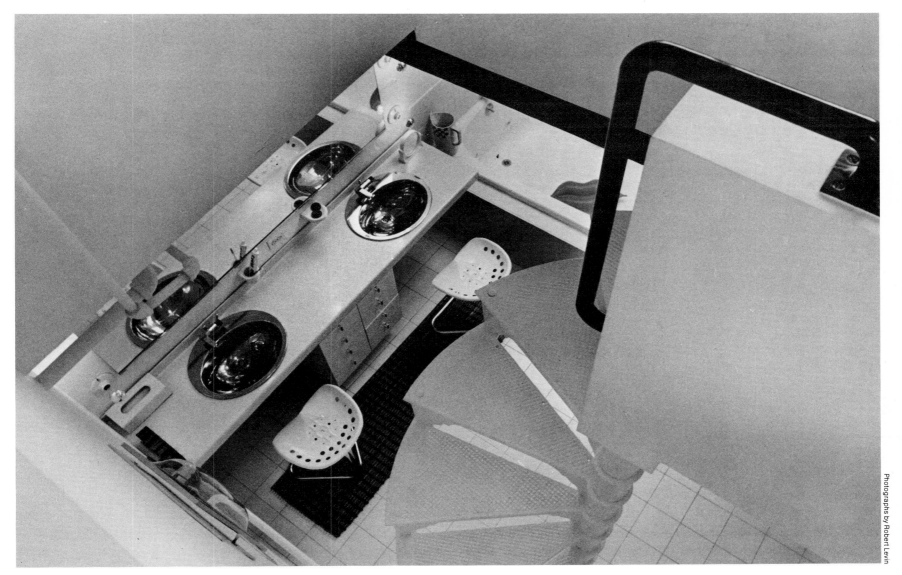

Photographs by Robert Levin

ing two accesses to the bedroom: one leading directly and privately to the bathroom, the other to the living area. The diagonal stairway to the bedroom has cantilevered treads that seem to be built into the wall. "They look as if they are floating," Lee said, "and are meant to lead the eye upward. Making the stair such a prominent feature was a way of letting people know there was a room upstairs." The stair treads, four-by-twelve-inch beams, were from an old building and have "a lot of character," Armenakis observed, adding that the metal spiral stair connecting the lavish

bathroom to the austere bedroom is "purely functional."

Faced with completely redesigning two apartments in a brownstone, John Stedila and his partner, Tim Button, of Stedila Design, used two unusual bridging devices. "The whole idea was to get light into the brownstone," said Stedila. In the duplex apartment, the designers wanted to keep the openness of the two-story living room yet take advantage of an odd-shaped space on the top floor. The designers had a four-foot-wide subway-grating bridge installed to connect the master bedroom to the space,

which is now a glass-walled study. Although the spaces between the railings of the bridge have been left open, the four-foot width inspires confidence.

In the second apartment, which occupies a floor and a half, a spiral stair, shown on page 138, links the living room and the upstairs mezzanine. A stock metal spiral stair was altered to curve around, then reach the top floor in a straight run. The adjacent wall niche was mirrored to reflect light from a skylight.

For other multilevel schemes, see pages 108 to 113, and 132 to 135.

In a brownstone renovation by Stedila Design, a bridge connects the bedroom to a study, far left. In a loft by architect Frederick Lee, a spiral stair links the bedroom to the bathroom, above.

Gilles de Chabaneix

A wooden stair was assembled from a mail-order kit for this Long Island house, above. A metal spiral stair was altered with wooden treads, right. Architect Peter Coan had a functional white metal stair installed in a Manhattan loft, far right.

Robert Levin

Gilles de Chabaneix

Ordering spiral stairs

Spiral stairs require approximately one-third the space that would be taken up by a conventional stairway. Sources include:

• American Ornamental Metal Company of Austin, Route 3, Box 136-B, Volente Road, Leander, Tex. 78641; 512-258-2227 or 713-692-5931.

• American Stair Corporation, 1 American Stair Plaza, Willow Springs, Ill. 60480; 312-839-5880.

• Duvinage Corporation, Box 828, Hagerstown, Md. 21740; 301-733-8255. Sales office: Spiral Stairs, 240 Grand Avenue, P.O. Box 285, Leonia, N.J. 07605; 201-944-6650.

• Logan Company, a division of ATO, 200 Cabel Street, Louisville, Ky. 42026; 502-587-1361.

• Studio Stair, by American General Products, 1735 Holmes Road, Ypsilanti, Mich. 48197; 313-483-1833.

• Woodbridge Stairways, by Woodbridge Ornamental Iron Company, 2715 North Claybourne Avenue, Chicago, Ill. 60614; 312-935-1500.

• The Iron Shop, Department 595, Box 128, 400 Reed Road, Broomall, Pa. 19008; 215-544-7100.

Raeanne Giovanni

Raeanne Giovanni

Robert Perron

Peter Fine

Security in open spaces

No matter what the dramatic possibilities of large open spaces, inevitably there are those who still need a small, secure place in which to retreat—to sleep, to read, to relax. Designers and loft-dwellers are particularly adept at devising such intensely private environments, which may range from a tiny mini-library to a soaring indoor pyramid structure. Some of these special spaces are more temporary than others; some are created for sheer visual effect rather than function. But all in all they allow for privacy and meditation and encapsulate the idea of a house within a house.

Designer Peter Stamberg devised a translucent tent for a bedroom, top left. Textile artist Moki Cherry designed a "truck" bedroom for son Eagle-Eye, top right. Byron Bell in his cube-like library, far left. Peter Fine's glass-doored bedroom has cloud-decorated walls, left center. Artist Diana Carulli's flowing sail-like veils are environmental partitions, left.

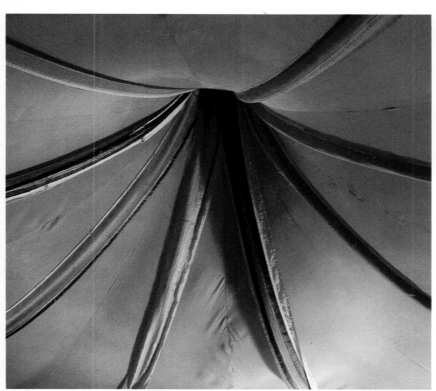

Indoor tent: private bedroom

Future Tents, a pioneer firm in the relatively unexplored field of fabric structures, has designed many outdoor structures for concert pavilions, exhibition halls, and circuses. But the company's partners—Todd Dalland, his brother Ross, Nicholas Goldsmith, and Denis Hector—have also experimented on a smaller scale with a different kind of indoor tent design.

"Tents no longer have to prove themselves," said Goldsmith. "We want to say, 'Yes, they stand up, but now you can make architecture with them.'"

While it is not unknown to use tents indoors, their recent interior projects, including a bedroom enclosure, are unusual applications of their theories, and have allowed the group, which is based in lower Manhattan, to turn its attention to projects that have more practical applications on a day-to-day basis.

"Our tensile structures are directly descended from traditional tents," said Ross Dalland. "But until now, seldom has tent design dealt

with the traditional architectural considerations of scale and decoration." He also felt that much of the appeal of tensile structures is in their ability to assume complex shapes and offer dramatic effects.

Goldsmith had the opportunity to experiment with a tent shape when he moved into an empty loft and needed a separate, and warm, bedroom. He decided on a tent bedroom chamber—the shape of which was determined in the same way the shape of a large-scale structure would be. A machine that used soap film demonstrated in a miniature space the ideal form for the tent. A computer was used to match the form and determine the cutting pattern for the fabric tent. Made of cotton duck with a silk and rayon interlining, the tent is more than a bed. It is a 10-foot-square room that provides a sense of enclosure and security. At a cost of about $2,500, it suggests a return to the canopied beds of past centuries as well as a revival of a voluptuous interior sense of fabric.

For an open loft, Future Tents devised a tensile structure suspended from the ceiling to create a private bedroom chamber, opposite left. Detail of the roof of the tent structure is above.

Photographs by Robert Perron

The loft divided: once and again

The first time the architect looked at the loft, he saw that the strongest feature of the sixty-foot-long and twenty-foot-wide space—a long line of windows— was not being played to its best advantage. "The secret of making a relatively small space feel big is to allow one to see a long way," explained Yann Weymouth of Redroof Design, who with his partner, Peter Coan, restructured Gerald Sussman and Elaine Louie's West Village loft.

What the architects came up with was a new circulation pattern for the long, narrow space, one that allows the occupants to get from one end to the other in more than one way. A central structure with a series of sliding pocket doors was built. With the doors pushed back into their recesses, two long hallways are created: one along the windows, the other connecting the kitchen to the living area. The bedroom—actually just a bed cantilevered between two walls—was situated opposite the dressing room and close to the bathroom.

With the doors open, the loft becomes a series of small, train-like compartments, which afford a necessary and flexible system of private and open spaces. Because Louie specializes in Chinese cooking, the kitchen was centered around the stove and left open to the dining and living areas. A small space was carved out to provide a private work area for the occupants, both of whom are writers.

But suddenly, the unexpected news of an impending arrival—Anna Louie Sussman—made the about-to-be parents reconsider their about-to-be-finished renovation. The architects were recalled. "Soundproofing became very important," Weymouth explained. "Luckily, we were able to borrow space at one end for two small but separate work cubicles, and turned what was the office into a tiny baby's room, conveniently close to the parents' bedroom."

Robert Levin

In a loft by Redroof Design, the kitchen has been left open to the living and dining areas and lined with a series of shelves. A stainless steel hood allows for high heat cooking.

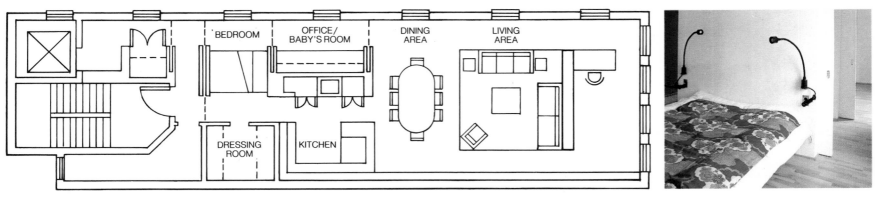

BEDROOM OFFICE/ DINING LIVING
BABY'S ROOM AREA AREA

DRESSING KITCHEN
ROOM

Photographs by Gilles de Chabaneix

146

Making room for baby Anna

For the arrival of baby Anna Louie Sussman, above, the loft had to be rearranged further. Since both the occupants are writers who work mainly at home, the architects borrowed space near the windows at one end to create two separate small offices. Gerald Sussman's is totally soundproofed with double walls and insulation in between. An oval door, similar to those used in submarines, adds to the airtightness of the small space. Meanwhile, the baby is ensconced in the former work area, which is conveniently located near her parents' bedroom. Eventually, it is planned that she will move into one of the new office spaces, where she will be able to play her stereo as loudly as she wants and entertain her friends without disturbing the rest of the household.

Plan of the loft, opposite top left. The bedroom, opposite top right, is cantilevered in the central structure. The dining area, opposite left, is close to the open kitchen. A long vista was created along the window wall, left.

150   **164**   **168**

Materials

190

The choice of materials is one of the most important decisions made in an interior. In few other areas can the designer or architect set off his talent as well as when he deals imaginatively with the finishing textures and colors.

Some designers are inspired by and drawn to a specific material because of its inherent properties—the suppleness and richness of leather, the crispness of shredded paper, the texture of stucco. Tile, mirror, and vinyl—all ordinary decorating materials by reputation—are attracting new consideration and are being reinterpreted in ways that offer a more economical means of producing a customized look.

New problems also inspire new uses; translucent glass block, for example, once used nearly exclusively for exterior architectural applications, is becoming an important light refracting source for interior partitions and enclosures.

The postmodernist movement has had an impact on the use of such traditional materials as marble, granite, and plaster. As columns, pediments, and archways are being praised for their decorative and evocative qualities, the materials associated with these classical elements are also being celebrated.

This interest has extended even to reproductions, with trompe l'oeil artists much in demand and a growing popularity for plastic laminates that copy stone finishes. This avant-garde predilection for the frankly fake has cheerfully confused the boundaries of what are, in terms of interior design, good and bad taste.

A solid scheme in stone

For designers who revamp high-rise city apartments, a commission often includes the mandate to create a distinctive and luxurious dwelling from a space that has little, beyond its location and availability, to justify its astronomical price. The Manhattan duplex apartment shown here had, however, the advantages of an extraordinary view plus owners with open minds and an ample budget with which to address the problem.

The challenge of transforming the small, low-ceilinged rooms into a unique, sumptuous home was the responsibility of Michael Schaible and Robert Bray, a design team who, during the 1970s, established a name for themselves with minimalism, a something-out-of-nothing esthetic that, at least in this country, became synonymous with glossy white walls, gray commercial carpeting, and platforms.

"The space was claustrophobic and shoddily constructed," said Schaible, recalling the apartment before its redesign. "But because of its location on the Upper East Side, it was very expensive. Frankly, except for the view, it had nothing you could call luxurious."

"The windows were wonderful," Bray added, "but there were no vistas—nowhere that one could stand back more than fifteen feet."

Especially when contrasted with the designers' earlier work, their wholesale renovation of this apartment is a series of surprises. First, it is a complex, lavish scheme that bears little resemblance to minimalism. Second, its primary material is pink stone, a durable variety called Kasota that is native to Min-

The entrance view of a stark interior landscape, with sloping walls of Kasota stone, offers no clue to the use of the space by designers Robert Bray and Michael Schaible.

Behind the stone walls are pillowed banquettes and stone-topped tables, above right. Electronic controls are incorporated into sleek, black units, above. In the living room, the stone slabs are on slanted walls, far right.

nesota. Finally, this stone, which is most often used for building exteriors, is employed as though it were paneling or veneer. It covers the floors, the bathroom, most of the tabletops, and especially the sloping, freestanding partitions in the living area. "Everything these days is so flimsily made," said Bray, "that we decided to do the opposite—rip out all the frail, current building materials and rely on a solid material for the design."

Because the ceiling height was only eight and a half feet, the designers decided to reshape and open up the space, by removing all the nonload-bearing walls and punctuating the ceiling with cutouts and mirrors to give an illusion of extra height. Soundproofing was

installed under the floor, and all the elaborate wiring was concealed in the ceiling.

But the owners wanted more than simply an apartment restyled to meet the needs of their family, their entertaining schedule, and their art collection. They also wanted drama. This Bray-Schaible achieved with an extravagant, bold scheme, an interior landscape that, at first glance, seems desolate, nearly lunar in reference. "It's the transition areas that are awesome," observed Bray. "They create a great mystery." The entrance, for example, offers a monolithic view of sloping walls that form a tunnel, as if one were entering a shrine. It is an effect that has been referred to as "a minitemple of Dendur."

Qualities of the pink stone

Kasota stone is a kind of limestone that is mined in Minnesota. It is softer than both marble and granite and is cleaned with soap and water. It can take a rough-grain or sawn finish, be honed with a 120-grit stone, or rubbed—for a more eggshell-like texture, similar to that shown here. The price ranges from $40 to $45 a square foot installed. Two sources are:
● Fordham Marble Company, 1931-1933 West Farms Road, Bronx, N.Y. 10460; 212-893-3380.
● Furlong and Lee, 41 East 42nd Street, New York, N.Y. 10017; 212-986-3828.

Photographs by Jaime Ardiles-Arce

In the master bed-room, slabs of the same pink stone are used for an oversize oval desk top, above. In one bathroom, the floor, counter top, and bathtub are all of Kasota stone, far right.

"The idea was to create a series of real contrasts," explained Schaible. To this end, the designers used spatial effects—"the contrast of the big open spaces to the small, intimate ones." Then, on a more subtle level, they juxtaposed the hardness and grainy texture of the stone with the softness and smoothness of the canvas that upholsters the seating banquettes, which are tucked behind the freestanding stone walls. It is not as rigid a design as one might expect from a scheme executed in stone; there is a surprising feeling of relaxation, even serenity, to the apartment.

And there is an undeniable sense of luxury to the space. Upstairs in the master bathroom, the stone tub was carved, sloped, and tapered to be comfortable, and set under the window to take advantage of the spectacular view. "Just a pure luxury," said Bray.

Linen: a natural solution

He calls linen "the sexiest of fabrics." She is more taken with its practical qualities. So when the Italian designers Massimo and Lella Vignelli renovated their Manhattan apartment, they used linen throughout the house. Walls, bookshelves, blinds, drapes, upholstery, platforms, bedcovers, pillows, and cabinetry have all been made of or covered with the same natural fiber—a total of about four hundred and fifty yards of linen.

"Linen can be wrinkled without losing elegance," Vignelli said, and elegance was an important factor for the couple, whose new apartment combined dramatic spaces with intimate ones. Smaller private rooms juxtaposed to soaring public ones offered a variety of spatial experiences. And, while the designers wanted a unity of color, they were intrigued with the range of possibilities in the different rooms.

The Vignellis also faced a range of design problems, however. The two-story apartment, on a street with a fire station, was noisy; the old windows leaked so badly that heat and air-conditioning were inefficient, the bedrooms were small and undistinguished. But, apart from turning the staircase around, the Vignellis were reluctant to make any architectural changes. Instead, they alleviated their problems by exploring the various uses of linen fabric. Because the spaces are large, the Vignellis said, they couldn't afford to have all the walls covered in natural linen. "When we had to retrench," Vignelli said, "we did only half in linen." In the double-height living room, for example, they used sand paint on the walls, colored to match the linen-covered walls elsewhere. Other rooms had walls covered in stucco. "These would have needed to be completely resurfaced," he said. "It was cheaper and faster to cover it all up." The guest room, facing a courtyard, was small and dark. Vignelli decided to have the ceiling lowered,

In the guest bedroom of their Manhattan duplex, designers Lella and Massimo Vignelli have used natural linen fabric on the walls, as well as for the tented ceiling, curtains, bedcovers, and headboards.

but instead of dropping a flat ceiling he had a tented one created. The curtained room has a linen-covered headboard and vertical blinds and linen bedcovers.

The fabric was padded and then stapled to the wall, primarily for sound absorption. In the master bedroom, the window curtain is quilted, and the walls and ceiling look as if they are. "They're not," Mrs. Vignelli confided. Because the room has many built-in cabinets and doors, a more complicated treatment was chosen. The linen fabric was made up into individual strips, but not all exactly the same sizes so that the breaks at the doors are not obvious visually.

For the library, the couple had slotted metal bookshelf standards put on the walls and then padding inserted between them. Then linen was stretched across the entire wall and the standards. The bookshelves themselves were also covered in linen and hung on brackets attached to the standards through the fabric. "Because linen doesn't absorb dirt," Mrs. Vignelli said, "we only had to put a piece of glass on the lowest shelf, where people put their drinks down." The low plywood platforms were also covered in linen, and the soft seating was upholstered in linen. "You get a good feeling of sitting down in a softly lit place that's very intimate," Vignelli said.

In addition to linen's characteristic of absorbing very little dirt, durability was also a factor. "Belgian linen will last forever," said Mrs. Vignelli, who researched the material when she designed the upholstery for St. Peter's Church in Manhattan's Citicorp building. "But for apparel," she added, "Italian linen is the best."

Photographs by Norman McGrath

Putting linen material to use

The greatest amount of linen flax, one of the oldest cultivated natural fibers, is produced in Belgium, but it is also grown in Ireland, France, Poland, Italy, and England. Ireland has traditionally specialized in linen that was treated to be crease-resistant, but the popularity of the "wrinkled look" has made untreated linen a viable alternative for both fashion and home applications. Linen is less dust-absorbing than cotton and less costly than wool.

Covering walls and ceilings with linen fabric is a job done by upholsterers, and the installation costs can more than equal the cost of the fabric yardage, which runs from $12 to $35 a yard for plain fabric, and up to $99 a yard for finely embroidered material. For better sound insulation, the linen can be padded and then stapled to the wall, rather than glued directly to the surface.

Linen, available in different weights, is often blended with cotton, or sometimes with polyester. Quality and cost depend on coarseness of weave. Sources for 100 percent linen, through architects and designers, include Brunschwig & Fils, 979 Third Avenue, New York, N.Y.; 212-838-7878, and Vice Versa, 979 Third Avenue, New York, N.Y.; 212-477-9877.

Information can be obtained by writing to the International Linen Promotion Commission, 280 Madison Avenue, New York, N.Y. 10016; 212-685-0424.

Strips of padded linen cover the walls, cabinets, and ceiling in the master bedroom, far left. In the library, above, the walls were done in linen, as were the bookshelves, platforms, and upholstery.

Visual play with one-way mirror

It was a rather ordinary one-bedroom apartment, but it featured a bright living room with a large window and a small dining area. Alan Buchsbaum and German Martinez, two architects with Design Coalition, the firm that took on the renovation, felt that the space needed a striking design feature. So they installed a large piece of one-way mirror between the living room and dining room.

One-way mirror is the translucent, reflective glass usually used in institutions, supermarkets, and, when specially treated for weather protection, on the exteriors of modern office buildings. The material is rarely used in residences. In this interior, the glass was hung from the ceiling as a partition between the living room and the dining room. Depending on the time of day and the amount of light in each room, the panel reflects or lets one see through to the adjacent space —creating a somewhat disorienting but still intriguing partial view of the furniture in both rooms.

In general, the side of the glass that is brighter is the more reflective and mirrorlike; the darker side is more transparent. If the light is equally bright on both sides, the glass looks the same on both surfaces. "But," Buchsbaum explained, "during the day, because the living room is very bright, that side is always mirrorlike. And if you turn on

A six-foot-high, eight-foot-wide panel of one-way mirror that is both reflective and transparent hangs between the dining and living areas, right. Reflection detail, above.

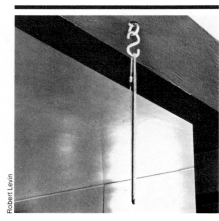

Hanging the mirror

Installation of the unwieldy two-way mirror usually requires professional assistance. In the project shown here, two sections, totaling six feet in height and eight feet in width, were needed. Because it was to be hung from the ceiling with crimp hooks, holes were drilled in the tempered glass. Because it would not be surrounded by a frame, the edges had to be polished to remove any rough spots. Called Mirropane, the two-way mirror is manufactured by Liberty Mirror, a division of Libbey-Owens-Ford, 851 Third Avenue, Brackenridge, Pa. 15104; 412-224-1800. It can be ordered through any local glass supplier. Depending on special requirements, such as polishing and drilling, you may spend about $20 a square foot.

When the dining room side is darker, one can see through to the living room, while dining chairs and lamps are reflected in the glass, right.

a light in the dining room, then that light can also be seen through the mirror." The installation is most effective at night, and all the lamps are on dimmers, Buchsbaum said, "so that one can play with the transparencies and reflections."

Ordinary mirror glass was used in the cabinet doors in the living room to create even more reflections. Painting the walls in darker or lighter tones also heightened the play of light in the apartment. The space consisted of a dark, long entryway that opened onto three areas: dining room, living room, and bedroom. "We assigned a color to each area that was meant to reflect its actual situation," Buchsbaum said. "So the dark hallway was painted black, the dim dining room gray, and the bright, light-filled living room white."

"The mirror reinforces the division we wanted to create between the living and the dining areas. It's very conceptual," added Martinez. The abstract quality that resulted from the changing quality of light in the apartment did not end with the mirror.

In the living room, there is a seemingly disjunctive assemblage of furniture; "Nothing is the same color," Buchsbaum said of the furniture. For the dining room, Buchsbaum designed a pear-shaped, polished green marble table. "We thought the apartment was getting too serious," said the architect. "But, when you do something a little silly," he said, referring to the fruit shape, "you have to contrast it with a textured and grained material like marble to bring it off.

"When you walk into this apartment, you somehow forget about ordinary things, like asking where the kitchen is," added the architect. The overall effect and the surreal qualities created by the use of the mirror reminded him of the work of the painter René Magritte. "That was accidental," said a pleased Mr. Buchsbaum.

A flair
for paper
designs

In designer
Jim McWilliams's
small Manhattan
duplex, shredded
waste paper is
hung in bales on
the walls in the
living room, right,
and dining room,
far right. The cof-
fee table, above
right, is made of
stacks of colored
paper, topped
with glass.

In his small apartment, with its bright palette and comfortably mismatched chairs, Jim McWilliams, a designer, has meticulously illustrated the possibilities of using paper "without being boring about it."

His seemingly whimsical uses of paper are meant to be taken seriously, even as they poke fun at some accepted forms of interior design. "I wanted to have people get excited about the different kinds of paper," he said, "and to show how paper comes in lots of colors and textures and has never been replaced by any synthetics." McWilliams's past association with a paper manufacturer gave him access to all the raw material he needed; the paper he worked with is treated to be flame-retardant.

In one corner of the living room stands his paper interpretation of a palm tree. "What all artificial trees should look like," he decreed. "And much easier to maintain." For a low table, McWilliams placed stacks of eighteen-inch-square pieces of different colored paper on small wood skids and topped each stack with a square piece of glass. "It can be moved in small increments," he explained. "I've drawn a pattern for my housekeeper so that when it's moved it can be put back in the same way."

He has been known to tear off a piece of paper from a large roll, jump on it, squash it, fold it, and sculpt it into a lamp shade. "It's surprisingly stable," he explained. One of the apartment's most startling design elements is the cascading series of large paper pieces on the living room wall. "It's what I think of when I hear the word 'wallpaper,'" said McWilliams, referring to the huge accumulations of paper strips that are gray on one side and white on the other.

In one of the most appealing applications, there are tiny square bits of paper strewn over the floor—scattered like confetti after a sum-mer wedding. "The new wood floor had none of the spirit of the paper," he recalled. So he painted the floor with high-quality gray deck paint; special confetti, made out of half-inch squares in ten pastel shades, was strewn on it while the paint was still wet. As the top layer gets dirty, McWilliams vacuums up the loose multi-colored pieces of paper and sprinkles on a new supply, kept conveniently at hand in a glass bowl on a nearby table.

"For a while I was looking for ways to protect the floor surface," he said. "After a while I realized that the paint is more likely to chip than the paper."

Paper Projects

Paper for most of designer Jim McWilliams's projects can be obtained from any wholesale paper merchant or printer. In New York City, Allan & Gray, 111 Eighth Avenue, New York, N.Y. 10011, (212) 741-5522, carries a wide selection of paper.

• To make the table: Have heavyweight paper cut in sheets and stacked. There is usually a minimum purchase of $50; trimming costs $5. The stacks are placed on skids (look in the Yellow Pages under Pallets and Skids). Glass or clear plastic can top the stacks.

• For the confetti: Have the paper cut into half-inch squares before sprinkling on the floor.

• For wall bales: Made from shredded waste paper, the bales are usually packaged in two-and-a-half-inch cubes.

• For the palm tree: Telescope a roll of wall paper for the trunk, then tear off large sections from another roll and insert them into the top for the drooping branches.

• To fireproof: Spray the paper with aerosol fireproofing spray. Because of their density, the wall bales are naturally fireproof and do not need to be sprayed.

In the living room, far left, bunches of paper cascade from the wall. The painted floor is sprinkled with small squares of pastel-colored paper, above left and left.

Clear choice: glass block

Slightly curved glass block shower enclosure was designed and built by architect Parker Zaner Bloser for the spacious bathroom of his Manhattan loft.

Glass block is a material that has for decades had a special appeal to designers and architects. As an element that is both structural and decorative, it lends itself to either exterior or interior applications. Because of its translucent quality it is often used as a window, creating a changing pattern of light between the outside of a house and its interior.

Despite the fact that there are few remaining manufacturers of the material, glass block has enjoyed a renaissance in the loft interior. The necessity of building partition walls while maximizing the light from distant windows has encouraged its use, and designers tend to turn to glass block particularly when planning bathrooms. It is suitable for bath and shower enclosures, and the material provides a functional yet esthetically pleasing wall.

While the square is the most common shape, rectangular and curved blocks allow for unusual configurations. The translucent blocks are also available in a range of patterns, from a wavy to a carved-glass surface.

For another application of glass block, see page 56.

Robert Levin

Robert Levin

**Giuseppe Zambo-
nini used glass
block to frame
the doorway, right,
and as an interior
window in a loft
bathroom, above.
Curved wall of
glass block in a
room by Charles
Boxenbaum, far
right, acts as a
dramatic light
source.**

Glass block sources

There are only a few companies
that still manufacture glass block.
Two that do are:

• Circle Redmont, 819 East Main
Street, Stamford, Conn. 06902; 203-
323-2103. This company sells made-
to-order concrete and aluminum
frame panels. Concrete costs $35 to
$40 a square foot, while aluminum
costs $110 for a one-by-six-foot
area, about $420 for a six-by-six-
foot area.

• Pittsburgh Glass and Block
Company, 2100 Babcock Boulevard, Pittsburgh, Penn. 15237; 412-
821-4940. Preassembles loose
blocks into given measurements,
then prepares the window and in-
stalls the glass. Costs are about
$130 for a two-by-four-foot area,
$300 for a four-by-five-foot area.

Robert Levin

Stucco: texture in the rough

"We didn't want it to look luxurious," Charles Swerz said. "Admittedly the space is luxurious, but we think the 80s are not a time to show one's wealth." With Jerry Van Deelen, his partner in a space and lighting design firm, Swerz had come from sunny California to a dark, inhospitable space in New York City's garment district. They found an 1,800-square-foot space on top of an office building and "totally demolished" it to create a living/working space for the two designers. "Everything is new," Van Deelen said, "but we went to great lengths to hide that."

The bare, cool, gray space appears minimal, at first glance. But on further inspection, it presents a varied contrast and accumulation of textures—rough, cementlike walls; nubby upholstery; grainy carpeting; a slick, striated marble table. "The idea was to keep the living space in character with the experience of the city and the rest of the building—all cement and metal," Mr. Swerz said.

The inside-outside feeling is crucial to the interior, which plays on surfaces and textures. The open space, divided only by a curving, sloping wall, behind which the kitchen was installed, offers long vistas, devoid of domestic touches. The sleeping area, in an L-shaped space off the living area, is especially stark looking. A mattress has been simply placed on a carpet-upholstered platform, and a television set sits on the floor.

Nothing is as it seems. The gray industrial carpeting resembles a gravel walkway. The roughly surfaced walls look ageless and historic. The soft upholstered seating looks as if it was carved out of rock. The thick, solid legs of the marble dining table suggest that it was fixed in one position a long time ago. A stone statue, placed demurely between the elevator doors, might have been pinched from a Parisian park. The textured plaster on the walls and the ceiling is the space's main innovation. "It's called California stucco," said Van Deelen, who added that when they were finally able to find a plasterer, he kept insisting, "I don't take any responsibility for this."

The designers relied on lighting effects to change the mood of the space, installing separate light controls for each of the floor's areas. "I like to use elements that are available to everybody," said Van Deelen, who is the lighting specialist. "And to get special effects by assembling basic hardware items in a new way." So in the kitchen a slim light bulb is hung on a cord, while near the daybed, a similar bulb is plugged directly into the wall socket. At night, colored lights are plugged into the recessed ceiling plug mold to change the overall color and atmosphere of the living room area.

For friends and visitors, the space is controversial. Some say it feels too empty, too cold, too minimal; others ask about dankness and dampness as if the cavelike quality of the walls could in fact produce a climatic change. But then there are those who sense that there is something rarefied and special about the space—a serene, almost placid atmosphere that results from the rough, urban, concrete envelope the designers created. This is especially true when it's been tidied up. "That's when people say that it really looks as if humans couldn't possibly live here," Mr. Swerz said.

Photographs by Raeanne Giovanni

A gray-stuccoed space by Charles Swerz and Jerry Van Deelen is minimally furnished. The marble dining table is near work area, far left. Colored lights vary monochromatic scheme, above.

In the sleeping area, left, the emphasis was on textures: nubby fabric, grainy carpeting, and rough walls. The pink lighting and small television set on a stone column, above, contribute to surreal effect.

Photographs by Raeeanne Giovanni

In the kitchen, above, a rounded-edge plastic laminate counter sits behind a sweeping stucco partition. The formal seating arrangement is in the living area of the 1,800-square-foot loft, right.

Mixing stucco

To obtain the cementlike stucco, designers Charles Swerz and Jerry Van Deelen mixed together in a wheelbarrow one-half cup of lamp-black powdered dye for each fifty-pound bag of California stucco that was used. It is not necessary to mix the cement uniformly as the various shades of gray add to the character of its final appearance. Both California stucco and lamp-black powdered dye are generally available in local home improvement stores or lumberyards. Apply the cement mixture to walls and ceiling with a trowel. It will dry overnight. Leave the stucco unpainted for a modeled claylike quality. Cracks will form when the cement dries, giving the surfaces the desired stonelike look.

Inventive uses for mundane finishes

It seemed at first to be simply a perfect decorating job—glossy, glamorous rooms with mirror-lined walls, softly carpeted floors, and perfectly arranged furnishings. It is an interior similar to many other urban renovations—a slick living room, a small but efficient kitchen, and a sparse office/den that doubles as a guest room. But the designer, Juan Montoya, was making another point. His choice of materials and the way they were handled proved to be worth a second look. While the materials themselves were mundane, and not new to the current design vocabulary, what the designer chose to do with them was noteworthy.

The renovation of the apartment, in a turn-of-the-century building in Manhattan, hinged on a big square column that had once been part of a wall separating two rooms. Years ago, when the original apartment was divided into a smaller unit, the column became a freestanding element. Montoya was aware that, in this time of the postmodernist interior, a column was not a bad thing to have; many architects and designers have even installed them as decorative elements. "Why put something in a space if it doesn't belong there?" he asked. "Mine was there, so I had to confront it."

The designer tried to make a pattern around the square column, but that approach failed. "Too timid," he said. "My column wasn't doing anything." But when he decided to make it into a round element, "it got bigger and bigger," he exclaimed. Then he began thinking about the uses of hard and soft materials. "That's when I decided to use vinyl," he recalled. So the column was padded in Dacron and upholstered in vinyl. To avoid unsightly seams, he created black plastic laminate inserts. The client decided on the bright red color. The designer went along with it. "I have used red in the past," he explained. "I am not tired of it yet."

The lined, fifty-four-inch-wide vinyl material was also used by the designer to cover the apartment's door frames and on part of the wall separating the living room from the kitchen and hall. Its appeal derives both from its shine and its cushiony, resilient surface. The method of installation was the same as in furniture upholstery. "An expensive process, but it can be done," said the interior designer.

Montoya designed a table to be incorporated into the column, making it even more of a focal point. The tabletop looks like black lacquer, but it is actually black industrial glass, often used in laboratories, that has been edged in wood.

The treatment of the under-window banquette in the dining room is also unusual. Instead of lacquered wood, the frame was covered with plastic laminate, which was also used for the floor-to-ceiling storage wall in the small office. "Wood in a room that size would have been claustrophobic," Montoya said of the office. "Wood is a veneer, and so is plastic laminate. I like to use a material that's honest and that works." The hardware-free storage cabinets create a flat wall with an overall grid pattern. Each of the panels is a door, and office equipment and stereo components are stored behind them. The white plastic laminate was also chosen because of its shiny surface. "And this way, I'm sure the walls won't warp," Montoya added.

For the backs and seats of the banquette upholstery, Montoya chose a light gray chintz and had it quilted. "I wanted it to have a certain elegance," he explained. "And not to wrinkle." One has to touch the upholstery to make sure it is not leather, but chintz was not chosen as a cheaper solution. "I felt," the designer said, "that because one is used to seeing chintz on dainty Louis XV chairs, this would be a little unexpected. Who wants to have the expected?"

In an apartment by Juan Montoya, a black industrial glass tabletop extends from a structural column covered in shiny vinyl fabric. The banquette has a plastic laminate base and chintz upholstery.

Robert Levin

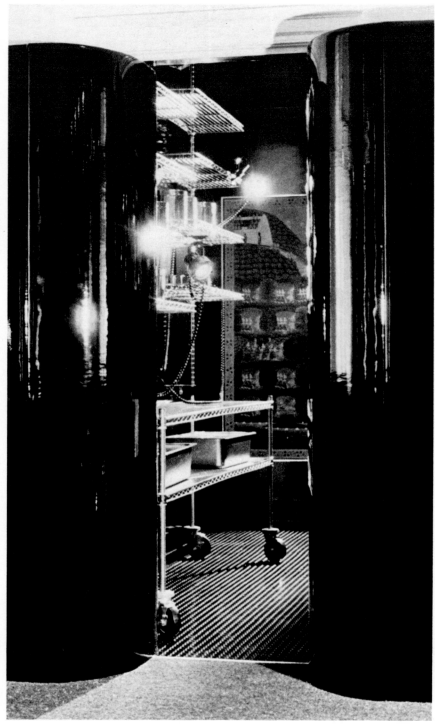

Industrial wire glass was used as a surface for the metal shelving units in the kitchen, above.

The door frame and the wall between the living room and kitchen, above, were covered in vinyl.

Office supplies and the stereo are kept in plastic laminate cabinets in the guest room, above.

Unexpected materials

Vinyl:
• J.M. Lynne Company Inc., 59 Gilpin Avenue, Hauppauge, N.Y. 11787; 516-582-4300 or 212-895-6222. Shiny vinyl is about $16 a yard.
• Janovic/Plaza, 1292 First Avenue, New York, N.Y. 10021; 212-744-3846. Shiny vinyl is $23 a yard.
• Wolf-Gordon Vinyl Fabrics, 132 West 31st Street, New York, N.Y. 10036; 212-255-3300. A to-the-trade source.

Wire and black industrial glass:
• A & C Glass Company, 1746 First Avenue, New York, N.Y. 10028; 212-534-1584. Industrial glass costs from $10 to $15 a square foot, wire glass a little bit less.
• Sundial Fabricators, 1491 First Avenue, New York, N.Y. 10021; 212-734-0838. Both types of glass range between $10 and $20 a square foot.

Solid-colored chintz:
• Clarence House, 40 East 57th Street, New York, N.Y. 10022; 212-752-2890. Through designers and architects.
• Etalage, 979 Third Avenue, New York, N.Y. 10022; 212-752-0120. Eighty colors available through designers and architects.
• Lee/Jofa, 979 Third Avenue, New York, N.Y. 10022; 212-889-3900. Plain chintz from $22 list a yard, through designers and architects.

Plastic laminate:
The most common trade names for plastic laminate are Formica, Wilsonart, Nevamar, and Lamin-Art—all available at lumberyards, home building centers, and custom cabinet shops. Two sources in the New York area are:
• Design Supply, 134 Morgan Avenue, Brooklyn, N.Y. 11237; 212-497-3700.
• Laminator's Supply, 6303 Fifth Avenue, Brooklyn, N.Y. 11220; 212-745-4540.

Shiny plastic vinyl comes in a range of colors and offers practical and inventive possibilities.

Finding a variety of imported tiles

Imported ceramic tile ranges from about $2.75 to $4.50 a square foot, and most tile installation begins at about $3 a square foot. Below are sources for both domestic and imported tiles. Prices quoted are per square foot.

• Amsterdam Corporation, 750 Third Avenue, New York, N.Y. 10021; 212-644-1350.

• Country Floors, 300 East 61st Street, New York, N.Y. 10021; 212-758-7414. Imported, hand-painted tiles from $2.80 to $15.

• Hastings Tile and Il Bagno Collection, 964 Third Avenue (trade showroom), New York, N.Y. 10021; 212-755-2710, and 404 Northern Boulevard, Great Neck, N.Y. 11021; 516-482-1840. Specializes in Italian tiles; from $4 to $7.

• American Olean Tile Co., 150 East 58th Street, New York, N.Y. 10021; 212-683-1177. Wall and floor tiles, Tuscany tiles, ceramic mosaics, and quarry tile, from $2.

• Agency Tile Inc., 979 Third Avenue, New York, N.Y. 10021; 212-832-8193 and 430 East Westfield Avenue, Roselle Park, N.J. 07204; 201-245-3020. Italian tiles from $2 to $14.

• Ceramica Mia, 405 East 51st Street, New York, N.Y. 10022; 212-759-2339. Italian tiles from $4.50.

• Rico Tile, 979 Third Avenue, New York, N.Y. 10021; 212-755-6590. To-the-trade source for imported tile.

• Tile Selections by Amaru, 961 Third Avenue, New York, N.Y. 10021; 212-755-3818, and 400 Northern Boulevard, Great Neck, N.Y. 11021; 516-487-4750.

• Design-Technics Ceramics, 160 East 56th Street, New York, N.Y. 10022; 212-355-3183.

• Quarry Enterprises, 183 Lexington Avenue, New York, N.Y. 10016; 212-679-2559. About sixteen hundred samples of American and imported tiles; wall tiles from $1.40; imported ceramic tiles from $2.50.

• Vedovato Brothers, 246 East 116th Street, New York, N.Y. 10029; 212-534-2854. Wall tiles from $1.80; floor tiles from $1.95.

• Tile Distributors Inc., 275 Madison Avenue, New York, N.Y. 10016; 212-792-0900. Ceramic tile from $1.50.

• Nemo Tile Inc., 177-02 Jamaica Avenue, Jamaica, N.Y. 11432; 212-291-5969. European and American tiles from $.50 to $20.

• Tilerama, 156-40 Grossbey Boulevard, Howard Beach, N.Y. 11414; 212-843-6622. Italian tiles from about $1.90 to $4.50.

• Mondial Tiles Inc., 1492 65th Street, Brooklyn, N.Y. 11219; 212-232-0800.

• Parma Tile Co., 14-38 Astoria Boulevard, Long Island City, N.Y. 11102; 212-278-3060. Italian wall tiles, from $1.75 each.

• Bari Tile and Ceramics Inc., 1748 86th Street, Brooklyn, N.Y. 11214; 212-837-3500.

• Crown Tile, 4722 Sunrise Highway, Massapequa Park, N.Y. 11762; 516-798-2457. About nine hundred American and imported tiles; $1.50 to $10.

• Canco Tiles Inc., 801 Old Country Road, Westbury, N.Y. 11590; 516-334-5700; 853 West Main Street, Riverhead, N.Y. 11901; 516-727-1034; 1050 Portion Road, Farmingville, N.Y. 11738; 516-736-0770; and 223 Main Street, Westhampton, N.Y. 11977; 516-288-2233. American, South American, and imported tiles from about $1.50.

• United Ceramic Tile, 1992 East Jericho Turnpike, East Northport, N.Y. 11731; 516-499-7801; 61 East Sunrise Highway, Lindenhurst, N.Y. 11757; 516-888-5550. More than two thousand items from $1 to $14.

• Maxsam Sales Inc., 2 Claire Road, East Brunswick, N.J. 08816; 201-238-2700.

• Joseph Fuda Tile Co., 157 West Fort Lee Road, Bogota, N.J. 07603; 201-342-8200. Imports from $1.35.

Robert Levin

Toying with tile

There are, realistically, few opportunities in the world of designer-and-client relationships for budget-free tiling schemes. Price and high installation costs tend to make tile applications a luxury.

If given the chance, there are few designers who would not jump at the opportunity of doing whatever they pleased with tile—including unusual combinations of colors and shapes; contrasting grout; oversize square tiles; and floor tiles used on walls, platforms, and mantels.

When Allen Scruggs and Douglas Myers of Scruggs-Myers & Associates were given a free rein to design a room for an Italian tile promotion, they remembered a summer picnic in the Italian countryside. "There was a wonderful house in the distance, and we wanted to re-create that memory indoors in a stylized way," said Scruggs. Their design is a dining room with a fourteen-foot-long mural of Cerdisa tile, in which the glazed and decorated tiles, combined with terra cotta and navy blue tiles, have been cut into various shapes and composed into an abstract geometric design, suggesting a window opening, a balustrade, and a crown molding. Along with a picnic basket and a bottle of wine, the designers placed an ant farm on the trompe l'oeil marble table. "What's a picnic without ants?" asked Myers.

Allen Scruggs and Douglas Myers had tiles cut out for dining room walls, left.

Fake marble finishes

Jane Kaplowitz and Robert Rosenblum had a twenty-foot-long cabinet in glossy onyx laminate made for their living room.

A pale blue
marbleized plastic
laminate was
used for the doors
in an apartment
dressing room,
right.

Interior designers and architects have been faking it for quite a while—faking materials like marble, granite, and onyx. But now, instead of being associated only with traditional grand interiors, illusionistic surfaces are being championed by the more avant-garde designers.

Postmodernism has boosted the popularity of the past, so that even minimalist designers look differently at ornamentation—adding a Greek column or two, reproducing the patterns of Italian marble, or finding a place for a classical statue. Classical references are also a way to give a touch of elegance or a humorous note to interiors done on a limited budget.

Surprisingly, the stone patterns once popular only for bathroom vanities are now favored for their frankly undisguised fake look. Plastic laminates, including those in the newly developed grid patterns and pastel, metallic, and textured surfaces, offer architects and designers a way to extend the limits of acceptable design and have a bit of fun at the same time. "I would call it the Coney Island School of design," said Alan Buchsbaum, an architect with Design Coalition, a New York firm. "Often, it has to do with being a deliberate mismatch; a kind of tongue-in-cheek design."

"We wanted something new and different, but didn't want to spend a lot of money," said Susan Silverman, who with her husband, Stuart, hired Peter Maase to redo their 1,250-square-foot residence in Mahattan. With the couple doing most of the painting, $16,000 was spent on the project, including furniture, cabinetwork, the faux finishes, and all the materials.

"The clients were unclear as to what they wanted, and I didn't have any ideas about what to do there," admitted the thirty-two-year-old interior designer. But the Silvermans' plaster bust reminded Mr. Maase of Italy, as did the high

Architect Charles Boxenbaum specified an onyx-like, matte-finish laminate for the work island and shelves of a loft kitchen, above.

Fake marble plastic laminate sources

Many plastic laminate reproductions of stone and marble finishes are available. Formica, Wilsonart, Lamin-Art, Westinghouse, and Nevamar are some of the trade names that are widely available at lumberyards, home building centers, and custom cabinet shops. The cost is about $1 to $1.50 a square foot.

Plastic laminates are veneers and are usually applied to cabinetry as specified by an architect or designer. Although it is quite possible for a do-it-yourselfer to apply

the plastic laminate on, for example, a plywood cabinet top, it usually requires a bit of practice to learn how to cut the veneer neatly. A router or a laminate trimmer will be required. Two sources are:
• Design Supply, 134 Morgan Avenue, Brooklyn, N.Y. 11237; 212-497-3700. Standard textured finishes, $1.35 a square foot; standard gloss finishes, from $1.65 a square foot.
• Laminator's Supply, 6303 Fifth Avenue, Brooklyn, N.Y.; 212-745-4540. Fake marble plastic laminate, about $.90 a square foot.

ceilings, pronounced beams, and a row of large windows. So Mr. Maase hired David Fisch, an artist who specializes in classical imitation, to paint a few of the surfaces to look like different kinds of marble and stone. The designer also had half of the floor area covered with a black-and-white vinyl tile, chosen because it looked like marble terrazzo. A sliding door looks like a rolling slab of marble, and a free-standing bar has a porphyrylike surface and painted black marble trim.

Mr. Maase added a floor-to-ceiling column near the entrance and had it painted to look like blue-gray granite. "It is meant to set people up, to stop them as they come in, and to create a foyer," he said. Although the faux finishes are decorative, the idea was to use them to make inexpensive materials seem more substantial. The "black marble" sliding panel that closes off the bedroom and bathroom is a hollow-core door and the bar is made of chipboard. "Although it's brittle, it's an underused material," said Mr. Maase. "I see it as terrazzo made out of wood."

In another project, Robert Rosenblum, an art historian and critic, observed, "We're not living in seventeenth-century Rome, but in late twentieth-century America. This is the age of reproduction and it's vulgar and witless to show real materials. Instead of thinking that plastic laminate is chintzy, why not make it classy?"

So he and his wife, Jane Kaplowitz, a painter, chose green-onyx-pink-veined patterned laminate in a shiny finish for a custom-made, twenty-foot cabinet in their living room. "I like anything that's fake—and it's very practical," Kaplowitz said, noting that the surface could not be marred by the couple's toddler, Sophie. "Once installed, you don't have to think about it," she explained. Some of their friends suggested that the couple would tire quickly of the onyx pattern. "Absolutely not," said Ms. Kaplowitz. "It's things like beige I get tired even thinking about."

Durability and cost were the reasons for Charles Boxenbaum's choice of a marble-patterned Formica plastic laminate for a loft kitchen work island and shelves. The architect chose the material because the space was large, the budget was small, and the pattern had a lot of detail. The architect was sensitive to the reproduction quality of the marble itself. "It's just another surface," he said. "But there are just few affordable materials that have any visual interest. People shouldn't look at it as a substitute for the real thing, but as an alternative when you can't afford to do it real," Boxenbaum said.

Artists who can fake it

The following artists can create the illusion of marble with paint. Prices vary, with $30 a square foot a low-to-average figure.
• David Fisch, 550 West 43rd Street, New York, N.Y. 10036; 212-695-0912. A muralist who specializes in architectural trompe l'oeil, including painted marble surfaces.
• Robert Jackson, 498 West End Avenue, New York, N.Y. 10024; 212-873-1920. A muralist who works only on through-the-trade commissions. In addition to trompe l'oeil marble, the artist specializes in architectural illusion.
• Louis Molina, 401 East 62nd Street, New York, N.Y. 10021; 212-751-1148. An artist who paints several finishes in addition to fake marble, including trompe l'oeil woods, stones, and malachite.
• Richard Lowell Neas, 157 East 71st Street, New York, N.Y. 10021; 212-772-1879. An artist who specializes in garden and floral motifs.

Tom Fox and Joey Nahem had a trompe l'oeil door frame painted in a Brooklyn house, far left. In loft by Peter Maase, below, columns, partitions, and sliding door, left, were painted by David Fisch.

Photographs by Robert Levin

Leather for zany designs

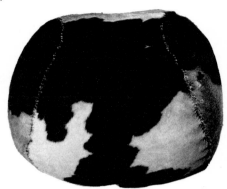

In Bobby Breslau's apartment, strange red, black, and silver, patterned, stenciled, stitched, and appliquéd objects—many with long, Medusalike fringes—are clustered in corners, piled around plants, or hung from the ceiling. One searches desperately for a point of reference. Africa and India come to mind, as well as a lunar landscape, a dense forest, or a lagoon. "Tropical Star Wars" was the way Issaye Miyake, the Japanese fashion designer, once described it. Many visitors, however, find themselves simply speechless.

For Breslau, a designer of fashion accessories, it all started more than ten years ago when Halston, the fashion designer, asked him to make a fringed toy and some fringed pillows. Breslau went out and bought a baseball and looked very closely at its construction. "Two pieces of leather stitched together to form a sphere with one continuous seam," he observed. "Actually two figure eights." He then made a pillow using leather that had been cut in the same pattern. "But instead of the finishing normally used on a baseball, I hand-fringed the pillow," explained the designer.

Fernando Sanchez, a fashion designer, mistook the pillow for a handbag. "So I put a strap on it and turned the concept into a handbag," Breslau said, and that unconstructed bag became the handbag of the 1970s. But while the handbags came to be mass-produced, the pillows remained at home. "It's a craft thing," the designer said. "They're each a one-of-a-kind object."

His first piece of furniture, made more than ten years ago, was a silver leather bag made up to ottoman-size. "I feel that, as far as the pillows are concerned, I'm a sculptor and that my medium is leather," Breslau said. "It's the play of textures against colors in which I'm interested, a suede against a glossy leather, or a bit of metallic that adds

Designer Bobby Breslau in his leather pillow strewn living room, left. An example of the type of pillows he has been making for the past twelve years, above.

In the bedroom, right, with its underwater mood, fringed rainbow-colored leather pillows hang from the ceiling or sit clustered on the white leather bedspread.

A piece of silver leather, cut out like a spider web, is stretched over a window, right. A bleached redwood table, far right, is surrounded by chairs with quilted silver leather pads. Stitched floor pillow, far right bottom, is another Breslau design.

Photographs by Robert Levin

depth to snakeskin." He works with a variety of leathers— printed suedes and ostrich skin, cowhide, bronze, and silver leathers, alligator and black leather decorated with black patent leather drops. "You are to leather what Cellini was to gold," Diana Vreeland, the former editor of *Vogue* who is now with the Metropolitan Museum of Art, once wrote to him.

He built platforms in the living room and dining/conference room on which to put the growing collection of pillows. "You throw them anyplace and they become a seating arrangement," he said. "In terms of pure shape and line they are still just like baseballs. It might sound outrageous, but I do like to keep things simple."

In the bedroom, the colors are softer. Instead of red and black, the pillow objects are pink, turquoise, yellow, and pale lilac. Pillows sit on a piece of white coral on top of the television set, looking like jellyfish in a lagoon, or are clustered on the white leather bedspread—a luxurious but effective use of leather and one which Breslau subsequently made a version of in black for Elsa Peretti, the jewelry designer.

Although Mr. Breslau's environment is bizarre by most standards, his designs are more practical than a visitor might expect. The largest seating pieces recall the bean bag chairs that were popular in the 1960s. Breslau sees the roomy, soft chairs used in groups and also upholstered in leather. His bag chairs are sometimes wedge-shaped, and can be stacked in piles to look like rocks or grouped in follow-the-leader descending sizes.

The apartment windows offered Breslau more opportunities for inventiveness. A spiderlike web of silver leather is stretched across one; the other windows and the doorway are covered with curtains of silver leather that recall old-fashioned beaded curtains.

Visitors to the apartment still enter gingerly and tend to make for the more recognizable pieces of furniture, shying away from the fringed pillows. "They take a bit of coaxing," Mr. Breslau said. "They seem to say 'Touch me but don't sit on me.' Sometimes I just have to force people."

198

204

214

Furnishing

In the past, when it came time to furnish an interior, many architects turned to the interior designer or decorator. But as the roles of these professionals have blurred—with architects doing more work in the field of interiors and many designers taking on ambitious renovating projects—furnishing an interior has become an intrinsic and important part of the design process.

There are, of course, many possibilities. We live in an era of cross-cultural furnishing, best exemplified by the acceptance of an eclectic style in which antiques are successfully mixed with modern pieces. But the actual choice of furnishings has of late taken on more importance. A collection of primitive or folk art pieces, an obsession with one type of chair, a predilection for a particularly favored era in design—all can be used to set the tone.

There are few hard and fast rules. Furnishings can be built-in, like banquettes, or freestanding; tables, lamps, and chairs can be as imaginative and colorful as art works.

Furniture is also a factor in giving scale to a room, but, surprisingly, the designs that work the best are often ones that depart from the ordinary. Small rooms do not necessarily look bigger when filled with delicate, tiny pieces. On the contrary, oversize accessories can create a striking and surprisingly contemporary style all their own.

220

Bringing back the Shaker style

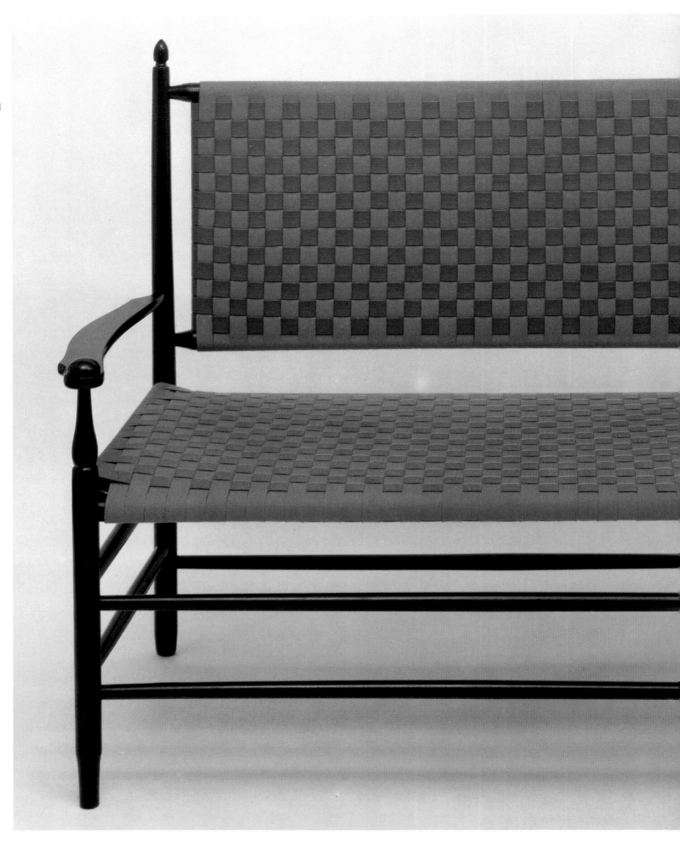

Reproductions of a rock maple New Lebanon settee, right, and weaver's chair, far right, are available in either kit form or completely assembled from Shaker Workshops in Concord, Mass.

The scenario goes something like this: A furniture craftsman with little or no experience sees a piece of Shaker furniture in a museum or antiques shop, or perhaps even in a book. The simplicity of the design encourages him to try his hand at copying it. Whether the task turns out to be as simple as the style or not, he is hooked on Shaker.

It seems that from Maine to Kentucky, in many of the same areas where the Shaker religious communities flourished in the nineteenth-century and then died out because they required celibacy, independent craftsmen are busily re-creating Shaker designs for twentieth-century applications. Although most of the new pieces do not have the patina and evocative beauty of the originals, they do offer practical furniture alternatives.

Originally made for the austere needs of a rural people, Shaker-style pieces are suited for urban apartment dwellers appreciative of small-scale, space-saving characteristics. The stepladders, for example, seem ideally designed for reaching high kitchen cabinets; the drop-leaf or flip-top tables offer an ingenious solution for extra dining or working space; the simple pegged boards that kept chairs off the floor and out of the way can easily be converted for clothes storage or shelf supports.

Trim little cabinets that are gracefully proportioned, unadorned bookshelves, tripod candle-stands, and beds on wheels, as well as many pieces of clever kitchen gear, are eminently practical. It is furniture that is refreshingly direct, appealing to modernists and traditionalists alike. The contemporary producers of Shaker and Shaker-style pieces make up in diligence what they lack in originality. "It happened to me ten years ago, when I saw some Shaker furniture in a museum and felt that I wanted to try and make some," said David Margonelli, a craftsman who, with

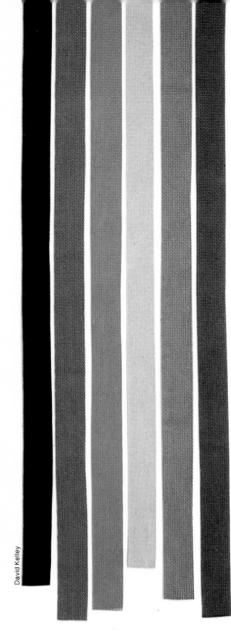

Cotton tapes, above, in a range of colors and patterns are available from the Shaker Workshops. The reproduction convertible bed, right, was made by Kipp and Margot Osborne of Wooden Furniture.

Ordering reproductions

- The American Country Store, 969 Lexington Avenue, New York, N.Y. 10021; 212-744-6705. Special orders on side, arm, and rocking chairs, small tables.
- Boston Museum Shop, P.O. Box 1044, Boston, Mass. 02120; 617-427-1111. Oval Shaker boxes in five sizes.
- The Country Loft, South Shore Park, Hingham, Mass. 02043; 800-225-5408. Pantry boxes, pine jelly cupboard, small storage units.
- Ian Ingersoll, Main Street, West Cornwall, Conn. 06796; 203-672-6334. Chairs, rockers, and clocks.
- Raimundo Lemus, 125 Christopher Street, New York, N.Y. 10014; 212-691-4035. Interpretations of classic Shaker pieces, designed and made-to-order by this master wood craftsman.
- David and Susan Margonelli, R.F.D. Box 84, Dover-Foxcroft, Me. 04426; 207-564-7552. Stepladders, chairs, chests.
- Robert Olsen, P.O. Box 451, Putney, Vt. 05346; 802-387-4288. Wall-mounted shelf units, candle-stands, tables, and boxes.
- Shaker Community Industries, P.O. Box 898, Pittsfield, Mass. 01202; 413-422-8381. Furniture, tinware, brooms, cloaks, shirts.
- Shaker Workshops, Box 1028-CJ91, Concord, Mass. 01742; 617-646-8985. Chair and furniture kits, preassembled pieces.
- Shakertown at Pleasant Hill, Route 4, Harrodsburg, Ky. 40330; 606-734-5411. Sconces, tables, boxes, stools, chests.
- Wooden Furniture, 510 Broome Street, New York, N.Y. 10013; 212-431-7075. Kipp and Margot Osborne produce custom-order pieces, including beds.
- The Guild of Shaker Crafts, 401 West Savidge, Spring Lake, Mich. 49456; 616-846-2870. One of the oldest makers of Shaker furniture.

The storage box on legs, far left, the desk/cabinet, left, and the work table, below, are all Shaker-type reproductions made of American pine by Raimundo Lemus, a New York craftsman.

Pegrail, above, is a copy of a unit that hangs in the infirmary of the Brick Dwelling at the Hancock Shaker Village in Hancock, Mass. The candle sconce, wall cupboard, rack, and mirror are also reproductions. A space-saving tilt-top table, right, and an eight-drawer chest, far right, were both made of American pine by Raimundo Lemus.

his wife, Susan, produces in a Maine workshop what he calls Shaker offshoots.

Some craftsmen choose to do their own interpretations. One of them is Raimundo Lemus, a Havana-trained woodworker with twenty-nine years' experience. In the last three years he has produced more than thirty-six pieces with Shaker antecedents. "They were so simple yet at the same time so elegant," said Lemus, who works out of a cluttered Greenwich Village showroom. "There was nothing pretentious about them." His pieces are made mostly of pine. They are all dovetailed and hand-pegged and polished to look like new. "I never use any metal," he said. "You can't imagine how long it takes to actually finish a piece."

Kipp Osborne remembered the time he made a trestle table "and it took us over." He and his wife, Margot, run Wooden Furniture in Manhattan, where they produce Shaker-style pieces. A settle bed and a variety of cupboards are included in their designs. They are working on Shaker-style kitchens and a couch bed. "That's our own design," Osborne said. "The Shakers didn't have couches." Nor did they worry about where to store wine bottles or keep the stereo, two more contemporary uses for the adaptable cabinets.

Many of the furniture makers do not produce Shaker-style pieces exclusively, and most of their output must be specially ordered or ordered by mail. It is not unusual to have a piece of furniture made specifically for a particular room and a special function. But keep in mind that some have year-long waiting lists; others sometimes stock the simpler pieces.

For a listing of places to find reproduction Shaker furniture, see page 200. Some sources for original Shaker pieces are on this page, at right.

Antique sources

The following are some of the most prominent antiques dealers on the East Coast who specialize in Shaker material. It is advisable to telephone for appointments.

• Charles Brown & Company, Trinity Pass Road, Pound Ridge, N.Y. 10576; 914-764-8392.

• Ed Clerk, Bethlehem, Conn. 06751; 203-567-5093.

• Charles Flint, 81 Church Street, Lenox, Mass. 01240; 413-637-1634.

• Edwin Pawling, Greenwillow Farms, Raup Road, Chatham, N.Y. 12037; 518-392-9654.

• Douglas Hamel, R.F.D. 10, Concord, N.H. 03301; 603-798-5912.

• Richard Rasso, Route 295, East Chatham, N.Y. 12060; 518-392-4501.

• John Keith Russell, Spring Street, South Salem, N.Y. 10590; 914-763-3553.

• Two folk-art dealers who stock some Shaker antiques are Gerald Kornblau, 790 Madison Avenue, New York, N.Y. 10021; 212-737-7433; and Thomas K. Woodard, 835 Madison Avenue, New York, N.Y. 10021; 212-988-2904.

Furniture pieces by the Dutch architect Gerrit Thomas Rietveld look deceptively easy to reproduce, prompting amateur cabinetmakers as well as professional designers to try their hand at making the angular designs. The interest in Rietveld has also been growing among architects and manufacturers. "There is a greater number of classic reproductions now being made," said Stephen Kiviat, president of Atelier International, a to-the-trade furniture showroom. "And Rietveld's pieces are among the oldest and the most significant."

A member of the De Stijl radical design movement in the Netherlands in the early decades of this century, Rietveld created designs that were more experimental than practical. His 1917 Red and Blue Chair, with its interlocking planes and primary colors, is his most widely known design. The chair is an example of the geometric principles that the artists Piet Mondrian and Theo Van Doesburg had investigated in painting, which Rietveld applied to the three-dimensional fields of interiors, architecture, and furniture. Use of color was usually restricted to the primaries: red, blue, and yellow; gray, white, and black were added when needed.

The original chairs are extremely rare and copies were not available in great number until 1973, when Cassina, the Italian furniture manufacturer, began making reproductions. Cassina entered into an agreement with the Rietveld estate to manufacture pieces under its supervision, with royalties from the sales to be paid to the estate. Included is the crate series, which was Rietveld's concept of knockdown furniture for mass production. This was a pioneering idea in the early 1930s, and the furniture was meant to be sold in kits.

Leon Barth, who runs the architectural research laboratory at Princeton University, makes the unpainted chairs on special order, using poplar with plywood for the seat and back. Among the architects who have bought the chairs are Peter Eisenman, Michael Graves, and Paul Segal. "I painted mine very accurately," said Segal. "While I was in school, I used the chair for reading because I knew I couldn't fall asleep in it." But if Segal doesn't appreciate the chair for comfort, he admires the way it is put together. "It requires a good dowel," he said. "Rietveld was a cabinetmaker before he was an architect."

Interest in the De Stijl look is not limited to precise reproductions of Rietveld's designs. The modern designer Koni Ochsner has interpreted Mondrian's paintings on a series of cabinets for the German company Tecta. Sections of the cabinet front, delineated by the Mondrianesque panels, open to reveal storage compartments.

Sometimes, dedication to a style can be taken to the extreme. In a suburban house outside London, Dr. Edward Cooper, an English art historian, did his whole kitchen in the De Stijl style. "I enjoy pastiches," he explained. "I tried to make a working evocation of a De Stijl interior, using only the colors available to the De Stijl artists." The room cost only the price of the paint. He found the furniture—even the refrigerator, which he dubbed "De Frij"—on the street. "I painted the walls and ceiling first," Cooper said, "then adjusted the primary colors to avoid the creation of secondary colors in the angles. That was the hardest part."

His housemate at the time, the design historian Stephen Bayley, was not happy with the new decor. "He was horrified," said Cooper, unperturbed. "When he saw what I had done, he didn't speak to me for a week."

For other reproductions of architect-designed furniture classics, see pages 34 to 35 and 222 to 225.

Bringing back the De Stijl look

Revivals of the Rietveld style

Original Rietveld pieces sometimes turn up in auctions and antiques shops but are extremely rare. Copies were not widely available until 1973, when Cassina, the Italian furniture manufacturer, began making reproductions of the original designs.

• Atelier International, a to-the-trade firm, 595 Madison Avenue, New York, N.Y. 10022; 212-644-0400. Imports the Cassina collection, including the Red and Blue Chair for $2,400 list.

• The Museum of Modern Art bookstore, 37 West 53rd Street, New York, N.Y. 10019; 212-956-7264.

Accepts mail orders only for the Red and Blue Chair, which costs about $1,600.

• Furniture of the Twentieth Century, 154 West 18th Street, New York, N.Y. 10011; 212-929-6023. A to-the-trade firm that imports the made-in-Italy, Ecart black and white design chairs by Sybold Van Ravesteyn for $670 list and the dining set by J.J.P. Oud for $3,150 list.

• Some craftsmen make their own copies. Leon Barth, 17 North Rochdale Avenue, Roosevelt, N.J. 08555; 609-448-1870. Makes unpainted Rietveld chairs on special order for $350 apiece.

In London, art historian Dr. Edward Cooper painted the walls, floor, furniture, and appliances in his kitchen, far left, in the De Stijl style. Cassina's Red and Blue Chair, above left, is a reproduction of a 1917 Rietveld design.

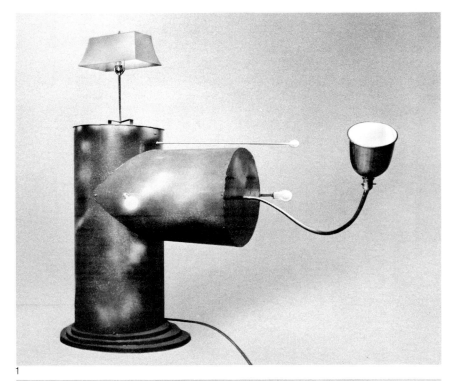

1

2

3

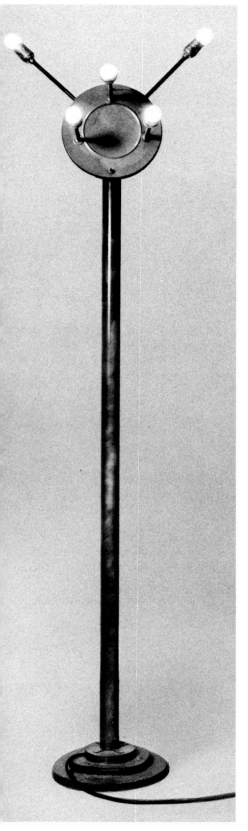

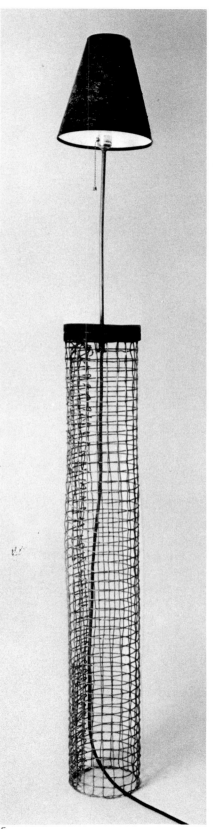

Artists and functional objects have always had an intertwined history, but recently many contemporary sculptors and painters are using household furnishings as a way to express their artistic and personal points of view. "I wanted to force viewers to deal with their cultural conditioning and play that up in a theatrical situation," said R.M. Fischer, a New York-based artist and sculptor whose works, which exhibit more than a few lamplike characteristics, are icons, characters, presences.

They also have bulbs, stand on the floor or a table, or are hung, sconcelike, on the wall or from the ceiling. One might guess that they are lamps. In any case, they are hard to ignore. Some are colorful, others steely. But most of all, they are wacky.

How did Fischer come to choose a lamp as the object of his current affections? "I wanted one object to be able to represent everything," he explained, noting that lamps come in different styles. "We all know what a lamp is, and what to expect of it. I decided to take that preconception and play with it." Fischer's intent is to take on the imagery of television, movies, advertising, the 40s and 50s, science fiction, and *Star Wars.* "I want to force the viewer into a confrontation," he said, "but not a hostile one."

But what are these for, one may be tempted to ask. They're not exactly ordinary bedside reading lamps—they're not reading lamps at all, for that matter. "They're environmental, reaching outside of themselves to light up the room," Fischer said. And they're entertaining, even lovable, in the way of some outer space monsters. These are lamps to keep one company.

For other examples of furniture by artists, see pages 36 to 37; a number of galleries that represent the artists are in the catalog under "Artists' Furniture."

Wacky lamps: function and art

1. "The Hog" is one of the lamps concocted by artist R.M. Fischer.

2. "The Multiple" is a three-bulb table lamp with a film can base.

3. "Warrior Lamp" is a one-of-a-kind lighting fixture made from found objects.

4. The "Mouse Lamp" floor fixture has a circular light bulb and two antennae.

5. Floor lamp has a tiny old-fashioned shade atop a wire-mesh base.

5

Classic
custom
seating

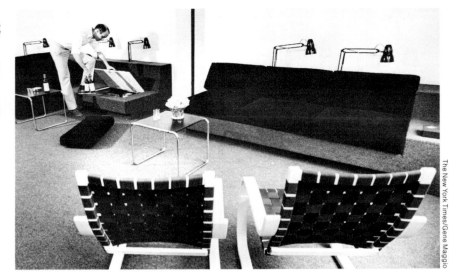

The New York Times/Gene Maggio

The banquette was once only a lowly bench—according to the French definition, a backless seating unit. Often used in large spaces when dozens had to be seated at dinner, the term banquet hall is a reminder of one of its original functions. Restaurants celebrated the legless banquette, which simplified cleaning, and traditionally women were seated there, protected from the possible clumsiness of waiters.

Today's banquette turns up in studio apartments and lofts and opulent living rooms, upholstered in velvet or canvas, plumped with pillows or straight and spare. It is the designer's shorthand for seating that can be practical or luxurious. "It can look very plain and architectural," said Michael Byron of Patchel, Byron and Associates, who with his partner, Estelle Patchel, designed an L-shaped banquette for a 350-square-foot apartment. "The main requirement was to be able to store extra sleeping mats," Patchel said. The solution was a sixteen-foot banquette along one wall, an eight-foot one along the other. The banquette—gray wool upholstery on a wood frame, thirty-one inches deep—is massive. "But it makes the room look bigger," said Patchel. "Because of its large size, we made the cabinet underneath it white," added Byron. A stainless steel grip functions as a drawer pull. The unit cost about $3,500.

Michael Rubin, of Rubin and Smith-Miller Architects, saw a banquette as the only solution for David and Valerie Itkin's living room. "The doorway was on a direct axis with the fireplace, and if we had done the usual sofa and chairs in front of it there would have been no space left in the room," he said. The result was a two-part banquette, "eighteen feet of straightforward seating—like pulling a ribbon around the periphery of the room." A plywood platform was covered in gray commercial carpeting, and velvet-covered pillows were placed on it. Hinged doors allow the platform to be used as extra storage space. It cost about $1,500, not including the carpeting or pillows.

"This is an informal dining room, and a banquette was absolutely the only answer," said Richard Mervis, who planned the renovation of what was once a foyer in an apartment. The stationary dining table has a carpeted base and a burl wood lacquered top. "Dining banquettes should be twenty-seven inches deep," he said, "but these are twenty-nine. I thought that the two extra inches would make the seating more versatile as extra lounge seating." An upholsterer made the velvet-covered banquette and the pillows for about $1,000. He also took a safety precaution and had the edge of the table curved. "A sharp table edge near a banquette is deadly."

For carpeting that can be used to cover platform-banquettes, look in the catalog under "Carpets and carpeting." Some sources for banquette builders are listed under "Cabinetry."

Two mattresses are stored in the base of a banquette by Patchel, Byron and Associates, left. Michael Rubin shows use of a platform banquette for wine storage, far left top. The dining alcove by Richard Mervis has a velvet-covered banquette, left top.

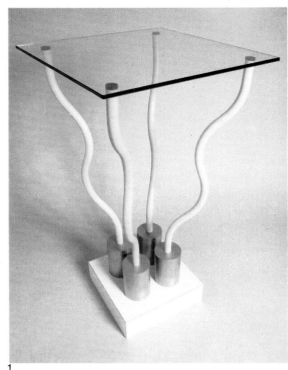

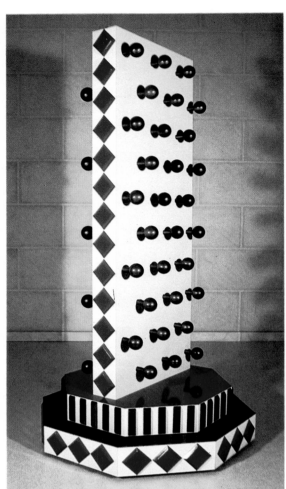

1

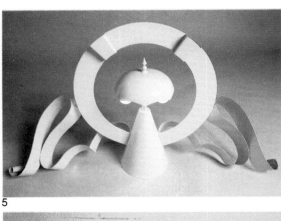

2

3

5

6

4

7

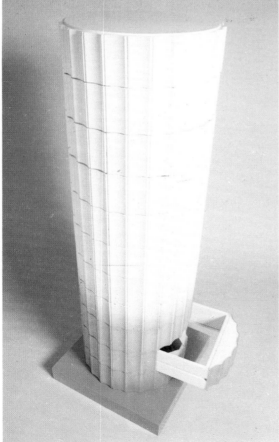

8

1. **Ettore Sottsass, Jr., designed glass-topped side table for Studio Alchymia.**

2. **Clock, by George James Sowden for Memphis, has a plastic laminate pedestal base.**

3. **Revolving coat rack was Paola Navone's design for Memphis.**

4. **Sofa by Andrea Branzi for Memphis has a convex seat cushion and plastic laminate base.**

5. **Sinerpica lamp, part of the Studio Alchymia collection, is by Michele De Lucchi.**

6. **Alessandro Mendini painted Proust armchair as a takeoff on antique furniture.**

7. **Casablanca cabinet, by Ettore Sottsass, Jr., for Memphis, has outstretched arms for storing bottles.**

8. **Colonna columnlike cabinet for Studio Alchymia is by Trix and Robert Haussman.**

"Memphis—The New International Style," a collection of furniture first unveiled in Milan in 1981, combines the lore of Egypt with the pop imagery and associations of American art and rock-and-roll music. And the name seems just right for a disparate collection of over fifty designs that have nothing in common except an effervescent sense of humor, a very definite verve, and an underlying serious intent.

Under the aegis of the iconoclasitc Ettore Sottsass, Jr., a celebrated Italian designer, the new lamps, tables, chairs, sofas, storage pieces, ceramics, clocks, and television sets were created by an international group of avant-garde architects and designers. Although experimental, the pieces are meant to be produced industrially and to function not as art objects but as real furniture. "Memphis does not deny functionality, but looks at it with eyes wide open, more as an anthropologist than as a marketing man," said Barbara Radice, the coordinator of the collection.

The pieces of furniture are meant to both comment on and be in radical opposition to what we know or think of as furniture. Cabinets sprout arms, desks look out of proportion, chairs and lamps are more like outer space pets than more practical counterparts. The colors are bound to set any interior on its side, and the use of materials—plastic laminate, glass, metal tubing—has already been influential and represents a radical visual departure from what we have already been used to in Italian design. The Memphis designs, like the pieces produced previously by the Studio Alchymia group, are furniture that is meant to be reacted to, and also to be functional—but never to go unnoticed.

Some of the Studio Alchymia and Memphis pieces are available at Art et Industrie and Furniture of the Twentieth Century.

The outré Italian style

The client rarely even makes coffee for herself and can't boil the proverbial egg. Yet she entertains a lot. So when she decided to renovate her apartment kitchen, she had it built not to her specifications but for those who would be cooking there—caterers and their professional chefs. The design decisions, however, have many home kitchen applications.

The architect Robert Rodin worked with Philip Idone, a designer and builder, on the project. "This was an opportunity for us to come up with a purely commercial solution in a home environment," Rodin said. "Our client didn't have a personal attachment to the kitchen, because she wasn't planning to spend a lot of time in it," Idone agreed. "It was up to us to see that it would work." Renovating the ten-by-twenty-foot kitchen, plus the pantry, cost about $50,000 for materials, labor, new wiring and lighting, and commercial appliances (which cost somewhat more than their domestic counterparts).

The plan developed for the narrow galley kitchen included placing the sinks, a dishwasher, and refrigerator on one side and the stove and cutting and pastry-making areas on the other. All was done with the idea that in some circumstances up to four people might be preparing a meal at the same time. The original pantry area was converted into a bar area, with a separate ice maker and storage space for glasses, linens, and silverware.

Unlike a home kitchen, intense cooking is done only on a weekly basis and food storage can be kept to a minimum. There was no need for a separate freezer, or for an elaborate larder. Storage was necessary, however, for cooking utensils and equipment. Knives, for example, are kept dust-free in divided drawers instead of being stored in a butcher block stand or against a magnetic strip. The designers also were careful to insure that all storage areas could be reached from a standing position.

On the side of the kitchen that was reserved for food preparation, pastry-making, and cooking, a powerful exhaust system was installed. The counters are topped with butcher block in the preparation area, marble in the pastry-making area, and Corian, a plastic material that can be sanded down, in the other areas. "Each station has its own setup for utensils," Idone said.

The kitchen was equipped with a six-burner, two-oven restaurant stove and two commercial dishwashers—one for pots and pans, the other for glasses and china. Easy maintenance was the major factor in choosing the surface materials. The floor was covered in nonslip tile; it was understood that if a chef were to spill something when he was working, he wouldn't stop to clean it up. The walls were covered with white ceramic tile to the unusual height of eight feet; the surfaces of the cabinets and appliances are brushed stainless steel laminate. There is very little exposed hardware. "It's a wipe-down kitchen," said Rodin.

A small cart on wheels solved the problem of a flexible work station. But another detail was not so easily solved. "Everyone wants garbage cans to be under the sink," said Idone. "But a professional can't deal with that. He needs a movable can. It sounds silly, but it's important." So an oversized garbage can on wheels was ordered for the kitchen. But, uncharacteristically, the client was adamant. "We still have to supply her with a garbage can under the sink," said Idone. "It'll be there, eventually."

For sources for professional ranges and kitchen equipment, see catalog under "Kitchen, commercial equipment." Under "Kitchens, European" are listed a number of sources for imported cabinets and equipment.

A chef's kitchen to order

Supplies are brought in directly from the service elevator, above. All-commercial equipment was specified, as were brushed stainless steel cabinets and white ceramic tile walls, left.

Photographs by Robert Levin

Learning from the hotel school

In Charley Gold and Peri Wolf-man's apartment, shelves are stocked with white restaurant china, left. The commercial stove is the focus of the kitchen, above. Bowls and baskets hold produce, top.

Peri Wolfman and Charley Gold's apartment blends the countrified design popular on the West Coast with a kind of East Coast sophistication, not a surprising combination considering that Wolfman is a New Yorker who has spent the last eight years in California.

The space itself, on a high floor in an older building, is gracious. A big square living room opens onto a small, flower-filled terrace. All the rooms were painted white—the kitchen and the shelving in semigloss, the rest in matte—and carpeted in taupe. After deciding to have an all-white apartment, Wolfman carried her simplification plan to its logical extreme by eliminating any furnishings or accessories that did not fit into her fresh, monochromatic color scheme.

"I went the restaurant supply route," she said, "but I add things to it; otherwise it's institutional and hard-edged." There are, for example, three armoires, all bleached to light wood tones, as well as the late nineteenth-century billiards table light over the dining table. Her yellow flowered china is now hidden in an armoire, and the shelves are filled with white coffee-shop mugs, hotel platters, stacking restaurant cups and saucers, and lots of wine glasses. Her predilection for hotel paraphernalia is not new. She first started using restaurant china when she furnished three restaurants in the Sonoma Mission Inn, a luxurious resort hotel in California's wine country.

Now, Wolfman sets her own table with ornate nineteenth-century silverware, which is grouped with heavy American restaurant china, Chinese cotton embroidered napkins, and straw cheese platters used as place mats. But nowhere is her hotelière's touch better illustrated than in the bathroom, where soft white towels are stacked in tall piles on a brass rack over the sink—an amenity worthy of a four-star hotel.

Commercial wares

Hotel and restaurant china and glassware are often sold by the case. Cookware, linens, and flatware are also available.
• Cook's Supply Corporation, 42 Cooper Square, New York, N.Y. 10003; 212-598-4100.
• Federal Restaurant Supply, 202 Bowery, New York, N.Y. 10012; 212-226-0441.
• Manhattan Ad Hoc Housewares, 842 Lexington Avenue, New York, N.Y. 10021; 212-752-5488.
• The Professional Kitchen, 18 Cooper Square, New York, N.Y. 10003; 212-254-9000.
• Turpan Sanders, 386 West Broadway, New York, N.Y. 10013; 212-925-9040.
• Wolfman-Gold & Good Company, 484 Broome Street, New York, N.Y. 10012; 212-431-1888.

A ceiling fan, a bleached pine armoire, and white linens recreate the hotel room scheme in the bedroom, left. A brass shelf and hardware spruce up the bathroom, above. The generous towel supply is another luxury hotel touch.

Return of the rustics

Rustic furniture made of birch, willow, hickory, apple branch, pine, or maple is part of a tradition that goes back to the eighteenth century, when woodsy pieces were commonplace in the English garden. Recently they have been enjoying a revival. The furniture doesn't appeal to everyone, but it does have committed admirers. As the pieces become rarer, even collectors' items, antiques shops are scoured for used pieces, and craftsmen in Connecticut, Louisiana, Pennsylvania, and Maine are making new versions of the natural wood designs intended to be used indoors.

"The concept of a rustic chair is unusually sophisticated, not primitive, as it would appear at first sight," writes Sue Honaker Stephenson in *Rustic Furniture* (Van Nostrand Reinhold, 1979). "It requires a built-in ambiguity in the visual interplay between the naturalistic materials and the unmistakable evidence of the wit of its human builder."

Rusticated chairs, tables, beds, and stools were usually made by anonymous craftsmen, and were found in country houses, log cabins, and in that American naturalistic classic, the Adirondack camp colony. Unfortunately, pieces left outdoors all year round did not always survive.

Ed Stiffler, a florist, is an aficionado. "Not everyone relates to them," he admitted. "A rusticated piece is handmade, more original, and personal. I look for a chair that's good and sturdy, so that it can be used."

Twig-based and swamp willow furniture is still being made, and is even used as inspiration for other furniture collections, made of hand-carved beechwood or banana-leaf to look as ingenuous as their rustic antecedents.

For other country furniture, see pages 226 to 229, and the catalog under "Americana," or "Furniture, bistro and country French."

Old painted rocking chair, far left, is a one-of-a-kind find from Ed Stiffler. Swamp willow settee, left, is among the pieces from Added Oomph currently being crafted in Louisiana. Log twig square stool, left below, is from Potcovers.

Ferreting out rustic pieces

Sources for old and new rustic furniture include:

• Added Oomph! 270 South Wrenn Street, High Point, N.C. 27260; 919-886-4410. Adirondack twig and new Kentucky rockers, bookcases, canopy beds. Mail order available.

• America Hurrah, 316 East 76th Street, New York, N.Y. 10021; 212-535-1930. Small antique pieces.

• The American Country Store, 969 Lexington Avenue, New York, N.Y. 10021; 212-744-6705. Country-style furniture and accessories, including new twig pieces.

• The Country Loft, South Shore Park, Hingham, Mass. 02043; 800-225-5408 or 617-749-7766. Americana and country pieces, plant stands, lamps. Mail order.

• Mary K. Darrah, 33 Ferry Street, New Hope, Pa. 18938; 215-862-5927. Adirondack twig, rockers, plant stands, tripod tables.

• Kelter-Malcé, 361 Bleecker Street, New York, N.Y. 10012; 212-989-6760. Antique Adirondack twig furniture.

• Mabel's, 1046 Madison Avenue, New York, N.Y. 10021; 212-734-3263. Small pieces of furniture.

• Potcovers, 101 West 28th Street, New York, N.Y. 10001; 212-594-5075. New woven-twig tables.

• Ed Stiffler Flowers, 1190 Third Avenue, New York, N.Y. 10021; 212-628-4404. Antique tables, rockers.

• The Place For Antiques, 993 Second Avenue, New York, N.Y. 10022; 212-475-6596. Adirondack twig pieces.

Big things for small rooms

In the living room, right, a forty-eight-inch galvanized steel drinking trough has been made into a coffee table. The dining area, far right, has been furnished with a stone table and wicker chairs.

For Richard Holley, a Houston-based designer, putting big things in small rooms is as much a matter of preference as it is a problem-solving technique. "Maybe it's a very personal point of view," admitted Holley. "But bigger and fewer objects in a small space really help give the sense of a larger space. And I also like the way they look."

Judging from the 800-square-foot apartment shown here, it seems his choice does work. In what was a relatively banal space, Holley has created a dramatic interior. "It was done very quickly," he added. The dining area is furnished with a table, whose top is made of fossilized stone quarried in Texas, and generously proportioned wicker chairs. In the living area, two side tables near the sofa, which is upholstered in a mix of unbleached flax and linen, are covered with movers' blankets edged in contrasting fabric and topped with oversize plaster urns. The hard-edged painting is by Texas artist Jane Allensworth.

The pièce de résistance is the forty-eight-inch-diameter, twenty-four-inch-high coffee table—actually a galvanized steel drum used for horses and cattle, which has been topped with mirror. "It's a vernacular thing," Holley explained. "I like to mix simple and expensive things together, like steel and gold leaf, for example."

For other ways of dealing with scale, see pages 12 to 15 and 114 to 115.

1. Tubular steel and canvas Thonet B55 armchair dates from 1928–29.

2. Tubular steel and canvas side chair was designed around 1927.

3. Coiled springs connect the back and seat of a 1928–29 Thonet tubular steel and rattan lounge chair.

4. The widely copied Thonet B32 tubular steel and cane side chair came to be known as the "Cesca" chair.

5. Oak armchair, 1922, reflects the influence of Rietveld designs.

6. Lightweight band steel and wood chair dates from the early 1930s.

7. Isokon side chair, from 1936–37, was an experimental use of plywood.

8. Cane and plywood side chair was designed in 1940 for a Museum of Modern Art competition.

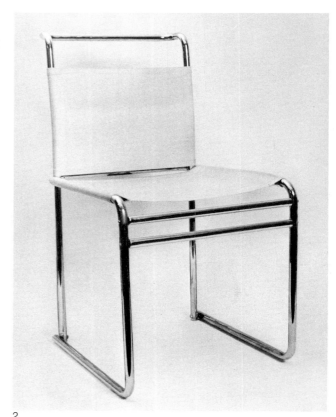

1

2

3

4

5

6

Breuer's enduring chair designs

Ellie Beckhard

Portrait of Marcel Breuer, above, was taken in 1979. The architect and designer died in 1981 at the age of seventy-nine.

7

8

Photographs by The New York Times/Gene Maggio

1

2

1. Tubular steel, metal, and painted wood Thonet tea cart, the B54, dates from 1929.

2. Tubular steel and glass table known as the B19 was made by Thonet in 1928.

3. Tubular steel and canvas club armchair, now known as the "Wassily," was first made in late 1927 or early 1928.

4. Small-scale wood and aluminum lounge chair is from 1933.

3

Marcel Breuer's chairs, modern classics that have become a symbol of twentieth-century design, represent a rare achievement in the history of furniture design. "Breuer simply changed the course of twentieth-century furniture," said J. Stewart Johnson, curator of design at the Museum of Modern Art. "He is seminal. He started it all and made everything happen." "Breuer invented modern tubular steel furniture in 1925," added Christopher Wilk, the author of *Marcel Breuer: Furniture and Interiors* (Museum of Modern Art, 1981), a monograph on the furniture and interiors designed by the celebrated Hungarian-born architect, who died in 1981 at the age of seventy-nine.

The contemporary architecture of the late 20s and early 30s made the furniture of the time look awkward and out of place. "The only thing that looked right was Thonet bentwood chairs," Wilk said, "because they were simple, visually transparent, and mass produced."

Breuer's most influential chair designs are the ones from the mid-1920s. The tubular steel club armchair—the "Wassily"—was designed in 1925. "Breuer was the first person to do a heavy upholstered club chair as a lightweight, tensile, architectural tubular steel structure," Wilk said. In 1928, Breuer developed the tubular steel, wood, and cane side chair, now widely known as the "Cesca" chair. According to Wilk, although this cantilevered two-legged chair was claimed by Breuer, Mart Stam, a Dutch architect, built the first model and copyrighted the design in Germany before Breuer's chair was subsequently made by Thonet as the B32.

Among Breuer's lesser known designs is the Thonet B35 cantilevered lounge chair of 1928–29, described by Johnson as "completely logical, and one of the most interesting." Of the Thonet B25 chaise, which is a 1929 tubular

steel and rattan chair whose seat is suspended by two coiled springs, he commented, "A piece of sculpture, but I wouldn't want to sit in it."

Other surprises include the Thonet B54 three-wheeled tubular steel tea cart, with visible nuts and bolts hardware; the Thonet B19 table, with rubber plumbing connectors; the remarkable, sinuous, and nearly completely unknown 1932–33 aluminum and wood lounge chair with riveted wood slats; and a pleasantly gawky 1932 small band steel and wood desk chair.

In Breuer's early interiors, he specified the exact placement of every piece of furniture, and minimalist designers have been influenced by these rather austere, stark rooms ever since. "A sense of openness and a freedom of movement distinguish the interiors," Wilk said. "If there is upholstery, it is thin and taut and all the structural members of the furniture are very narrow." Many interior design details from the 30s and 40s that we now take for granted turn out to be Breuer signatures: the inevitable Persian rug or natural sisal carpeting on bare floors; the imaginative mix of wood and metal. Even the plants. "The rubber tree and the cactus were acceptable," said Wilk.

Marcel Breuer's chairs are among the most widely plagiarized modern designs, and "knockoffs" have proliferated since the 1920s. Tubular steel chairs sold well in the 30s, but not in the 40s, when there was a reaction against their severity. The designs were revived in the 60s when Gavina, the Italian furniture company, reproduced the club armchair and the tubular steel chair, naming them the "Wassily," for the painter Kandinsky, and the "Cesca," after Breuer's daughter Francesca, who was born decades after the original design.

Breuer chair sources are at right. For other revival designs, see pages 34 to 35 and 204 to 205.

4

Photographs by The New York Times/Gene Maggio

Reproductions and look-alikes

In the 1960s Gavina, the Italian firm, reproduced the tubular steel chair and the club armchair, naming them the "Cesca," after Breuer's daughter Francesca, and the "Wassily," for the painter Kandinsky. International Contract Furnishings, Knoll International, Stendig, and Thonet make reproductions of the originals.
• Conran's, 160 East 54th Street, New York, N.Y. 10022; 212-371-2225.
• Door Store, 210 East 51st Street, New York, N.Y. 10022; 212-753-2280.
• International Contract Furnishings, 305 East 63rd Street, New York, N.Y. 10021; 212-750-0900.
• Knoll International, 655 Madison Avenue, New York, N.Y. 10021; 212-826-2400.
• Stendig, Inc., 410 East 62nd Street, New York, N.Y. 10021; 212-838-6050.
• Thonet, 305 East 63rd Street, New York, N.Y. 10021; 212-421-3520.
• Workbench, 470 Park Avenue South, New York, N.Y. 10016; 212-481-5454.

In the guest bedroom, right, the walls have been stenciled by Virginia Teichner, who adapted a number of traditional patterns. The appliquéd spreads are from the mid-nineteenth century. The stenciling on the stairs, far right, is based on a Victorian pattern.

A house with a Shaker feeling

Although many collectors and historians would, if given the chance, match a period house to its furnishings, there are few opportunities to do so. One alternative is the approach chosen by folk art dealers Thomas Woodard and Blanche Greenstein when they renovated a cottage on Long Island and filled it with some of their Shaker and early folk art.

Built in 1939 by a local family, the house was dark and had a series of small rooms, low ceilings, few windows, and an attic, but no upstairs. The couple hired Peter Paul Muller to help them with the renovation. The goal, according to Woodard, was to achieve "the idea of the clear Shaker feeling of light and space." Whenever possible, stock elements for floors, stairs, and windows were ordered from catalogs. The attic was converted into a master bedroom, tiny guest room, and bathroom. The widest available boards were chosen for the floors and were pickled and polyestered. Woodard insisted on square nails.

One detail that reinforced the feeling the couple was after was the meticulous stenciling that was done in many of the rooms and on the stair treads. Virginia Teichner, an artist from upstate New York, came to live in the house for a week and adapted traditional stencil motifs, applied with custom colors, to the different rooms. The renovated house became a backdrop for some of Woodard and Greenstein's choice antiques—including a pair of mid-nineteenth-century appliquéd cotton spreads, a rare mid-nineteenth-century tree of life appliquéd quilt that was placed over the fireplace, two late-eighteenth-century Windsor chairs, and a mid-nineteenth-century painted cupboard filled with a collection of Shaker and Indian baskets, and spongeware.

For more sources of Shaker furnishings see pages 198 to 203.

A mid-nineteenth-century painted cabinet, far left, holds Shaker and Indian baskets and spongeware pieces. Quilt from the mid-nineteenth century is hung over a bleached wood fireplace, left center. Two late-eighteenth-century Windsor chairs are in front of the living room windows, left.

Finding the woven chairs

A limited number of original Lloyd Loom chairs, hampers, settees, and tables are available at:

• Richard Camp, Montauk Highway, Wainscott, N.Y. 11975; 516-537-0330. Lloyd Loom chairs, hampers, settees, and tables, from $75 to $125 apiece.

• Prince Street Limited, 106 Prince Street, New York, N.Y. 10012; 212-966-7235.

• The Yankee Peddler, 519 Hudson Street, New York, N.Y. 10014; 212-243-2005. Chairs are about $195 each.

Newly made reproductions are being made by:

• Jack Lenor Larsen, 232 East 59th Street, New York, N.Y. 10022; 212-674-3993. A to-the-trade source that is reproducing the original designs. Armchairs in quantities from one to twenty-four are $335 list apiece.

A group of original Lloyd Loom chairs assembled by a New York dealer, right. Patented in 1922, the chairs, of woven paper fiber reinforced with 18-gauge steel, were made until 1962. Close-ups of one of the many versions, far right.

English easy chairs

The story began on a "cold and rainy English day," when David Utz, an antiques dealer, walked into a furniture shop in London and sat down in a small gold-painted woven chair. "It was so comfortable," he said, "that I stayed there for a couple of hours, and ended up by buying thirty similar chairs." Back in New York, he mentioned the chairs to a friend who was leaving for England and asked him to look for more. In fifteen months, Utz found himself the proud owner of more than 550 chairs—and firmly committed to what he referred to as his "Lloyd Loom obsession."

The original manufacturing process for the woven chairs was patented in 1922 by an American company and then taken to England by two brothers, who set up a factory. The Lloyd Loom Wicker Company made the chairs in what was then a new material: woven paper fiber reinforced with 18-gauge steel. The factory closed in 1962.

"The largest market for these chairs in the 1930s was the English Army," Utz said. "Every soldier who retired at that time was given a chair and a hamper to go home with." At its peak, Lloyd Loom produced five thousand chairs a week. "Lloyd Looms were usually the housekeeper's favorite chairs," Utz said. That may have been because they were comfortable and easy to live with. The way they fit into many current decorating schemes is a testimony to their popularity.

"We started out small," said Andrea Gould, who married Utz and his hundreds of chairs in 1980. "I don't even notice them anymore," she said. "And anyway, there's always somewhere to sit down." There are Lloyd Looms in the living room, in the dining room, in the bedroom, and piled up everywhere from floor to ceiling. There are pink, green, and blue chairs, some with their original silver or gold underpainting, some with cushions, most without, some repainted in primary colors, all with arms but in many sizes, some with full or half skirts. To the uninitiated, the chairs look very much alike. "But," Utz said, "we know each of them intimately."

Catalog

This catalog of designers and architects and home furnishings shops and services is primarily based on material that has appeared in "Home Beat," a weekly column, as well as a number of service and source-oriented articles published in The Home Section of *The New York Times.*

The material has been brought up to date, and, in the case of service articles, includes a short text explaining the background and reasons for the current interest in particular categories—Americana, artists' furniture, inexpensive and functional glassware and stainless steel cutlery, chintz fabric, objects from the Fifties.

New York, as well as many other cities in the United States, offers an ever-changing cornucopia of design-related sources. This catalog is not, nor was it intended to be, a complete listing of such services and wares. We have tried to be selective, not all-inclusive. Stores change hands and move, while others open up, on a seemingly continual basis. The catalog and its varied entries are meant to be used as a general shopping guide that can offer readers a starting point—a way to introduce them to unusual and in some cases hard-to-find merchandise as well as custom or to-the-trade sources.

The catalog is also designed to be used as a cross-reference to the projects and interiors illustrated in the other sections of this book. Short biographies of most of the architects and designers whose work is shown are also included. Every effort has been made to be accurate. But if mistakes do occur, every endeavor will be made to make the necessary corrections in future editions of this book.

Americana, antiques

In the past few years there has been a resurgence of interest in Americana, particularly folk art and quilts. Listed below are some sources that carry selections of these wares.

• The Antique Furniture Newsletter, Box 524, Adams Street, Bedford Hills, N.Y. 10507; 914-232-8687. Informative bimonthly newsletter for beginning and more sophisticated antiques collectors. Topics include design, crafstmanship, materials. Write to above address to get rates for subscription information.

• American Antiques and Crafts Society, Fame Avenue, Hanover, Pa. 17331; 717-632-3535. Members are entitled to discounts on books from the annual catalog, covering everything from paper dolls to Rockwood pottery.

• Added Oomph! 270 South Wrenn Street, High Point, N.C. 27260; 919-886-4410. Adirondack twig furniture, quilts, advertising memorabilia.

• America Hurrah, 316 East 70th Street, New York, N.Y. 10021; 212-535-1930. One of the largest collections of antique American and Amish quilts, plus antique weather vanes, hooked rugs, and primitive paintings.

• A.S. Perry Antiques & Design, 29 Northern Boulevard, Greenvale, N.Y. 11548; 516-621-3594. Contemporary and antique pieces in the rusticated style.

• The Collector's Choice, 63

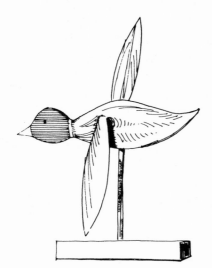

Duck whirley-gig,
Made in America Country
Antiques and Quilts

Illustrations by Greg Ryan

Thompson Street, New York, N.Y. 10012; 212-226-3677. Braided rugs designed by Elizabeth Eakins.

• Eggs & Tricity, 979 Third Avenue, New York, N.Y. 10022; 212-371-6728. Renée Leonard and Audrey Chatsky operate this source of antique accessories, including quilts, pillows, bed linens, baskets, and folk art.

• Mary K. Darrah, 33 Ferry Street, New Hope, Pa. 18938; 215-862-5927. Adirondack twig furniture, including rockers, plant stands, hat racks, umbrella stands, chairs, bedside stands, and smoking and tripod tables.

• Equator, 459 Broome Street, New York, N.Y. 10013; 212-925-5805. A to-the-trade source for American folk art, antiques, and eccentric collectibles.

• Kelter-Malcé, 361 Bleecker Street, New York, N.Y. 10014; 212-989-6760. Adirondack twig furniture, including antiques and trunk tables. See Rustic Furniture, pages 218 to 219.

• The Manhattan Art and Antiques Center, Second Avenue and 56th Street, New York, N.Y. 10022; 212-355-4400. Art and antiques complex, with seventy-three independent shops and galleries. Prices range from $10 to $300,000.

• Mill House Antiques, Route 6, Woodbury, Conn. 06798; 203-263-3446. A country estate that offers eighteenth- and nineteenth-century antique furniture.

• Thomas K. Woodard American Antiques and Quilts, 835 Madison Avenue, New York, N.Y. 10021; 212-988-2906. Antique quilts, furniture, baskets, rag rugs, folk art, sponge wear, and cotton calicos.

• See pages 226 to 229.

• See pages 198 to 203 for sources on Shaker material.

Americana, new

The taste for collecting antique Americana and folk art has also developed an interest in craftspeople who make traditional or traditionally derived American crafts pieces, including weather vanes, furniture, and decorative accessories.

• The American Country Store, 969 Lexington Avenue, New York, N.Y. 10021; 212-744-6705. New handcrafted furniture and accessories on a country theme, including Shaker reproductions.

• Robert Goodwin, Ltd., 31 Ferry Street, New Hope, Pa. 18938; 215-862-2381. Adirondack twig furniture, including loop baskets.

• Mabel's, 1046 Madison Avenue, New York, N.Y. 10021; 212-734-3263. Pottery, ceramics, and handcrafted rugs and throws.

• Made in America Country Antiques and Quilts, 1234 Madison Avenue, New York, N.Y. 10028; 212-289-1113. Baskets, hooked rugs, pottery, and quilts.

• Museum of American Folk Art, 49 West 53rd Street, New York, N.Y. 10019; 212-581-2474. Blanket chest, jelly cupboard, door chest.

• American Craft, Hunt Hill Farm, RR 3, New Milford, Conn. 06776; 203-355-0300. All forms of crafts, including tea tables and toys.

• See also listings under "Craft galleries" and "Quilts."

• See pages 218 to 219.

The American Museum of Natural History, Central Park West at 79th Street, New York, N.Y. 10024;

212-799-8958. In addition to miniature replicas of many museum exhibits, the museum gift shop offers such items as jewelry, dolls, Japanese fans, and African masks.

Antiques, rentals

• Newel Art Galleries, 425 East 53rd Street, New York, N.Y. 10022; 212-758-1970. Antique resources and interiors, both furnished and rented, appraisals, and estates purchased.

Apartment Appearance, 1465 South King Street, Honolulu, Hawaii 96814. Provides thorough cleaning of private residences, including pulling out the refrigerator, cleaning cupboards, window screens, air-conditioning filters, floors, faucets, and lighting fixtures. Cost is $1,500 per day.

Appalachian Art, 26 Montauk Highway at Baiting Hollow Green, East Hampton, N.Y. 11937; 516-324-5353. Shop that specializes in Appalachian arts and crafts, including blankets and statuettes.

Aquarium Design, 251-21 Northern Boulevard, Little Neck, N.Y. 11363; 516-225-6815. Firm that works with architects, designers, and builders to design, manufacture, install, and maintain custom aquariums all over the country.

Architectural details

The postmodern style in interior design is one of the current styles that have contributed to the interest in architectural artifacts — including columns and archways, cast-iron pieces, plasterwork, and remnants of sculpture and decorative detailing that adorned the exterior of many buildings. Listed below are a number of sources where one can find such items.

• Architectural Antiques Exchange, 715 North Second Street, Philadelphia, Pa. 19123; 215-922-3669.

• Architectural Sculpture, 242 Lafayette Street, New York, N.Y. 10012; 212-431-5873. Produces sharply detailed, fine-quality architectural details and ornaments, as well as custom reproduction and renovation of capitals, ceiling columns, brackets, and stairs.

• Oliver Bradley, P.O. Box 272, Jim Thorpe, Pa. 18229; 717-325-2859. Architectural dealer; offers a selection in ironwork of railings, brackets, fencing, urns, and fountains.

• Art Directions, 6120 Delmar Boulevard, St. Louis, Mo. 63112; 314-863-1895. Mail-order architectural dealer.

• American Column Company, 913 Grand Street, Brooklyn, N.Y. 11211; 212-782-3163. Oldest and most complete source for columns. Free catalog.

• Evelyn Croton, 51 Eastwood Lane, Valley Stream, N.Y. 11581; 516-791-4703. Antique architectural ironwork.

• Irreplaceable Artifacts, 526 East 80th Street, New York, N.Y. 10021; 212-288-7397. Architectural objects.

• Focal Point, 2005 Marietta Road NW, Atlanta, Ga. 30318; 404-351-0820. Designs and manufactures architectural ornamentation, including cornices, ceiling medallions, recessed domes, and mantels.

• Kenneth Lynch and Sons, Box 488, Wilton, Conn. 06897; 203-762-8363. Custom ironwork; catalogs of outdoor metal furniture, sundials.

• Niedermaier, 435 Hudson Street, New York, N.Y. 10014; 212-675-1106. A supplier of sculptural objects for department store displays, including a Venus de Milo, huge jugs, pillars made from plasterlike composition, and fiberglass in a range of colors.

• Old-House Journal Catalogue, Old House Journal Corporation, 69A Seventh Avenue, Brooklyn, N.Y. 11217; 212-636-4514. Listing of architectural dealers.

• United Housewrecking Corporation, 328 Selleck Street, Stamford, Conn. 06902; 203-348-5371. Stock is always changing, but includes window guards, railings, register grills, old radiators, decorative fencing, and antique architectural ironwork.

• Urban Archaeology, 137 Spring Street, New York, N.Y. 10012; 212-431-6969. All varieties of architectural antiques: large selection of iron and stonework, much of it from city buildings. One-of-a-kind items, including capitals, gargoyles, keystones.

• See pages 30 to 33 for postmodern interior design schemes in which architectural elements play an important role.

Artists' furniture

The boundaries between art and furniture used to be very clear-cut. Artists painted pictures or made sculptures, often to be looked at only. For functional furniture, one shopped department stores. Nowadays many artists have turned to everyday objects to express themselves. Below is a list of galleries that carry such works.

• Anichini, 7 East 20th Street, New York, N.Y. 10003; 212-982-7274.

Sculptured plaque, Architectural Sculpture

Scott Burton stone chair, Max Protetch Gallery

Balans kneeling chair, Menash

Gallery that features work by contemporary American artists.

• Art et Industrie, 464 West Broadway, New York, N.Y. 10013; 212-777-3660. Functional and decorative accessories for the home, all designed by artists.

• Leo Castelli Gallery, 420 West Broadway, New York, N.Y. 10013; 212-431-5160. Richard Artschwager is one of its artists.

• Marian Goodman Gallery, 38 East 57th Street, New York, N.Y. 10022; 212-755-3520.

• Frank Kolbert Gallery, 724 Fifth Avenue, New York, N.Y. 10022; 212-541-6006.

• Frank Marino Gallery, 489 Broome Street, New York, N.Y. 10012; 212-431-7888.

• Multiples, Inc., 24 West 57th Street, New York, N.Y. 10019; 212-977-7100. Work by Larry Bell.

• Max Protetch, 37 West 57th Street, New York, N.Y. 10019; 212-838-7436. Work by Scott Burton.

• Holly Solomon Gallery, 392 West Broadway, New York, N.Y. 10013; 212-925-1900. Painted patterned sofas, chairs, lamps, and coffee tables designed by Kim MacConnel.

• Stefanotti, Inc., 30 West 57th Street, New York, N.Y. 10019; 212-757-6712. Ron Fischer lamps.

• Barbara Toll Fine Arts, 146 Greene Street, New York, N.Y. 10012; 212-431-1788.

• See pages 36 to 37.

• See also listings under "Craft galleries" and "Furniture, custom."

Artists' supplies

• Arthur Brown & Brothers, 2 West 46th Street, New York, N.Y. 10036;
212-575-5555 or 575-5544. A wholesale and retail source for artists' materials.

• Charette Drafting Supply Corporation, 212 East 54th Street, New York, N.Y. 10022; 212-593-1649; and 215 Lexington Avenue, New York, N.Y. 10021; 212-683-8822. Furniture, file cabinets.

• Fuller Office Furniture, 45 East 57th Street, New York, N.Y. 10022; 212-688-2243; and 10-16 44th Drive, Long Island City, N.Y. 11101; 212-688-2243.

• Menash, 2305 Broadway, New York, N.Y. 10024; 212-877-2060. Commercial stationery, office supplies, and a complete line of graphic artists' materials.

• New York Central Supply Co., 62 Third Avenue, New York, N.Y. 10003; 212-473-7705. Artists' materials, printmaking supplies, imported papers and stationeries.

• Sam Flax, 111 Eighth Avenue, New York, N.Y. 10011; 212-620-3000; and 55 East 55th Street, New York, N.Y. 10022; 212-620-3060. Art supplies, including chairs, easels, tables, stacked drawers, multi-file drawer units, and paints.

Laura Ashley, 714 Madison Avenue, New York, N.Y. 10021; 212-371-0606. Retail source for fashion designs, home furnishings, home decorative accessories of floral print fabrics. See also listings under "Catalogs," "Fabrics, retail," and "Chintz."

Atelier International, 595 Madison Avenue, New York, N.Y. 10022; 212-644-0400. A to-the-trade company that imports furniture from Italy, including designs by Le Corbusier and Gerrit Rietveld. See pages 204 to 205.

Bathroom accessories

There are many companies that manufacture and retail accessories for the bathroom. Listed below are a few that offer special items.

• Allibert Inc., 182 Madison Avenue, New York, N.Y. 10016; 212-685-1733. A to-the-trade source for modern bathroom hardware and cabinets.

• Alter Bath & Kitchen Company, 137 Lexington Avenue, New York, N.Y. 10016; 212-683-1682. Vanities, medicine cabinets.

• Bakit Bathrooms, 32 East 30th Street, New York, N.Y. 10016; 212-683-6093. Company that will install and design bathrooms and supply medicine cabinets, bathtub enclosures, and vanities.

• Deweese Woodworking Company, Department A, P.O. Box 576, Philadelphia, Pa. 39350; 601-656-4951. Manufacturer of bathroom accessories, including an oak toilet seat.

• The Elegant John, 401 Third Avenue, New York, N.Y. 10016; 212-725-5770; and 812 Lexington Avenue, New York, N.Y. 10021; 212-935-5800. Stores that carry a wide selection of bathroom hardware and accessories.

• George Terranova and Son, 159 Chrystie Street, New York, N.Y. 10002; 212-228-4910. Ceramic and porcelain fixtures and marble vanities.

• Caroma, manufactured and distributed by Vivid International, 5726

West Washington Boulevard, Los Angeles, Calif. 90016; 213-934-1100. Bathroom accessories, including toothbrush and toothpaste holders, soap dishes, towel racks.

• Wedgwood Artistic Brass, a division of Norris Industries; 3136 East 11th Street, Los Angeles, Calif. 90023; 213-264-2818. Faucets and other bathroom accessories, featuring pale blue Wedgwood Jasper Ware.

• See also listings under "Cabinetry" for people who can build special storage, "Housewares," and "Gift Stores."

Bauhaus lighting. See pages 34 to 35 and listing for "George Kovacs Lighting."

Bed linens

Customized linens, a luxury once reserved for the bride's trousseau, seem to be back in style. Sources range from established stores to trendier and more recent arrivals. Monograms, special fabrics, and coordinated linens are part of what these expensive and exclusive shops can offer. Many department stores, including Bloomingdale's, Saks Fifth Avenue, and Macy's, also have custom linen shops.

• E. Braun & Company, 717 Madison Avenue, New York, N.Y. 10021; 212-838-0650.

• Brook Hill, 698 Madison Avenue, New York, N.Y. 10021; 212-688-1113.

• Descamps, 723 Madison Avenue, New York, N.Y. 10022; 212-355-2522. French bed and table linens by Primrose Bordier.

• Frette Fine Linens, 787 Madison Avenue, New York, N.Y. 10021; 212-988-5221.

• Léron, 745 Fifth Avenue, New York, N.Y. 10022; 212-753-6700.

• Maison Henri, 617 Madison Avenue, New York, N.Y. 10021; 212-355-5463.

• Porthault, 57 East 57th Street, New York, N.Y. 10022; 212-688-1660.

• Pratesi Shop, 829 Madison Avenue, New York, N.Y. 10021; 212-288-2315. High-quality linens, sheets and towels by Athos Pratesi.

• The Upstairs Shop, 238 East 60th Street, New York, N.Y. 10021; 212-751-5714.

Bienaimé, 231 East 51st Street, New York, N.Y. 10022; 212-688-4643. Furniture designed primarily for small spaces. The style is a mixture of modern and country; includes stereo racks, benches, chairs, tables, platforms, and wall systems. See also listings under "Furniture, contemporary."

Belcic & Jacobs Architects, 50 West 96th Street, New York, N.Y. 10025; 212-222-2201. Victor Belcic was born in Rumania in 1941, was educated in Bucharest, and lived in France. "I look for design that is related to the client," he explains. "I want to have the clients see themselves in my work." See pages 78 to 79.

Eric Bernard Interiors, 177 East 94th Street, New York, N.Y. 10028; 212-876-9295. The principal of the company, Eric Bernard was born in New York City in 1943. Before being an interior designer, his career was in the beauty industry and in theater set design. His philosophy is "to provide a dynamic atmosphere within a minimal and supremely functional space." See pages 26 to 29.

Parker Zaner Bloser, 13 Worth Street, New York, N.Y. 10013; 212-966-6177. Architect, b.1937 in Columbus, Ohio. Studied at Harvard University School of Architecture. Believes that design should form a consistent whole and aims for placidity, a look without too much "visual excitement." See pages 84 to 87.

Bon Marché, 1060 Third Avenue, New York, N.Y. 10021; 212-620-5592; and 74 Fifth Avenue, New York, N.Y. 10011; 212-620-5588 (lighting accessories); and 55 West 13th Street, New York, N.Y. 10011; 212-620-5550 (main store). Furniture and accessories. See also listings under "Furniture, contemporary."

Books, architecture and design

• Lee & Lee Booksellers, 424 Broome Street, New York, N.Y. 10013; 212-226-3460. Rare fine art, architecture, and furniture books.

• Morton, Interior Design Bookshop, 989 Third Avenue, New York, N.Y. 10022; 212-421-9025.

• Prairie Avenue Books, 711 South Dearborn Street, Chicago, Ill. 60605; 312-922-8311. Architectural books and magazines; stocks out-of-print books and sends catalogs.

• Jaap Rietman, 167 Spring Street, New York, N.Y. 10012; 212-966-7044.

• Rizzoli International Bookstore, 712 Fifth Avenue, New York, N.Y. 10019; 212-397-3706.

• Taunton Press, 52 Church Hill Road, Box 355, Newtown, Conn. 06470; 203-426-8171. Publishers of woodworking books and magazines.

Eric Bernard

*R. Scott Bromley
and Robin Jacobsen*

*Michael Schaible
and Robert Bray*

• Urban Center Books, 457 Madison Avenue, New York, N.Y. 10022; 212-935-3595.

• Weyhe, 794 Lexington Avenue, New York, N.Y. 10021; 212-838-5466.

Charles Boxenbaum, 1860 Broadway, New York, N.Y. 10023; 212-586-5778. Architect, b.1942 in New York City. Received Master of Architecture degree in 1967 from Harvard University. Enjoys speculating with the client about possibilities that "in the end define the limit of design." See pages 168 to 171 and 184 to 187.

Brass beds

• Bedlam Brass Beds, 19-21 Fair Lawn Avenue, Fair Lawn, N.J. 07410.

• Isabel Brass Furniture, 120 East 32nd Street, New York, N.Y. 10016; 212-689-3307.

• Kleinsleep, 962 Third Avenue, New York, N.Y. 10022; 212-755-8210; and 149 West 24th Street, New York, N.Y. 10011; 212-807-1989.

Bray-Schaible Design Inc., 80 West 40th Street, New York, N.Y. 10018; 212-354-7525. Partners since 1972, Robert Bray and Michael Schaible have been leaders of the minimalist movement. They describe their new work, which includes residential and commercial projects in the United States and Europe, as "rational glamour." See pages 150 to 155.

Bobby Breslau, 45 East 7th Street, New York, N.Y. 10003; 212-473-4277. Artist/sculptor, b.1942 in Brooklyn, N.Y., who studied graphic and package design at New York Community College. See pages

190 to 195.

Marcel Breuer, architect and furniture designer. See pages 222 to 225 and listing for "Galerie Metropol."

Bromley-Jacobsen Architecture & Design, 242 West 27th Street, New York, N.Y. 10001; 212-620-4250. R. Scott Bromley, an architect, and Robin Jacobsen, an interior designer, have been partners since 1977. Their work includes commercial and residential projects, including discotheques and shops as well as private homes. See pages 4 to 7.

Butcher block

• J&D Brauner, 298 Bowery, New York, N.Y. 10012; 212-477-2830. Six different sizes of pantry bars, cut to size but with no installation.

• Great North Woods, 425 Fifth Avenue, New York, N.Y. 10036; 212-889-0983; 683 Lexington Avenue, New York, N.Y. 10022; 212-593-0423; 160 East 86th Street, New York, N.Y. 10021; 212-369-6555; 636 Eleventh Avenue, New York, N.Y. 10036; 212-541-4304. Butcher block furniture and wall units.

Cabinetry

Unless one is handy, just getting a wall of bookcases or a series of cabinets built in one's home can be a frustrating experience. Listed below are a number of cabinet shops and cabinetmakers who can help you get organized.

• Neal Andrews Limited, 152 Madi-

son Avenue, New York, N.Y. 10017; 212-683-4292. Plastic laminate cabinets, wood cabinets, architectural hardware.

• Guild Furniture, 30 West 36th Street, New York, N.Y. 10018; 212-695-3266. Frames and cushions for banquettes.

• Laszlo Szoecs, 2575 33rd Street, Long Island City, N.Y. 11102; 212-726-6463. Cabinetmaker of custom furniture, including frames for banquettes.

• 3K Cabinet Corp, 360 Great Neck Road, Great Neck, N.Y. 11021; 516-487-8988. All kinds of cabinets, including kitchen furnishings.

• See also listings under "Closets."

Camping

Camping equipment is often well designed, lightweight, efficient, and easy-to-use. Chairs, water bottles, coolers, portable stoves, lighting, and showers and canteens can be as useful at home, at the beach, or in the backyard as in the woods. Even a gadget-crazy cook will be impressed by the simplicity and compactness of camping tableware and cooking implements. In the area of lighting, at-home campers can choose between propane-fueled lights, waterproof flashlights, and battery-operated lamps that come with both fluorescent and incandescent bulbs. Listed below are some mail-order sources that specialize in camping and outdoor wares, as well as a few high-tech and industrial-minded stores that supplement their regular stocks with such items. See also the listing of shops under "Housewares."

• Eddie Bauer, 1330 Fifth Street, Seattle, Wash. 98124; 206-622-2766.

• L.L. Bean, Freeport, Me. 04033; 207-865-3111.

• Eastern Mountain Sports, 13403 Vose Farm Road, Peterborough, N.H. 03458; 603-924-7276.

• Herman's World of Sporting Goods, 135 West 42nd Street, New York, N.Y. 10036; 212-730-7400.

• Kreeger & Son, Ltd., 16 West 46th Street, New York, N.Y. 10036; 212-575-7825.

• Land's End, 105 Leffler Street, Dodgeville, Wis. 53533; 608-935-2788.

• Manhattan Ad Hoc Housewares, 842 Lexington Avenue, New York, N.Y. 10021; 212-752-5488.

• The North Face, 1234 Fifth Street, Berkeley, Calif. 94710; 415-524-8432.

• Outdoorsman, 2306 Broadway, New York, N.Y. 10024; 212-362-6880.

• Paragon Sporting Goods Company, 867 Broadway, New York, N.Y. 10003; 212-255-8036.

• Sportpages, 3373 Towerwood Drive, Dallas, Tex. 75234; 214-247-3101.

• Sears, Roebuck & Company, Department 139H, Chicago, Ill. 60607; 312-875-2500.

• Turpan Sanders, 386 West Broadway, New York, N.Y. 10012; 212-925-9040.

Carpets and Carpeting

Listed below are sources for commercial wool carpeting, both retail and wholesale. Most of the designer sources carry a very wide selection of both new and antique carpeting of all kinds.

• ABC Carpet, 880 Broadway, New York, N.Y. 10003; 212-677-6970.

• Samuel Aronson & Son, 135 West 17th Street, New York, N.Y. 10011; 212-243-4993.

• Carpet Loft, 161 Avenue of the Americas, New York, N.Y. 10013; 212-924-2400.

• Carpet Showroom, 979 Third Avenue, New York, N.Y. 10022; 212-832-7789.

• Dylan Carpets, 979 Third Avenue, New York, N.Y. 10022; 212-688-0345. Broadloom and Oriental rugs.

• Einstein Moomjy, Inc., 150 East 58th Street, New York, N.Y. 10022; 212-758-0900.

• G. Fried Carpet, 1285 Second Avenue, New York, N.Y. 10021; 212-737-3700. Wide selection of patterns, colors, and sizes of dhurrie rugs and other carpeting.

• Harmony Carpet Corporation, 979 Third Avenue, New York, N.Y. 10021; 212-355-6000.

• Helen Miller Rugs, Second Street, Stockholm, Wis. 54769; 715-442-5534. Handwoven rag rugs, some hand-dyed.

• Phoenix Carpet, 979 Third Avenue, New York, N.Y. 10022; 212-758-5070. Broadloom rugs.

• Rug Warehouse, 2222 Broadway, New York, N.Y. 10024; 212-787-6665.

• Saxony Carpet Company, 979 Third Avenue, New York, N.Y. 10021; 212-755-7100. Latex-backed Belgian sisals.

• Mark Shilen, 185 West Houston Street, New York, N.Y. 10014; 212-989-8664. Authentic Oriental rugs.

• Stark Carpet, 979 Third Avenue, New York, N.Y. 10011; 212-752-9000.

• See also listings under "Tapestries" and "Kilims."

Diana Carulli, 158 East 7th Street, New York, N.Y. 10009; 212-677-5970. Artist who designs and produces mobiles made of various materials, including sheer cotton, muslin, batik organdy, and rip-stop nylon. See page 141.

Catalogs

Many home-furnishings products, from gadgets to sofas, are available by mail-order. Included below is a listing of some of the most useful in this area. Some catalogs are free, some cost between 50¢ and $3 apiece. In many cases, the price is refundable against a purchase.

• Adam York Unique Products, 340 Poplar Street, Hanover, Pa.17331; 717-637-1600.

• Laura Ashley, 55 Triangle Boulevard, Carlstadt, N.J. 07072; 201-933-6611.

• Brookstone Company, 127 Vose Farm Road, Peterborough, N.H. 03458; 603-924-7181. Tools.

• The California Catalogue, 4344 Promenade Way, P103, Marina del Ray, Calif. 90291; 213-306-3882. Wares from small, exclusive California stores.

• Conran's, 145 Huguenot Street, New Rochelle, N.Y. 10805; 914-632-0515. Chairs, tables, sofas, kitchen equipment, lighting.

• The Country Loft, South Shore Park, Hingham, Mass. 02043; 617-749-7766 or 800-225-5408. Americana and country accessories, including plant stools, lamps, and pickle barrels.

• Crate and Barrel, 190 Northfield Road, Northfield, Ill. 60093; 312-446-9300.

Solar camping cooker, Manhattan Ad Hoc Housewares

*Chisel,
Garrett Wade*

• Edmund Scientific, 101 East Gloucester Pike, Barrington, N.J. 08007; 609-547-8900. Hobby accessories, school supplies, and industrial items.

• Garrett Wade, 161 Avenue of the Americas, New York, N.Y. 10013; 212-807-1757 or 800-221-2942. Variety of home accessories, including tools, books, and kits for Shaker-style furniture.

• Hammacher Schlemmer, 147 East 57th Street, New York, N.Y. 10022; 212-937-8181. A mail-order and retail source for unusual gadgets and furnishings.

• The Horchow Collection, 4435 Simington Road, Dallas, Tex. 75234; 214-233-1008. One-of-a-kind antiques, gifts, collectibles, decorative accessories.

• Martha M. House, 1022 South Decatur Street, Montgomery, Ala. 36104; 205-264-3558. Victorian reproduction furniture.

• The Nature Company Catalog, P.O. Box 7137 S, Berkeley, Calif. 94707; 415-524-8340 or 800-227-1114. Collection of gifts, tools, books, prints, and field gear designed to enhance enjoyment of the natural world.

• Orvis, 10 River Road, Manchester, Vt. 05254; 802-362-3434 or 362-3622. Hunting and camping-oriented items.

• The Paddle Wheel Shop, P.O. Box 12429, St. Louis, Mo. 63132; 314-993-9068. Gifts and home accessories with a Southern flavor.

• The Paragon, 35 High Street, Westerly, R.I. 02891; 401-596-0134.

• The Sharper Image, 755 Davis Street, San Francisco, Calif.

94111; 415-788-4747 or 800-622-0733 or 800-227-3436. Products include cordless telephones, calculators, exercise bicycles, and cassette holders.

• Trifles, P.O. Box 44432, Dallas, Tex. 75234; 800-527-0277. Home decorative accessories, novelties, and gifts.

• Lillian Vernon Corporation, 510 South Fulton Avenue, Mount Vernon, N.Y. 10550; 914-699-4131. Specializing in gifts, jewelry, housewares, games, gourmet needs, and stationery items.

• The White Pine Company, 1148 Williamson Street, P.O. Box 3512, Madison, Wis. 53704; 608-251-2303. Nature-oriented mail-order products, including fine herb teas, winter clothing, kitchen accessories, and books.

• Williams-Sonoma, P.O. Box 3792, San Francisco, Calif. 94199; 415-652-1515. Kitchen supplies, gadgets, and storage pieces.

Ceramics

• Chambers Street Pottery, 158 Chambers Street, New York, N.Y. 10013; 212-349-5991. Wheel-thrown, hand-built, one-of-a-kind, functional and decorative stoneware.

• Design-Technics Ceramics, 160 East 56th Street, New York, N.Y. 10022; 212-355-3183. Ceramics, including lamps, tiles for floors and walls, and dinnerware.

• Fireworks, 151 West 25th Street, New York, N.Y. 10001; 212-924-5479. Ceramics workshop studio where Carol Cutler, Joy Johnson, and Nancy Lowell offer a variety of courses for ceramics students of all ages and at all levels.

• David Heger Ceramics, 1335 Third Avenue, New York, N.Y. 10021; 212-249-8198. Crafts, ceramics, and glassware.

• For other crafts, see also listings under "Craft galleries."

Children, furniture and accessories

Furniture for children should be easy to maintain and wear well, as well as be safe. Be sure to check that the items you select follow the federal government's guidelines for safety, especially in the area of cribs and car seats.

• Albee's, 715 Amsterdam Avenue, New York, N.Y. 10025; 212-662-5740. Childcraft and Simmons cribs, carriages, and strollers.

• Au Chat Botté, 888 Madison Avenue, New York, N.Y. 10021; 212-772-3381. French furniture, linens, and storage pieces.

• Childcraft Center, 155 East 23rd Street, New York, N.Y. 10010; 212-674-4754; and 150 East 58th Street, New York, N.Y. 10022; 212-753-3196. Chrome-plated steel cribs; northern hard-maple cribs; inflatable tubs.

• Ben's Babyland, 87 Avenue A, New York, N.Y. 10009; 212-674-1353. Complete stock of Simmons cribs.

• Ben's For Kids, 1380 Third Avenue, New York, N.Y. 10021; 212-794-2330. Infant carriers; Childcraft bentwood cribs in white, honey oak, or natural oak.

• The Children's Room, 318 East 45th Street, New York, N.Y. 10017; 212-687-3868. Children's furniture, including loft beds and cribs.

• The Chocolate Soup, 946 Madison Avenue, New York, N.Y.

10021; 212-861-2210. Swings and decorative accessories.

● Descamps, 723 Madison Avenue, New York, N.Y. 10021; 212-355-2522. Straw-colored basket of woven reed; rocking bassinet.

● Domodidovo, Susan Sears and Kathy Garner, partners. A line of brightly colored accessories for babies and children. Available through Bergdorf Goodman (745 Fifth Avenue, New York, N.Y. 10020; 753-9500) and Lewis of London (see next listing).

● Lewis of London, 215 East 51st Street, New York, N.Y. 10022; 212-688-3669. European imports, including playpens, cribs.

● Motif Designs, 26 Pryer Terrace, New Rochelle, N.Y. 10804; 914-636-7973. Karen Sevell-Greenbaum, Iris Rosenblatt-Vanderputten, and Lyn Peterson produce and market Whimsical Walls.

● Scandinavian Design, 127 East 59th Street, New York, N.Y. 10022; 212-755-6078. Blond wood drawer units on casters.

● Schachter's Babyland, 81 Avenue A, New York, N.Y. 10002; 212-777-1660. Childcraft crib line, strollers, infant chairs.

Chimney sweeps

● Marty Butler promises to make homes safe from chimney fires. He can be reached at 212-283-6309.

● Tristate Chimney Sweep, P.O. Box 22, Hasbrouck Heights, N.J. 07604; 201-288-5209 or 212-724-9411. Harry Richart and his sons, Kevin and John, will clean your chimney professionally anywhere in the tristate area. Price depending on size and condition of chimney.

Chintz

Cotton chintz fabric is available in a myriad of patterns, based on Oriental, English, or French designs. Often the fabric can be obtained either with a glazed or unglazed finish. Apart from the painted and patterned fabrics, it is available in dozens of solid colors. Some of the sources, available through designers and interior decorators are listed below. Prices quoted are list prices.

● Fonthill Ltd., 979 Third Avenue, New York, N.Y. 10022; 212-751-8666. British, French, and American chintzes from $14 to $60 per yard.

● Decorators Walk, 160 East 56th Street, New York, N.Y. 10022; 212-355-5300. Plain and printed American chintzes, from $5 to $50 per yard.

● Zumsteg, 979 Third Avenue, New York, N.Y. 10022; 212-355-4010. Swiss and French cotton chintzes from $45 to $90 per yard.

● Donghia Textiles, 979 Third Avenue, New York, N.Y. 10022; 212-477-9877. Domestic printed chintzes; solid colored Swiss chintzes from $50 to $70 per yard.

● Stroheim & Romann, 155 East 56th Street, New York, N.Y. 10022; 212-691-0700. American, British, and Swiss chintzes from $14 to $60 per yard.

● I.D. International Fabrics & Wallcoverings, 979 Third Avenue, New York, N.Y. 10022; 212-688-3580. Solid-colored chintz in forty-five colors is $9.75 per yard. Printed English chintzes from $36 to $105 per yard.

● Alan Campbell, 979 Third Avenue, New York, N.Y. 10022; 212-688-1560. Printed domestic chintzes from $21 to $24 per yard.

● Scalamandré, 950 Third Avenue, New York, N.Y. 10022; 212-980-3888 or 361-8500. Patterned and solid glazed domestic and English chintzes from $11.50 to $69 per yard.

● Old World Weavers, 136 East 57th Street, New York, N.Y. 10022; 212-355-7186. French, British, and Italian chintzes from $12 to $75 per yard.

● Clarence House Imports, 40 East 57th Street, New York, N.Y. 10022; 212-752-2890. Source for Colefax & Fowler Designs Ltd., English chintzes based on documents from eighteenth & nineteenth centuries; also French and Italian chintzes from $30 to $120 per yard.

● Cowtan & Tout, 979 Third Avenue, New York, N.Y. 10022; 212-753-4488. British, American, Italian, Swiss. Mostly floral prints. The imported chintzes are about $40 to $50 per yard; hand-blocked chintz is up to $90 per yard.

● Yves Gonnet, 979 Third Avenue, New York, N.Y. 10022; 212-758-8220. French printed chintz from $30 to $54 per yard. Solid-colored chintzes are $22.50 per yard.

● Brunschwig & Fils, 979 Third Avenue, New York, N.Y. 10022; 212-838-7878. Traditional floral patterns from England and France from $40 to $100 per yard. Plain chintzes, $27 per yard.

● Rose Cumming Chintzes Ltd., 232 East 59th Street, New York, N.Y. 10022; 212-758-0844 or 758-1029. French, English, Italian, German, Swiss, and American chintzes in traditional documentary designs from $24 to $96 per yard.

● Schumacher, 939 Third Avenue,

Swedish crib, Scandinavian Design

New York, N.Y. 10022; 212-644-5900. English, French and German chintzes from $35 to $70 per yard. American chintzes from $15 to $40 per yard.

• Greeff Fabrics, 155 East 56th Street, New York, N.Y. 10022; 212-751-0200. Printed English chintzes, plain and patterned, from $8.25 to $27 per yard.

• Etalage Fabrics & Wallcoverings, 979 Third Avenue, New York, N.Y. 10022; 212-752-0120. Plain cotton/polyester chintzes in eighty colors, $12 per yard; also printed, quilted, and hand-painted chintzes, $60 to $160 per yard.

• Laura Ashley, 714 Madison Avenue, New York, N.Y. 10021; 212-371-0606. Patterned chintz is $15 per yard in retail collection. Decorator collection is $22.50 per yard.

• Lee/Jofa Inc., 979 Third Avenue, New York, N.Y. 10022; 212-889-3900. Plain and patterned chintzes from England, Italy, Switzerland, and America from $22 to about $100 per yard.

Closets

Getting one's closets in order can give homemakers a major sense of accomplishment. Listed below are people who can help organize closets, as well as suppliers of closet storage accessories.

• American Home Accessories, 686 Lexington Avenue, New York, N.Y. 10022; 212-688-6568. Cecil Rhodes specializes in customized closet interiors and accessories; he coordinates carpentry and redecorates closets.

• Bath and Closet Studio, 117 Middle Neck Road, Great Neck, N.Y. 11021; 516-487-3461. Custom

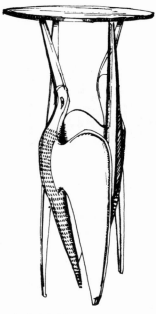

Judy McKie carved table, The Elements

designed storage space and closet accessories.

• The Closet King, 430 East 72nd Street, New York, N.Y. 10021; 212-734-2178; and 113 West 10th Street, New York, N.Y. 10011; 212-741-0027.

• Closet Masters, 67 Wintercress Lane, East Northport, N.Y. 11731; 516-368-4800.

• Closets and Spaces, 31 West 16th Street, New York, N.Y. 10011; 212-242-1174. David Eason works on storage problems in apartments and offices, accommodates all budgets. Initial consultation fee is $85.

• Closet Space Saver, 180 West 58th Street, New York, N.Y. 10019; 212-581-0572.

• Fabulous Closet Company, 51-19 Bell Boulevard, Bayside, N.Y. 11364; 212-423-2555. Vincent Bell, closet organizer, has designed swivel hangers and shelves to economize space. No construction. Free estimates.

• Placewares, 351 Congress Street, Boston, Mass. 02210; 617-451-2074. Specialty store for "places to put things," including products and ideas to help organize living and working spaces. Stocks cabinet hardware and wall and window coverings. Other stores in Concord and Wellesley, Mass.

• Up and Company, 190 Hubbell Street, San Francisco, Calif. 94107; 415-552-1025. Soft shelves, compartmentalized units, flying closets designed by Richard Pathman.

• White Carousels, P.O. Box 100, Kenilworth, N.J. 07033; 201-272-6700. Manufactures an automated

closet carousel, a push-button revolving modular wardrobe.

Birch Coffey, 105 East 88th Street, New York, N.Y. 10028; 212-725-0358. Architect/designer, b. 1947 in Tennessee. Received master's degree in architecture and urban design from Rice University. Interested in clients who "want to move into the twenty-first century in terms of space and how it is used. A $500 job could intrigue me if the problem were fascinating enough."

Comforters

• Samuel Beckenstein, 125 Orchard Street, New York, N.Y. 10002; 212-475-4525. A 63-year-old firm that stocks a wide range of domestic and imported fabrics and exclusive cloths, including silks, velvets, laces, draperies, and slipcovers.

• See also listings under "Futons."

Communications Center for the Disabled Customer, 1095 Avenue of the Americas, New York, N.Y. 10036; 212-395-2400. A branch of Bell Systems, which provides a range of special services for the hearing impaired, blind, and those with other physical disabilities.

Craft galleries

• John Bickel, 6 Grants Lane, Ossining, N.Y. 10562; 914-441-5408. Designer/woodworker whose work ranges from complete interior residential design to small, one-of-a-kind sculptural objects and furniture.

• Convergence Gallery, 484 Broome Street, New York, N.Y. 10013; 212-226-0028. Postmodern, nonfunctional craft objects.

• The Craftsman's Gallery, 16 Chase Road, Scarsdale, N.Y.

10583; 914-725-4644. Changing selection of contemporary American crafts.

• Departure Gallery, 1310 Madison Avenue, New York, N.Y. 10028; 212-860-0748. Work by American artists.

• The Elements, 766 Madison Avenue, New York, N.Y. 10021; 212-744-0890. Contemporary American artists.

• Folklorica Imports, 89 Fifth Avenue, New York, N.Y. 10003; 212-255-2525. A wholesale and retail source for traditional crafts, textiles, and jewelry from Africa and South America, including baskets, textiles, musical instruments, rugs, sculptures, masks, and decorative accessories.

• The Glass Store, 1242 Madison Avenue, New York, N.Y. 10028; 212-289-1970. Hand-blown ornaments by American artists.

• The Goodfellow Catalogue, P.O. Box 4520, Berkeley, Calif. 94794; 415-845-7645. A reference to the work of 680 craftsmen.

• Hadler/Rodriguez Galleries, 38 East 57th Street, New York, N.Y. 10022; 212-752-7734. Contemporary crafts.

• The Hired Hand, 1324 Lexington Avenue, New York, N.Y. 10028; 212-722-1355. Handcrafts, children's clothing, and calico fabrics.

• Sherley Koteen Associates, 2604 Tilden Place NW, Washington, D.C. 20008; 202-363-2233. Contemporary American art objects.

• Signature, The Village Market Place, Stevens Street, Hyannis, Mass. 02601; 617-771-4499; and One Dock Square, North Street, Boston, Mass. 02109; 617-227-

4885. Fine art and American crafts.

• Glenda Schwartzman Tanaka, 2700 Neilson Way, Santa Monica, Calif. 90405; 213-399-7554. Artist who designs large fans imprinted with paintings.

• Twenty Six Horses, Native American Arts, 484 Broome Street, New York, N.Y. 10013; 212-925-6346. Contemporary native American art, including pottery, jewelry, textiles, basketry, carvings, and paintings.

Custom furniture, see "Furniture, custom."

Robert Currie, Gloworm Inc., 954 Lexington Avenue, New York, N.Y. 10021; 212-628-1135. Born Paterson, N.J., 1948. Attended seminary for four years. Has no formal design training. Worked for the department store Henri Bendel as display director and is presently doing residential and commercial interiors and designing museum installations and catalogs. See pages 20 to 23.

D

Danish design

The Danish furniture available today in retail stores in the United States bears only a distant relationship to the classic pieces that earned Denmark its reputation as a leader in furniture design three decades ago. Although some of the classics of modern Danish furniture have survived, most are rare and as costly as antiques. The sculptural esthetic of the "Danish look," which for years was justly accepted as synonymous with "modern furniture," influenced both American and European manufac-

turers. Listed below are a number of stores that do carry Danish and Danish-inspired furnishings.

• Design Selections International, 150 East 58th Street, New York, N.Y. 10022; 212-751-1321. A to-the-trade source for imports by the well-known Danish designers, including Finn Juhl, Poul Kjaerholm, Hans Wegner, and Borge Mogensen.

• International Contract Furnishings, 305 East 63rd Street, New York, N.Y. 10021; 212-750-0900. Arne Jacobsen designs for Fritz Hansen, Hans Wegner chairs.

• Cado Royal System Inc., 979 Third Avenue, New York, N.Y. 10022; 212-593-0962. Wall systems, dining- and living-room furniture.

• Rudd International, 1066 31st Street NW, Washington, D.C. 20007; 202-333-5600. Designs by Johnny Sorensen and Rud Thygesen.

• Wim and Karen Scandinavian Furniture, 319 East 53rd Street, New York, N.Y. 10022; 212-758-4207. Danish tables, chairs, desks, bedroom and dining sets.

• Norsk, 114 East 57th Street, New York, N.Y. 10022; 212-752-3111. Platform beds, storage systems, lighting.

• Maurice Villency, 200 Madison Avenue, New York, N.Y. 10016; 212-725-4840. Teak platform beds, tables.

• Conran's, 160 East 54th Street, New York, N.Y. 10022; 212-371-2225. Mogens Kold dining tables, sideboards, and chairs.

• The Museum Store, 37 West 53rd Street, New York, N.Y. 10019;

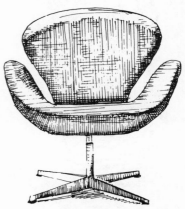

Arne Jacobsen Swan chair, I.C.F.

Joseph Paul D'Urso

212-956-7544. Ribbon chair by Niels Bendtsen; accessories by Johnny Sorensen and Rud Thygesen; stainless steel pieces by Arne Jacobsen.

• The Door Store, 1 Park Avenue, New York, N.Y. 10016; 212-679-9700. Furniture designed in Denmark, made in Malaysia, including a selection of chairs.

• The Workbench, 470 Park Avenue South, New York, N.Y. 10016; 212-481-5454. Kevi chairs.

• Good Design, 331 Route 4, Paramus, N.J. 07652; 201-343-5660; Monmouth Mall, Routes 35 and 36, Eatontown, N.J. 07724; 201-542-1750; 1807 Post Road East, Westport, Conn. 06880; 203-255-2855. Storage units and dining-room furniture.

• Peter Condu of Sweden, 19 Christopher Street, New York, N.Y. 10014; 212-242-1745. GNT telephone, Stelton Cylinda brushed stainless steel accessories.

• Liberty Music, 450 Madison Avenue, New York, N.Y. 10022; 212-753-0180. Bang & Olufsen stereo components.

• Royal Copenhagen, 683 Madison Avenue, New York, N.Y. 10021; 212-759-6457. China, stainless steel flatware, sterling silver.

• Rais & Wittus, Hackgreen Road, Pound Ridge, N.Y. 10576; 914-764-5679. Rais wood-burning stoves.

Decorating services

Although the companies and decorators listed below do work on complete design schemes, they are also available for more piecemeal and limited design advice. Many work on an hourly basis.

• Colorations, P.O. Box 264, Westport, Conn. 06880; 203-762-3399. Ann Deiters and Kit Watson are interior design consultants who develop an overall design plan, from color scheme to shopping ideas.

• Design Difference, 178 East 70th Street, New York, N.Y. 10021; 212-988-1867. A design shopping service operated by Sanna Mayo, who searches for anything in the area of interior design furnishings in addition to offering a decorating service.

• Lauri Ward, 145 East 74th Street, New York, N.Y. 10021; 212-628-8676. Use-what-you-have interiors. Designs interiors using what the client already has to create a unified image. One hundred dollars per room.

• See also listing for "Arthur Ferber."

Decorators Walk, 245 Newtown Road, Plainview, N.Y. 11803; 516-249-3100. Showrooms in New York City at 171 East 56th Street (212-355-5300, fabrics) and 160 East 56th Street (212-688-4300, furniture). Other showrooms in Atlanta, Boston, Chicago, Dallas, Houston, Miami, Los Angeles, San Francisco, Seattle, Denver, Philadelphia, and Washington, D.C. To-the-trade firm that markets furniture, fabrics, wall coverings, art, antiques, and accessories.

Design Coalition, 12 Greene Street, New York, N.Y. 10013; 212-966-3010. Founded in 1967. Alan Buchsbaum, Leslie Armstrong, and Stephen Tilley are drawn to the adventuresome client, one who is "interested in experimenting with design." See pages 160 to 163.

Dexter Design, 133 East 58th Street, New York, N.Y. 10022;

212-752-2426. Interior design firm with a staff of ten founded by Barbara Schwartz and Barbara Ross. Takes a project from empty space to a completely furnished interior. Says Barbara Schwartz: "Because we are dealing with taste, the client's preferences are vital to the design." See pages 12 to 15 and pages 46 to 47.

Disabled, See listings for "Communications Center for the Disabled Customer" and also "Sola."

D'Urso Design, 80 West 40th Street, New York, N.Y. 10018; 212-869-9313. Joseph Paul D'Urso, b.1943. Minimalist architect and furniture designer, whose collection is manufactured by Knoll International. See pages 108 to 113.

Eigen Arts, 579 Broadway, New York, N.Y. 10012; 212-966-5107. Ceramicist Barbara Eigen makes oven and freezer-proof casseroles, bowls, and platters that are fruit and vegetable or seashell lookalikes.

80 Papers, 80 Thompson Street, New York, N.Y. 10012; 212-966-1491. Japanese rice papers, including Mingei, a rare stenciled paper; papers from Sweden, Italy, France, and handmade American papers.

Energy Savers, manufactured by RD Associates, Box 99, New Rochelle, N.Y. 10804; 914-636-8699. Products for personal comfort that save heat, light, fuel, water, mileage, power, and time.

Espresso machines

Espresso machines have been on the market for many years, but in the last six years, sales of home machines have quadrupled, reflecting the current American taste for this strong and originally European brew. Manual, electric, stove-top, and automatic machines that make from one to a hundred cups are currently on the market. Some of the best units, both in terms of design, operation, and taste of the coffee, are Olympia Cremina, Krups Gaggia, Alessi Caffeteria Espresso, Olympia Maxi-Matic, Riviera, Sama, Italia, Morenita, Bialetti Moka Express and Vesuviana. Most department stores with gourmet or kitchen departments carry a good selection. These include Bloomingdale's, B. Altman & Company, Macy's, and Abraham & Straus. Hammacher Schlemmer, the Pottery Barn stores, Manhattan Ad Hoc Housewares, Turpan Sanders, Zabar's, and Dean & Deluca are also sources. See listings under ''Housewares.''

European kitchens, see ''Kitchens, European.''

Fabric, chintz, For a listing of companies that specialize in this glazed or unglazed cotton fabric see listings under ''Chintz.''

Fabric, hand-painted

Listed below are companies and craftspeople who custom paint fabric to match interior decorating schemes or by the yard. Most of their products are available through designers and architects.

• Art People, 594 Broadway, New York, N.Y. 10012; 212-431-4828. Organization of skilled artists who design hand-painted fabrics to be used as wall coverings, upholstery, and draperies. Made on base goods of 100 percent cotton duck, imported linen, or pure silk. Fifteen-yard minimum order on each design and coloration selected.

• Gretchen Bellinger, 979 Third Avenue, New York, N.Y. 10022; 212-688-2850. Textiles and fabrics, specializing in textured weaves made from natural fiber and unique colors.

• Brunschwig & Fils, 979 Third Avenue, New York, N.Y. 10022; 212-838-7878. Designed fabrics and textiles.

• California Drop Cloth, 233 West 26th Street, New York, N.Y. 10011; 212-929-3497; and 706 West Pico Boulevard, Los Angeles, Calif. 90015; 213-747-0669. Hand-painted fabrics and wallpaper, including patterns hand-screened on vinyl-coated paper.

• China Seas, 979 Third Avenue, New York, N.Y. 10022; 212-752-5555. Imported batiks and screen prints from Indonesia.

• Groundworks, 231 East 58th Street, New York, N.Y. 10022; 212-759-8250; and 79 Fifth Avenue, New York, N.Y. 10022; 212-620-0700. Contemporary line of designed, hand-printed, custom-colored fabrics and wallpaper.

Fabric, retail

• Fabric Scouts, 1375 Broadway, New York, N.Y. 10018; 212-391-2630; and 818 Lexington Avenue, New York, N.Y. 10021; 212-486-0708. Imported designer- and home-decorating fabrics, from such sources as Knoll International.

• Fabrications, 146 East 56th Street, New York, N.Y. 10022; 212-371-3370. Retail store that offers a wide variety of fabrics for home furnishings applications.

• Marimekko, 7 West 56th Street, New York, N.Y. 10019; 212-581-9616. Linens, stationery, clothing, and yardage made of the bold-patterned Finnish fabrics.

Fabric, fake marbleized

Along with the trend for faking trompe l'oeil marble surfaces with paint or using fake marble laminates, fabrics in different weights that reproduce marbleized effects are now widely available. Printed on a variety of fabric weights, and sometimes done by hand, these patterns either reproduce stone finishes or approximate the patterns of antique book endpapers.

• See also listings of fabric companies under ''Chintz.'' Some of the showrooms offer some custom or hand-painted materials.

• Mira-X International Furnishings, 246 East 58th Street, New York, N.Y. 10022; 212-753-3618. Collections of interior textiles, now carrying the work of Alfred Hablutzel's company, H-Design. The fabrics include trompe l'oeil patterns, grisaille designs, and architectural motifs by Trix and Robert Haussman.

• Ron Seff, 232 East 59th Street, New York, N.Y. 10021; 212-935-0970. To-the-trade. Hand-printed marbleized fabrics designed by Sandra Holzman.

• Lee/Jofa Inc., 979 Third Avenue, New York, N.Y. 10022; 212-889-3900. To-the-trade source for mar-

Barbara Ross and Barbara Schwartz

Espresso machine, Zabar's

bleized fabrics by Mary Smith Ashley on voile and cotton fabrics.

● See pages 184 to 189.

Arthur Ferber, 16 West 16th Street, New York, N.Y. 10011; 212-929-7757. Designer, b.1946 in New York City. With a background in business and painting, he began merchandising fabrics and wall-coverings, a field that eventually led him to design. His look ''incorporates modern, but not in the hard sense; it is rather eclectic modern.''

Fifties

Vintage 1950s collectibles — from Fiestaware and kidney-shaped cocktail tables to Disney souvenirs — are both an East and West Coast phenomenon. The fact that nearly every Los Angeles swimming pool, and many interiors, was furnished with modern furniture in the late 1940s and early 1950s contributed to the present number of pieces that crop up in California shops. Prices tend to be lower in California, and the diversity and availability of wares more plentiful. Many Los Angeles dealers are used to East Coast shop and gallery owners purchasing items from them and reselling them for many times their price in the East. Listed below are a number of East and West Coast stores that offer imaginative and interesting furniture and objects from the 1940 to 1960 period.

● Deanna Annis, Main Street, Eastport, N.Y. 11941; 516-286-1392. Antiques from 1880 to 1950.

● Buddy's California Pottery, 7208 Melrose Avenue, Hollywood, Calif. 90046; 213-939-2419. American commercial pottery from the 1930s to the 1950s, including California pottery, Hall china, Fiestaware, Rus-

Table lamp,
Fifty-50

sell Wright pieces.

● Fat Chance, 7716 Melrose Avenue, Hollywood, Calif. 90046; 213-653-2287. Designer furniture from the 1940s and 1950s, including pieces by Charles Eames. Some California pottery; airplane models on stands.

● Fifty-50, 72 Thompson Street, New York, N.Y. 10013; 212-598-4259. Designer furniture and artifacts produced from 1940 to 1960.

● Jadis Moderne, 2701 Main Street, Santa Monica, Calif. 90405; 213-396-3477. Art Deco-style furnishings, including lamps and accessories.

● Johnny Jupiter, 385 Bleecker Street, New York, N.Y. 10014; 212-675-7574; and 392 Bleecker Street, New York, N.Y. 10014; 212-741-1507. Old and new housewares, including 1940s and 1950s kitchenware and glassware, small appliances.

● Mark McDonald, 799 Broadway, New York, N.Y. 10003; 212-777-3208. Primarily American furniture from the 1930s and the 1950s, including Knoll and Herman Miller designs.

● Nostalgia City, 548 Hudson Street, New York, N.Y. 10014; 212-924-1329. China, pottery, and appliances from the 1940s and 1950s.

● Shary's, 8575 Melrose Avenue, Los Angeles, Calif. 90069; 213-659-7399. Some accessories, including ashtrays and lamps; mostly vintage plastic jewelry and knick-knacks.

● Topeo, 94 Christopher Street, New York, N.Y. 10014; 212-255-4523. American art, pottery, Art Deco and Depression glass, china

and accessories from the 1940s and 1950s. Some small pieces of furniture.

● Virginia's, 7223 Melrose Avenue, Los Angeles, Calif. 90046; 213-934-4524. Quality furniture from the 1940s and 1950s, including designs by Charles Eames, Harry Bertoia, and Isamu Noguchi.

Fireplace, accessories

● A.E.S. Firebacks, 27 Hewitt Road, Mystic, Conn. 06355. Reproduced seventeenth- and eighteenth-century cast-iron firebacks designed by Arthur Singer. Firebacks can be designed and made to order.

● Bennington Bronze, 256 Garfield Place, Brooklyn, N.Y. 11215; 212-788-0362. Mantels and accessories, cast of solid bronze or brass; also available with nickel plate.

● William H. Jackson Company, 3 East 47th Street, New York, N.Y. 10022; 212-753-9400. Vintage mantels of wood and marble, restored and ready for installation.

Floors

● Castle Burlingame, R.D.I. Box 352 Basking Ridge, N.J. 07920; 201-647-3885. Donald Burlingame operates this antique-flooring business out of a castle; thirty rooms have sample floors that illustrate the wood and workmanship.

● Designed Wood Flooring, 940 Third Avenue, New York, N.Y. 10022; 212-421-6170. Wholesale and retail painted floors; previous work includes the floors of the Metropolitan Museum and work by Stephen Kelemen.

Flotsam Furniture, 456 West 17th Street, New York, N.Y. 10011; 212-691-7772. A by-product of New York street ecology: crates and boxes become desks, tables, night-stands, chests, and cabinets.

Flowers, as design

While a bunch of flowers used to be bought at the corner flower store, the arrival of floral designers made flower arranging and presentation into a high and chic art form. Now, flower shops seem to be branching out into even more ambitious directions. Single and exotic blooms, terra cotta and hand-crafted containers, even accessories like pedestals, and party design, are features of this new type of store.

● Flowers on the Square, 399 Bleecker Street, New York, N.Y. 10012; 212-243-0218; and 1886 Broadway, New York, N.Y. 10023; 212-397-5882. Orchids.

● Goslee Associates, 1100 Madison Avenue, New York, N.Y. 10021; 212-737-0252. Glass beakers. Ceramic containers.

● Howe Floral Company, 171 West 23rd Street, New York, N.Y. 10001; 212-691-4381. Urns and chemical glass.

● Evan G. Hughes, 522 Third Avenue, New York, N.Y. 10016; 212-683-2441.

● Ronaldo Maia Flowers, 27 East 67th Street, New York, N.Y. 10021; 212-288-1049. Vases, potpourri, candles.

● Madderlake, 816 Madison Avenue, New York, N.Y. 10021; 212-879-8400. Terra cotta urns and planters.

● Perriwater Ltd., 900 First Avenue, New York, N.Y. 10022; 212-759-9313. Japanese eighteenth- and nineteenth-century antiques and prints.

● Persephonie, 1373 Third Avenue,

New York, N.Y. 10021; 212-734-1536. Dried flowers and potpourri.

● Renny, 27 East 62nd Street, New York, N.Y. 10021; 212-371-5354. Dinnerware and linens as well as planters, pots, and flowers.

● Salou Design, 452A Columbus Avenue, New York, N.Y. 10024; 212-595-9604. Plants, flowers, and party planning.

● Ed Stiffler, 1190 Third Avenue, New York, N.Y. 10021; 212-628-4404. Silk flowers and antique tables.

● Surroundings, 2295 Broadway, New York, N.Y. 10024; 212-580-8982. Ceramic crafts, pottery, and pedestals.

Michel Fortin, 351 West Broadway, New York, N.Y. 10012; 212-925-8383. Gallery for decorative arts of the Art Deco period from Europe, including Oriental pieces, painting, and sculpture.

Fox Nahem Design, 69 Fifth Avenue, New York, N.Y. 10010; 212-929-1485. Tom Fox, b.1952 in West Virginia, and Joey Nahem, b. 1955 in New York City, founded their interior design firm in 1975. Handles all types of projects within all budgets.

Frank Design, 699 Madison Avenue, New York, N.Y. 10021; 212-759-5512. Doug Frank, b.1946 in Virginia. After pursuing graduate studies in philosophy, he turned his interests to architecture and design, receiving his certificate from the New York School of Interior Design. He concerns himself "both with the architecture of a space and its decoration," but feels that "in matters of aesthetics, there is ultimately no right or wrong, just matters of personal taste and opinion." See pages

116 to 119.

Furnishings, children, see "Children, furnishings and accessories."

Furniture, bistro and country French

Listed below is a range of stores that offer both new and antique furnishings related to the French bistro style. These include French restaurant wares, marble-topped bistro tables, rattan and plastic-wire restaurant chairs, and lighting.

● Antiques International, 53 East 10th Street, New York, N.Y. 10003; 212-777-4360. Eighteenth- and nineteenth-century country furniture: bistro bars, desks, armoires, commodes, buffets, hutches, chairs.

● Jean-Paul Beaujard, 209 East 76th Street, New York, N.Y. 10021; 212-249-3790. Late-nineteenth-century tables and chairs, reproduction brass light fixtures.

● Bon Marché, 74 Fifth Avenue, New York, N.Y. 10011; 212-620-5588. French-style park chairs and bistro tables.

● Howard Kaplan's French Country Store, 35 East 10th Street, New York, N.Y. 10002; 212-674-1000. Reproductions of hard-to-find furniture and pottery, including copies of 1900s brass faucet fixtures, country baskets, and bistro furniture.

● Hubert des Forges, 1193 Lexington Avenue, New York, N.Y. 10028; 212-744-1857; 11 East 10th Street, New York N.Y. 10003; 212-674-0810. Decorative accessories and gifts.

● Pierre Deux, 870 Madison Avenue, New York, N.Y. 10021; 212-570-9343; and 369 Bleecker Street, New York, N.Y. 10014;

Doug Frank

212-243-7740 or 675-4054. Lampshades, cloth-covered boxes, pillows, and French Provençal fabric by the yard.

• La Remise du Soleil, 704 Sansome Street, San Francisco, Calif. 94111; 415-398-8646. French antiques, including bistro furniture.

• La Ville du Soleil, 556 Sutter Street, San Francisco, Calif. 94102; 415-434-0657. Bistro glassware, painted earthenware, candles, and vases.

• Williams-Sonoma, 5750 Nollis Street, Emeryville, Calif. 94608; 415-652-1553. Paris park furniture and bistro tables.

• See pages 88 to 89.

Furniture, contemporary

There are many stores that specialize in contemporary furniture, known as ''lifestyle.'' Listed below are those that seem to carry a particular kind of stock, from Italian modern to simple unpainted units.

• Conran's, 160 East 54th Street, New York, N.Y. 10022; 212-371-2225. Contemporary international home furnishings and accessories, including lamps, modular seating, and storage units. Mail-order catalog available for $2.50 by writing to 145 Huguenot Street, New Rochelle, N.Y. 10805. See also listing under ''Catalogs.''

• The Door Store, 210 East 51st Street, New York, N.Y. 10022; 212-753-2280. Finished and unfinished plain and functional furniture, including storage units, chairs, and tables.

• Furniture-in-the-Raw, 1021 Second Avenue, New York, N.Y. 10022; 212-355-7373. Simple modular wood furniture, including

Painted screen,
Susan Tarlov

cabinets, bookcases, chests, wall units, desks, and files. Mail-order catalog is $2.

• Jensen-Lewis Company, 89 Seventh Avenue, New York, N.Y. 10011; 212-929-4880. Canvas furniture.

• Naked Furniture, 10 West North Avenue, Lombard, Ill. 60148; 312-629-9293. Unfinished furniture.

Furniture, modern

• Theema, 10 Christopher Street, New York, N.Y. 10014; 212-242-8693. Home furnishings and accessories, including platform beds and cotton and satin moving blankets.

• Maurice Villency, 200 Madison Avenue, New York, N.Y. 10016; 212-725-4840.

• West Town House, 2276 Broadway, New York, N.Y. 10025; 212-724-5000. Home furnishings and accessories, including rag rugs, vinyl boxes, and chairs.

• Wim and Karen Scandinavian Furniture, 319 East 53rd Street, New York, N.Y. 10022; 212-758-4207. Features a line of Scandinavian-designed and -inspired furniture.

• Workbench, 470 Park Avenue South, New York, N.Y. 10016; 212-481-5454. Unfinished wood furniture, including oak cabinets, bed frames, and storage units.

• See also listings under ''Craft galleries'' and ''Catalogs.''

Furniture, custom

There are many craftspeople who are designing modern furniture on custom order. While most of these pieces are expensive, they are also sometimes closer to art works than furniture. Many of the designers listed below will work to your speci-

fications and needs.

• Christie Interiors, 114 West 27th Street, New York, N.Y. 10001; 212-929-5274 or 392-1488. A line of furniture and hand-painted fabrics, including knockdown tables and custom cabinetry, modular and nonmodular pieces, and fiberboard lacquered in red, black, silver, or white.

• Howard Crouch, 115 Avenue A, New York, N.Y. 10009; 212-673-6768. Sun trellis, geometric tables.

• Paul Evans, 30 East 61st Street, New York, N.Y. 10021; 212-753-8258. Electromechanical devices for the home.

• George Hollander, 340 West 22nd Street, New York, N.Y. 10011; 212-691-9838. Designer plans and executes interiors, as well as a line of furniture called Alumni, which includes tables with aluminum bases and various tops of bluestone or marble.

• Jeffrey Johnson, 119 Avenue D, New York, N.Y. 10009; 212-674-0245. Designer of lacquered furniture.

• Susan Tarlov, 2255 Broadway, New York, N.Y. 10024; 212-874-7872. Architecturally painted screens.

• See also listings under ''Artists' furniture.''

Furniture, Danish, see ''Danish design.''

Furniture of the Twentieth Century, 154 West 18th Street, New York, N.Y. 10011; 212-929-6023. A to-the-trade source of early-twentieth-century architect-designed furniture by René Herbst, Eileen Gray, Robert Mallet-Stevens, and J.J.P. Oud. See pages 34 to 35 and 70 to 73.

Futons

The traditional Oriental mattresses, called futons, are made up of layers of cotton batting covered with unbleached muslin or cotton fabric. Japanese futons tend to be thinner and more matlike than Chinese ones. All fold or roll up and are particularly useful for extra sleeping surfaces or guest room accommodations. Listed below are some Oriental shops that usually stock the mattresses as well as a number of places that will make futons on special order, and covered with special fabrics.

• Arise Futon Mattress Co., 37 Wooster Street, New York, N.Y. 10013; 212-925-7784.

• Beylerian Ltd., 305 East 63rd Street, New York, N.Y. 10021; 212-755-6303. Wholesale source for futons covered in solid-colored cotton.

• The Futon Shop, 178 West Houston Street, New York, N.Y. 10014; 212-620-9015. Handmade, natural fiber bedding produced by Nancy Wykstra.

• Mingei, 398 West Broadway, New York, N.Y. 10014; 212-431-6176.

• Miya Shoji, 107 West 17th Street, New York, N.Y. 10011; 212-243-6774. Authentic Japanese furnishings and accessories, including custom shoji screens, tatami mats.

• Shinera, 481 Columbus Avenue, New York, N.Y. 10024; 212-362-1367.

• Takony Form and Design, 38-25 Woodside Avenue, Queens, N.Y. 11377; 212-478-2426.

• Tansuya, 159 Mercer Street, New York, N.Y. 10014; 212-966-1782.

• Tony Koga Interiors, 116 Green-point Avenue, Brooklyn, N.Y. 11222; 212-383-8481.

Future Tents, Ltd., 37 Murray Street, New York, N.Y. 10007; 212-732-4691. An architectural and engineering design firm specializing in tensile structures. Founded in 1977 by architects Todd Dalland, Ross Dalland, Nicholas Goldsmith, and Denis Hector. Most of the company's work consists of large-span permanent structures for civic and corporate clients, but it will also design tents for smaller interiors on private commission. See pages 142 to 143.

Galerie Metropol 927 Madison Avenue, New York, N.Y. 10021; 212-772-7401. Furniture gallery that carries early-twentieth-century original pieces, including tubular steel furniture by Marcel Breuer, Josef Hoffmann, and Otto Wagner designs. See also listing for Harwood Galleries. See also pages 34 to 35 and 222 to 225.

Gift stores

Having a store of one's own is many small entrepreneurs' dream, and in the last few years, there has been a burgeoning of such establishments, particularly in the area of home furnishings. The selection of merchandise frequently reflects the owners' personal tastes; the rather idiosyncratic — and often exclusive — wares on display provide a satisfying diversity of objects. Listed below is a selection of such establishments, which can provide the New Yorker as well as the out-of-towner with a beginner's tour of interesting and imaginative shops all over town. They range from the industrial high-tech esthetic to the country home look.

• Accents and Images, 1020 Second Avenue, New York, N.Y. 10022; 212-838-3431. Home decorating accessories, including fine china and crystal, porcelain, sculpture, fragrances, and soaps.

• Stephen Anson, 1058 First Avenue, New York, N.Y. 10022; 212-888-0557. Store that carries crystal, dinnerware, toys, ceramics, potpourri, and soaps.

• Any Occasion, 209 Columbus Avenue, New York, N.Y. 10023; 212-580-1049. Home decorative accessories, china, glass, and ceramics.

• Lee Bailey at Henri Bendel, 10 West 57th Street, New York, N.Y. 10022; 212-247-1100. Home accessories, both decorative and functional, including first-aid kits, handcrafted tableware, and stainless flatware.

• Barney's Chelsea Passage, 111 Seventh Avenue, New York, N.Y. 10011; 212-929-9000. Many imported and well-selected wares, including Le Jacquard table linens and napkins.

• Cache-Cache, 758 Madison Avenue, New York, N.Y. 10021; 212-744-6886. Home decorative accessories, including scented, hand-painted pillows.

• Cherchez, 864 Lexington Avenue, New York, N.Y. 10021; 212-737-8215. Specializes in antique lace, including sachets, pillows, and table linens.

• Diversions, 905 Madison Avenue,

Futon,
The Futon Shop

New York, N.Y. 10021; 212-737-7073. Toys, stationery items, pillows.

• Fiorucci, 125 East 59th Street, New York, N.Y. 10022; 212-751-1404. A trendy clothing store that also stocks a few home accessories.

• Five Eggs, 436 West Broadway, New York, N.Y. 10012; 212-226-1606. Japanese home decorative accessories, including lanterns, lamps, shades, and bedding.

• Gwenda G, 1364 Lexington Avenue, New York, N.Y. 10028; 212-427-9672.

• Home Base, 2335 Broadway, New York, N.Y. 10024; 212-724-5959. Whimsical table-top wares, including mugs, placemats, and glasses.

• Jenny B. Goode, 1194 Lexington Avenue, New York, N.Y. 10021; 212-794-2492. Imaginative tableware and china, as well as toys and stationery.

• Diane Love, Inc., 851 Madison Avenue, New York, N.Y. 10021; 212-879-6997. Specializes in decorative accessories with a floral theme, including vases and antiques, artificial flowers, potpourri, and candles.

• Michel Designs, 1306 Second Avenue, New York, N.Y. 10021; 212-772-9259. Hand-painted and custom-made pottery, art objects, and furniture, including 1940s cookie jars and pitchers.

• Mixed Company, 10 Fifth Avenue, New York, N.Y. 10022; 212-475-1624; and 105 Christopher Street, New York, N.Y. 10014; 212-807-1570. Contemporary novelties and elegant accessories.

• Mythology, 370 Columbus Ave-

nue, New York, N.Y. 10024; 212-874-0774. Toys, posters, home decorative accessories.

• Of All Things, 900 First Avenue, New York, N.Y. 10022; 212-752-3628. Decorative accessories, including stationery, toys, glassware, porcelain, and vases.

• Pizazz, 1270 Madison Avenue, New York, N.Y. 10021; 212-860-2482. Home decorative accessories, including soap and potpourri.

• Robin Importers, 510 Madison Avenue, New York, N.Y. 10022; 212-753-6475. Table linens, table accessories.

• Seabon, 54 East 54th Street, New York, N.Y. 10022; 212-755-0422. Imported things from Scandinavia.

Glassware

One small revolution in the area of home entertaining is the availability of many different types of reasonably priced, hand-blown or machine-made glassware, including tumblers and wine goblets, double old-fashioneds and champagne flutes, squat shot glasses, and shapely brandy glasses. Decades ago, gas stations offered tumblers as premiums and thick-sided jelly glasses were recycled as juice glasses. But now commercially made glass can be delicate looking and find its place on the dining-room table — at a reasonable price. New drinking habits, particularly the flourishing interest in wine, have had an influence on the sale of specialized glassware. The all-purpose wine glass has evolved as the basic black dress of the glassware industry. While the department stores, including Bloomingdale's, Macy's, and B. Altman & Company, carry large selections of inexpensive glassware,

some smaller stores also have good selections — some domestic glass, some imported from the Middle European countries and the Far East. Listed below are a few of these sources.

• Conran's, 160 East 54th Street, New York, N.Y. 10022; 212-371-2225. Italian Campari glasses from Bormioli; wine glasses from Rumania.

• Manhattan Ad Hoc Housewares, 842 Lexington Avenue, New York, N.Y. 10022. 212-752-5488. Milk-shake glasses.

• The Pottery Barn, see listing under "Pottery Barn" for the addresses of this chain of stores that offers one of the best selections of glassware in the New York area. Included are cordial glasses hand-blown in China and tulip-shaped champagne flutes.

• Third Avenue Bazaar, 1362 Third Avenue, New York, N.Y. 10021; 212-861-5999. Fluted-stem wine glasses.

• Tiffany & Company, 727 Fifth Avenue, New York, N.Y. 10022; 212-759-9110. Hollow-stem champagne flutes.

• Turpan Sanders, 386 West Broadway, New York, N.Y. 10012; 212-925-9040. Classic martini glasses from Rumania; glasses from Finland.

• Wolfman-Gold & Good Company, 484 Broome Street, New York, N.Y. 10013; 212-431-1888. Restaurant glassware.

• See also listings under "Housewares."

Gloworm Inc., see Robert Currie.

Eileen Gray, Irish-born architect and furniture designer who lived in Paris most of her life (1879-1976). Her

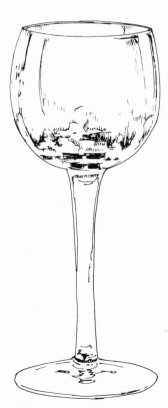

All-purpose wine glass, Pottery Barn

avant-garde designs have been rediscovered, and reproductions of her designs, including lamps, rugs, and chairs, are available from:

Furniture of the Twentieth Century, 154 West 18th Street, New York, N.Y. 10011; 212-929-6023.

Beylerian Ltd., 305 East 63rd Street, New York, N.Y. 10021; 212-755-6303.

Stendig, 410 East 62nd Street, New York, N.Y. 10021; 212-838-6050.

The Museum Store, 37 West 53rd Street, New York, N.Y. 10019; 212-956-7544.

Henri Charles Gueron and Associates: Architects and Planners, 343 East 30th Street, New York, N.Y. 10016; 212-532-4989. Born 1936 in Paris. Moved to the United States in 1948. Studied civil engineering and architecture at Pennsylvania State University. Started practicing in 1966. Current work is mainly commercial space and corporate interiors. Mr. Gueron likes the clean lines of modern design, believing that keeping the geometry simple saves space as well as cost. See pages 68 to 69.

Hammocks

Hammocks are a convenient, popular, and relaxing kind of seating for the outdoors as well as the large living room — and particularly appropriate for open loft spaces. Listed below are a number of sources for these often-woven seats.

• The Gentle Swing, 156 Calle Cristo, San Juan, Puerto Rico 00901; 809-724-6625. Mail-order source for all shapes and styles of handmade hammocks.

• The Hammock Way, 900 North Point, San Francisco, Calif. 93401; 415-776-6650. Hammock chairs.

• Lyon Hammocks, 41 Galen Street, Watertown, Mass. 02172; 617-923-2261. Mail-order source for handwoven cotton Mayan hammocks.

• Twin Oaks Hammocks, Louise, Va. 23093; 703-894-5126. Mail-order source for weather-resistant rope hammocks and sandles made from hammock fiber.

Hardware

• Ball and Ball, 463 Lincoln Highway, Extof, Pa. 19341; 215-363-7330. Hand-forged iron rat-tail hinges and other authentic hardware reproductions from 1680 to 1900.

• Forms and Surfaces, Pacific Design Center, Space 245, 8687 Melrose Avenue, Los Angeles, Calif. 90069; 213-659-9566.

• Hunrath Company, 153 East 57th Street, New York, N.Y. 10022; 212-758-0780. Wholesale and retail decorative bathroom fixtures and accessories in all finishes.

• The Ironmonger, 446 North Wells, Chicago, Ill. 60610; 312-467-4622.

• Simon's Hardware, 421 Third Avenue, New York, N.Y. 10016; 212-532-9220. Wholesale and retail source for a wide selection of hardware of all styles, as well as bathroom fixtures.

Harwood Galleries, 1045 Madison Avenue, New York, N.Y. 10021; 212-744-5062. Specialist in bentwood furniture, Thonet and J.J. Kohn.

Heaney/Magioncalda, 42 West 29th Street, New York, N.Y. 10001; 212-683-1571. Interior designers Ted Heaney, b.1945, and Alan Magioncalda, b.1942, create "eclectic designs that fit into hi-tech." See pages 88 to 89.

René Herbst, French architect and furniture designer. See listing for "Furniture of the Twentieth Century." See pages 34 to 35 and 70 to 73.

Josef Hoffmann, Austrian architect and furniture designer, a founder of the Wiener Werkstatte school. Reproductions of his furniture, accessories, and fabrics are sold through designers and architects at International Contract Furnishings, 305 East 63rd Street, New York, N.Y. 10021; 212-750-0900. Accessories are available at Sointu, 20 East 69th Street, New York, N.Y. 10021; 212-570-9449. Some of his lighting designs are at George Kovacs, 831 Madison Avenue, New York, N.Y. 10021; 212-861-9500, and available through designers and architects at Lighting Associates, 305 East 63rd Street, New York, N.Y. 10021; 212-751-0575.

Richard Holley, 2017 West Gray Street, Houston, Tex. 77019; 713-529-6112. Designer, b.1940 in Texas. Studied interior design at the Pratt Institute in New York. Practiced in London until 1977. Work ranges from residential to commercial, particularly executive suites and stores, such as the Zandra Rhodes boutiques in London and New York. Holley's style, which runs the gamut from minimal to postmodern, depends on the client and his or her needs, but space planning and a

René Herbst chair, Furniture of the Twentieth Century

sense of drama are emphasized. See pages 220 to 221.

Holloware

Holloware is best remembered as the often-scratched pieces of tableware that appeared on breakfast trays in the nicer European hotels. Today, the generously sized pieces are rarer and in many instances have been replaced by lighter stainless steel serving pieces. Holloware is the generic name for tableware that was originally made from a base metal, a nickel and copper alloy, and then covered with a heavy plating of pure silver. The electroplating process that made the pieces possible was patented in the mid-nineteenth century by two Birmingham, England, manufacturers who wanted to develop a cheaper substitute for sterling silver. While stainless steel holloware is still commonly found on many home tables, the hotel-grade ware, heavier and more durable, constructed of nickel silver, is fast disappearing. The International Silver Company, Oneida Silversmiths, and Reed & Barton are three of the remaining domestic suppliers of holloware. New pieces are to be found in stores that specialize in restaurant supply and hotel wares. These include:

• H. Friedman & Sons, 18 Cooper Square, New York, N.Y. 10003; 212-254-9000.

• Town Food Service Equipment Company, 351 Bowery, New York, N.Y. 10002; 212-473-8355.

• See also pages 212 to 217. See also listings under "Kitchens, commercial equipment."

Hot tubs

These originally Californian tubs are finding aficionados in the East — on decks, roofs, and in backyards. The seasons are shorter but many easterners are becoming increasingly out-of-doors addicts for this often-therapeutic mode of bathing and relaxation.

• The Bedpost, 5921 North High Street, Worthington, Ohio 43058; 614-885-5172. Waterbed kits, hot tubs, and mattresses. Available through mail-order; catalog is $1.95.

• Wet Rooms, 168 Garfield Place, Brooklyn, N.Y. 11215; 212-468-8827. Hot tubs and saunas.

Housewares

This category of wares for the home can run the gamut from a stockpot to a room heater. Listed below are a number of stores that usually have a wide selection of kitchen and gourmet items as well as appliances.

• Crosstown Glass and Shade, 200 West 86th Street, New York, N.Y. 10024; 212-787-8040. Bathroom accessories, window parts, and household appliances, including one- and two-inch wood blinds, measured and installed for free.

• Dean & Deluca, 121 Prince Street, New York, N.Y. 10012; 212-254-7774. Kitchen accessories and gourmet products.

• First Stop Housewares, 1025 Second Avenue, New York, N.Y. 10022; 212-838-0007. Lamps, professional lights.

• Bazaar de la Cuisine, 1003 Second Avenue, New York, N.Y. 10021; 212-421-8028. Kitchenwares and accessories.

• Gracious Home, 1220 Third Avenue, New York, N.Y. 10022; 212-535-2033.

• Manhattan Ad Hoc Housewares,

842 Lexington Avenue, New York, N.Y. 10021; 212-752-5488. Complete selection of kitchen and home accessories.

• The New Frontier Trading Corporation, 2394 Broadway, New York, N.Y. 10024; 212-799-9338. Oriental home accessories and kitchen supplies.

• The Pottery Barn. China, glassware, and kitchen equipment. See listing under "Pottery Barn" for all New York locations.

• Turpan Sanders, 386 West Broadway, New York, N.Y. 10012; 212-925-9040. Imaginative and intelligent selection of home furnishings, with products chosen more for function and quality of materials than for high design.

• Wolfman-Gold & Good Company, 484 Broome Street, New York, N.Y. 10013; 212-431-1888. All-white china, restaurant ware, antique linens.

• Zabar's, 2245 Broadway, New York, N.Y. 10024; 212-787-2000. Discount kitchen appliances and housewares, including Braun and Krups.

• See also listings under "Glassware," "Gift stores," and "Catalogs."

IPF International, 11-13 Maryland Avenue, Paterson, N.J. 07503; 203-345-7440. Antique reproductions, including a Louis XV chaise longue and French-style beechwood mantels.

Holloware,
H. Friedman & Sons

International Contract Furnishings, Inc., 305 East 63rd Street, New York, N.Y. 10021; 212-750-0900. To-the-trade source for imported furniture, including designs by Alvar Aalto, Josef Hoffmann, and Marcel Breuer. For other sources of designer furniture, see listings under the individual designers' names. See pages 34 to 35, 204 to 205, and 222 to 225.

Robin Jacobsen, see Bromley-Jacobsen Architecture & Design.

Jewelite Signs and Letters, 154 Reade Street, New York, N.Y. 10013; 212-683-4474. Specializes in custom-made signs and letters, including hand lettering on plaques, assorted Plexiglas, Lucite, acrylic, and various plastics. See also listings under "Plastic materials."

Eileen Joyce, see Richard Knapple, Inc.

Kaplan/Aronson, 156 Fifth Avenue, New York, N.Y. 10010; 212-242-0066. Manufacturer and distributor of kitchen utensils and gadgets, including corkscrews and bottle and jar openers.

Kenny Company, P.O. Box 9132, St. Louis, Mo. 63117; 314-724-3978. Source for the Plug-Lok, a device to lock the television set.

Kilims

There are many independent dealers, many of whom travel to the East periodically and sell out of their homes or small showrooms, who offer these Oriental rugs. Listed below are a number who specialize particularly in this kind of rug.

• Renée Gilodo, Kilims from Turkey, 799 Broadway, Room 608, New York, N.Y. 10003; 212-673-2197. Handwoven rugs and tapestries.

• Kamdin Designs, 791 Lexington Avenue, New York, N.Y. 10022; 212-371-8833. Indian dhurries.

• Kilims, 150 Thompson Street, New York, N.Y. 10012; 212-533-1677. Linda Miller sells rare, old, and antique flat-woven tapestry rugs from Morocco.

• M. Miller Kilims, 148 East 28th Street, New York, N.Y. 10016; 212-685-7746. Old kilims and kilim pillows.

• See also listings under "Carpets and carpeting," and "Tapestries."

Kitchen accessories, see "Housewares."

Kitchens, commercial equipment

Restaurant stoves and equipment, because of their gutsy looks and efficient operation, have found their way into many homes. Listed below are stores and suppliers of the well-known brands.

• AAA Restaurant Equipment, 284 Bowery, New York, N.Y. 10012; 212-966-1891.

• Ackley Mutual Equipment Company, 358 West 18th Street, New York, N.Y. 10011; 212-255-2220. All commercial appliances.

• American Metal Restaurant Equipment Company, 43-04 19th Avenue, Long Island City, N.Y. 11105; 212-932-0323.

• Crescent Metal Products, 12825 Taft Avenue, Cleveland, Ohio 44108; 216-851-6800. Restaurant ranges, ovens, warmers.

• Daroma Restaurant Equipment Corporation, 196 Bowery, New York, N.Y. 10012; 212-226-6774.

• Hobart Corporation, 48-48 Fifth Street, Long Island City, N.Y. 11101; 212-361-1010. Under-the-counter, four-minute-cycle dishwashers.

• Matas Restaurant Supply Corporation, 226 Bowery, New York, N.Y. 10012; 212-966-2251.

• New York Soda Fountain Company, 1399 Park Avenue, New York, N.Y. 10029; 212-534-2242.

• The Professional Kitchen, 18 Cooper Square, New York, N.Y. 10003. 212-254-9000.

• Vulcan-Hart Corporation, 200 Park Avenue South, New York, N.Y. 10003; 212-475-1120. Offices also in Baltimore, Louisville, St. Louis, Dallas, Miami, Detroit, Cleveland, and Boston. Commercial kitchen appliances, including refrigerators, convection oven-base ranges, rolltop dishwashers.

• See also pages 212 to 217.

Kitchens, European

Traditionally, in the United States, kitchens come with an apartment or house; in Europe, they belong to the tenant. When someone moves in, he or she buys a kitchen, as one might a sofa, and takes it along when moving out. The cabinets are not custom built, but hung on a wall, and each has its own back and can be disassembled. European kitchens are more like a moveable stor-

Restaurant stove, Vulcan-Hart

age system than equipment. Recent co-op, condominium, and loft renovations as well as rising prices and the difficulty of obtaining custom cabinetry have prompted a resurgence of interest in European kitchens. Listed below are the names of a number of importers of these units.

• International Contract Furnishings, 305 East 63rd Street, New York, N.Y. 10021; 212-750-0900. A to-the-trade company that imports the Italian-made Boffi Glacé kitchen units, which are available in plastic laminate, ash, elm wood, and polyester lacquer finishes.

• Euro Concepts Limited, 964 Third Avenue, New York, N.Y. 10022; 212-688-4910. To-the-trade showroom that carries the Allmilmo kitchens.

Joseph Lembo

• Architects Samples Corporation, 22 East 40th Street, New York, N.Y. 10016; 212-683-1400. Stainless steel Italian Alpes Inox kitchen components.

• Hastings Tile and Il Bagno Collection, 201 East 57th Street, New York, N.Y. 10022; 212-755-2710. The Poggenpohl units are available from this to-the-trade showroom.

• Nema Furniture, 150 East 58th Street, New York, N.Y. 10022; 212-758-0193. To-the-trade showroom for the Italian Salvarini kitchen units.

• Conran's, 160 East 54th Street, New York, N.Y. 10022; 212-371-2225. Knockdown pine kitchen available in this retail store or by mail order.

Richard Knapple, Inc. 18 East 53rd Street, New York, N.Y. 10022; 212-752-7201. Partners Richard Knapple and Eileen Joyce do residential and commercial design

work. See pages 20 to 21.

Knoll International, 655 Madison Avenue, New York, N.Y. 10022; 212-826-2400; and 105 Wooster Street, New York, N.Y. 10012; 212-334-1525. A to-the-trade designer furniture manufacturer, offering designs by Marcel Breuer, Joseph Paul D'Urso, Mies van der Rohe, and Eero Saarinen. See pages 222 to 225.

George Kovacs Lighting, 831 Madison Avenue, New York, N.Y. 10021; 212-861-9500. See also listing under "Lighting, retail."

Kulicke Frames, made by A.P.F. Inc., 35 East 76th Street, New York, N.Y. 10021; 212-988-1090; 601 West 26th Street, New York, N.Y. 10001; 212-924-6660; and 315 East 91st Street, New York, N.Y. 10028; 212-860-2500. Modern and reproduction frames, in stock and made to order.

L

LCS Inc., 1059 Third Avenue, New York, N.Y. 10021; 212-838-6420. To-the-trade showroom for unusual furniture, accessories, and fabrics.

Jack Lenor Larsen, 232 East 59th Street, New York, N.Y. 10022; 212-674-3993; 41 East 11th Street, New York, N.Y. 10003; 212-674-3993. To-the-trade source for designer fabrics, furniture, and floor coverings. See also pages 230 to 231.

Laundries, special

The laundries listed below offer special services for fine linens.

• Mme. Blanchevoye, 75 East 130th Street, New York, N.Y. 10037; 212-368-7272.

• Daniele, 1334 Lexington Avenue, New York, N.Y. 10028; 212-534-1483.

• Jeeves of Belgravia, 770 Madison Avenue, New York, N.Y. 10021; 212-570-9130.

• Park Avenue French Hand Laundry, 1305 Madison Avenue, New York, N.Y. 10028; 212-289-4950.

Frederick A. Lee, 682 Broadway, New York, N.Y. 10012; 212-473-1829 or 392-0656. Architect, b.1944 in New York City. Received Bachelor of Architecture and Master of Science degrees from Columbia University. Worked with Norman Jaffee for two years, and with Marcel Breuer for one and a half years. See pages 136 to 139.

Joseph Lembo, 116 West 29th Street, New York, N.Y. 10001; 212-279-4452. Designer, b.1953. Minimalist, designed Stillwende discotheque, New York City. See pages 8 to 9 and 128 to 131.

Raimundo Lemus, 125 Christopher Street, New York, N.Y. 10014; 212-691-4035. Store with furniture designed by Raimundo Lemus. See pages 198 to 203.

Lighting Associates, 305 East 63rd Street, New York, N.Y. 10021; 212-751-0575. To-the-trade lighting systems and lamps. See pages 34 to 35.

Lighting, designers

There's more to modern lighting than plugging in a lamp. And the newest catchwords in interior design are amps, wattage, lumen, low voltage, recessed and direct, wall washers, up and down lights, track, spot, or flood lights. Discotheques, the theater, new computer technology, and even the energy crisis have made consumers more aware of the possibilities and the choices that modern home lighting presents. The lighting designer, once called in after the fact, has taken center stage and has become integral to the planning of an interior design project. Lighting designers are neither electricians nor lighting salesmen; some come from the theater, where lighting design is an acknowledged profession, others have backgrounds in engineering, architecture, and interior design. Listed below are a number of lighting designers and consultants.

• Douglas Baker, 745 Fifth Avenue, New York, N.Y. 10022; 212-371-1960.

• Thomas L. Foerderer, 122 Remsen Street, Brooklyn, N.Y. 11201; 212-237-2131.

• Incorporated Consultants, 175 Fifth Avenue, New York, N.Y. 10010; 212-475-3810.

• Retina, 133 Greene Street, New York, N.Y. 10012; 212-226-3700.

• Ron Rezek/Lighting, 5041 West Pico Boulevard, Los Angeles, Calif. 90019; 213-931-2488. Designer lighting, perforated shades, diffused and focused light, hanging and floor systems.

• Say It In Neon, 444 Hudson Street, New York, N.Y. 10014; 212-691-7977. Custom-designed neon signs.

• Dana Simmons, East Main Road, Little Compton, R.I. 02837; 401-635-2657.

• Brian Thompson, 954 Lexington Avenue, New York, N.Y. 10021;

212-628-1077.

• Wheel Gersztoff Associates, 40 East 49th Street, New York, N.Y. 10022; 212-752-1590.

• See pages 58 to 63.

Lighting, retail

• Just Bulbs, 934 Broadway, New York, N.Y. 10011; 212-228-7820. Foreign bulbs, hard-to-find bulbs, and unusual function bulbs.

• George Kovacs Lighting, 831 Madison Avenue, New York, N.Y. 10021; 212-861-9848; and 230 Fifth Avenue, New York, N.Y. 10016; 212-683-5744.

• Lamp Warehouse, 1073 39th Street, Brooklyn, N.Y. 11219; 212-436-2207.

• Light, Inc., 1162 Second Avenue, New York, N.Y. 10021; 212-838-1130.

• Lighting Center, 1097 Second Avenue, New York, N.Y. 10021; 212-888-0571; and 353 East 58th Street, New York, N.Y. 10022; 212-752-6868. Lighting systems and accessories.

• Morsa, 247 Center Street, New York, N.Y. 10013; 212-226-4324.

• Novitas, 1523 26th Street, Santa Monica, Calif. 90404; 213-829-1822. Manufacturer of Light-o-Matic, an electronic helper that turns on interior lights when door is opened.

• Thunder and Light, 171 Bowery, New York, N.Y. 10002; 212-966-0757. Wholesale and retail company that imports exclusive Italian-designed lights and innovative lighting systems.

Linens, Bed, see ''Bed Linens.''

Mario Locicero, 343 West 71st Street, New York, N.Y. 10023;

212-873-2439. Interior designer Mario Locicero, b. 1942 in Brooklyn, is a fantasist and minimalist. See pages 18 to 19.

Manhattan Ad Hoc Housewares, see listings under ''Housewares'' and ''Glassware.''

Lee Mindel, see Shelton, Stortz, Mindel & Associates.

Miniatures

Miniatures are not only for children. On the contrary, collecting and making small-scale furnishings is a growing pastime. Listed below are a number of sources for these tiny pieces, from Victorian and bentwoodlike pieces to modern appliances on a tiny scale.

• Dollhouse Antics, 1308 Madison Avenue, New York, N.Y. 10028; 212-876-2288.

• The Enchanted Doll House, Manchester Center, Vt. 05255; 802-362-3030. A mail-order company featuring a 112-page catalog of collectors' dolls, play dolls, toys, books, and games.

• Minis by Me, 16 Broadway, Malverne, N.Y. 11565; 516-599-6608. Miniatures produced by Elaine Fleishman and Marilyn Davidson that are scaled one inch to the foot and based on life-sized furniture, including sofa, dining set, lamp, kitchen, and grandfather clock.

• Malcolm Thomas, 19 Bank Street, New York, N.Y. 10014; 212-255-1831. Dale Flick and Martin Stone

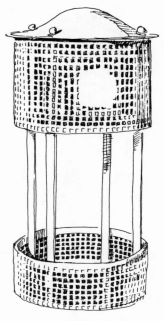

Josef Hoffmann lamp, George Kovacs Lighting

Juan Montoya

Richard Oliver

produce miniature versions of classic furniture.

• Tiny Doll House, 231 East 53rd Street, New York, N.Y. 10022; 212-752-3082.

Master Crafters, 42 Orchard Street, Manhasset, N.Y. 11030; 516-627-5484. A nonprofit community service project that markets crafts by elderly Nassau County residents. Products include folk art, wind chimes, pottery, and afghans.

Juan Montoya Design Corporation, 80 Eighth Avenue, New York, N.Y. 10019; 212-242-3622. Interior architect, b.1945 in Bogotá, Colombia. Began with a concept of ''elegant, precise, and comfortable'' design, which he has ''continually tried to hone and perfect on each successive assignment. My designs are comparable to a Chanel dress.'' See pages 12 to 15, 114 to 115, and 178 to 181.

The Phillip Mueller Company, P.O. Box 73, New York, N.Y. 10002; 212-834-9111. Artist who designs and produces lacquered objects for the home, including masks, platters and plates, baskets, lamps, bird cages, table mats, bar trays, candlesticks, cutlery, and fitted picnic baskets with utensils.

N

Neas, Richard , see page 185.

Novo Arts, 57 East 11th Street, New York, N.Y. 10003; 212-674-3093. A fine arts consulting service available to corporations, decorators, architects, and private clients. Services include the purchasing of art collections, advising private investors and organizing the presentation and placement of acquisitions. Maintains large inventory of contemporary American art. See pages 36 to 37. See also listings under ''Artists' furniture.''

O

Richard Oliver, 23 East 26th Street, New York, N.Y. 10010; 212-685-4620. Architect, b. 1942 in California. Received his Master of Architecture degree from the University of Pennsylvania in 1967. Taught at several universities and uses ''traditional and/or modern elements to create a solution which is specific to time and place.'' See pages 80 to 83.

P

P & K Products Company, 640 Church Road, Elgin Oaks Industrial Park, Elgin, Ill. 60120; 312-695-7070. Decorative products designed with sports logos from the NFL, NHL, NBA, and others, including wastebaskets, trays, helmets, and lamps.

Paneling

• Michael Alexander, 454 Union Street, San Francisco, Calif. 94133; 415-982-7980.

• Hanlen Organization, 401 North Michigan Avenue, Chicago, Ill. 60611; 312-222-1080.

• Yorkraft, P.O. Box 2386, 550 South Pine Street, York, Pa. 17405; 717-845-3666. Decorative panels for ceilings, walls, windows, and dividers. Colors are silk-screened on translucent acrylic panels for the effect of stained glass. Panels are available in standard and custom sizes.

Patchel Byron & Associates, 322 West 57th Street, New York, N.Y. 10019; 212-582-7340. Estelle Patchel, b.1956 in Wayne, N.J., and Michael Byron, b.1954 in Toronto, studied together at Parsons School of Design. In addition to residential projects, their firm does photographic styling, commercial showrooms. ''We think of an interior space as a three-dimensional collage, finding the most exciting spaces to be the ones that are never finished, where one can still participate by adding and subtracting accessories, and by changing the furniture arrangement.'' See pages 106 to 107.

Karl Pehme, 1175 Johnson Street, Brooklyn, N.Y. 11201; 212-875-8151. Sculptor of three-dimensional work for commercial projects and individual buyers, including display houses and props.

Pet Alert, made by Chroma, P.O. Box 3532, Annapolis, Md. 21403; 301-268-3050. Signs to alert firemen and neighbors about pets in case of fire.

Pierre Deux, see listing under ''Furniture, bistro and country French.''

Pillows, hand-painted

• Linda Braun, 237 East 26th Street, New York, N.Y. 10010; 212-659-3238. Designs and hand-paints pillows, floor cloths, upholstery, and wall hangings, primarily on canvas.

● See also listings under "Fabric, hand-painted."

"Places," published by Tenth House Enterprises, P.O. Box 810, Gracie Station, New York, N.Y. 10028; 212-737-7536. A directory of public places for private events, and private places for public functions.

Plaster

● Felber Studios, P.O. Box 551-U, 110 Ardmore Avenue, Ardmore, Pa. 19003; 215-642-4710. Plaster ceiling decorations, cartouches, cornices, brackets, capitals. A staff of sculptors and designers works from sketches, photographs, and architectural drawings. Will work from cast stone.

● Eugene Lucchesi, 859 Lexington Avenue, New York, N.Y. 10021; 212-744-6773. Art stone, plaster.

Plastic Materials

● Abacus Plastics, 102 West 29th Street, New York, N.Y. 10001; 212-947-8990. Line of contemporary Lucite furniture and accessories, including furniture, shelving, and carts.

● Ralph Wilson Plastics Company, Temple, Tex. 76501; 817-778-2711. Decorative laminate. See pages 184 to 187.

Playgrounds

● There are some artists and designers who tend to specialize in playgrounds for children. Listed below are a few who have recently completed such projects.

● Sheila Berkley, P.O. Box 501, Gracie Station, New York, N.Y. 10028; 212-722-7190. Designs and builds miniature metal sculptures, including playgrounds for children.

● Soft Space Playgrounds, 59 Carmine Street, New York, N.Y. 10014; 212-741-0433. Soft interior playgrounds: large geometric shapes made of solid foam covered in bright vinyls, including giant slides, giant steps, and huge pads.

● David Stiles, 161 East 91st Street, New York, N.Y. 10028; 212-427-2317.

Plexi-Craft Quality Products Corporation, 514 West 24th Street, New York, N.Y. 10011; 212-924-3244. Acrylic goods, including pedestals, cubes, shelving units, and magazine racks.

P. & G. Plumbing, 155 Harrison Avenue, Brooklyn, N.Y. 11206; 212-384-6310. Pedestal sinks, claw-foot tubs, pull-chain toilets from renovated apartments and houses.

Pop Art Stable, 132 Round Hill Road, Greenwich, Conn. 06830; 203-661-4889. Stuart Calle models ordinary games into extraordinary sizes, including huge backgammon and checker sets.

Pop Eye Gallery, 390 West Broadway, New York, N.Y. 10012; 212-925-7300. Oversized versions of everyday things, including paper clips, cups and saucers, and crayons.

Portraits, houses

● Susan Cohen, 364 West 18th Street, New York, N.Y. 10011; 212-741-7270. Artist who paints portraits of interiors and views from windows.

● Bess Schuyler, 246 West 16th Street, New York, N.Y. 10010; 212-255-4611. Artist who paints portraits of houses on colored ceramics. May be commissioned to do plaques of an entire facade on a scale of half an inch to the foot, or just the doorway. Also works from photographs.

● Trudi Frank, 1230 Park Avenue, New York, N.Y. 10028; 212-348-2908. Artist who paints portraits of people's favorite objects, paying particular attention to textures, patterns, and details.

● Michael Parkinson, 309 East 95th Street, New York, N.Y. 10028; 212-427-4837. Sculptor who designs and produces miniature replicas of homes and buildings.

Portraits, pets

● Robert Greene, 344 West 72nd Street, New York, N.Y. 10023; 212-724-5018. Miniature paintings of people and their pets.

Pot Covers, 101 West 28th Street, New York, N.Y. 10001; 212-594-5075. Imports from Haiti, Africa, Thailand, Brazil, China, and the Philippines. See pages 218 to 219.

The Pottery Barn, 231 Tenth Avenue, New York, N.Y. 10001; 212-741-9120. Other branches are:

117 East 59th Street, New York, N.Y. 10022; 212-741-9132.

2109 Broadway, New York, N.Y. 10023; 212-741-9123.

49 Greenwich Avenue, New York, N.Y. 10011; 212-741-9140.

1292 Lexington Avenue, New York, N.Y. 10022; 212-741-9134.

1451 Second Avenue, New York, N.Y. 10021; 212-741-9142.

250 West 57th Street, New York, N.Y. 10019; 212-741-9145.

Pritam & Eames, 29 Race Lane, East Hampton, N.Y. 11937; 516-324-7111. Furniture gallery that specializes in pieces by the crafts-

Giant toothbrush, Pop Eye Gallery

men who taught today's generation of artists. These include Wendell Castle, Wharton Esherick, William Keyse, and George Nakashima. See also listings under "Craft galleries" and "Artists' furniture."

Quilts

Collecting antique quilts, learning to make new quilts using traditional fabrics, and restoring and caring for old fabrics are all part of the current interest in Americana and folk art.

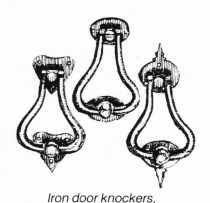

Iron door knockers, The Renovator's Supply

• Come Quilt With Me, P.O. Box 1063, Cadman Plaza Station, Brooklyn, N.Y. 11202; 212-469-0030. Pat Yamin, an experienced quilter and teacher, runs this mail-order quilting supply business and teaches quilting classes. Register for classes at Made in America, 1234 Madison Avenue, New York, N.Y. 10028; 212-289-1113.

• Draperies Direct, 112 Lincoln Avenue, Bronx, N.Y. 10454; 212-993-5668. Company that quilts bed-spreads, slipcovers, draperies, and accessories for greater durability and body.

• Judy King, 536 Highway 3A, Bow, N.H. 03301. King sews custom-made quilts, incorporating into her design any pictures, patterns, and quotations desired by the customer.

• Madison Quilt Shop, 2307 Grand Concourse, Bronx, N.Y. 10468; 212-733-2100. Hand-quilted comforters, pillows, and bolsters, stuffed with down feathers, wool, or synthetic material.

• The Textile Conservation Workshop, Main Street, South Salem, N.Y. 10590; 914-763-5805. Conservation of quilts of any kind.

• For antique quilt sources see listings under "Americana, antiques," and pages 198 to 203. For new quilts, see listings under "Americana, new."

Redroof Design, 30 East 20th Street, New York, N.Y. 10003; 212-598-0360. Yann Weymouth, b.1941 in California, and Peter Coan, b.1946 in New York City. Architects. "What excites us is translating people's needs and desires into an ordered, working reality. We build with durable materials and take an almost obsessive care in their detail and assembly. And when we succeed, the spaces we make have a kind of serenity to them." See pages 138 to 139 and 144 to 147.

The Renovator's Supply, 750 Northfield Road, Millers Falls, Mass. 03149; 413-659-3006. Mail-order catalog for renovation supplies, including brass lamps and side-bolt locks.

Rentals

While there are many professional party-rental concerns, listed below are a few companies that provide custom, and often expensive, entertaining services. For information for floral design, look at the listings under "Flowers, as design."

• Table Wraps, 959 Brush Hollow Road, Westbury, N.Y. 11590; 516-334-8833. Party cloths and napkins.

• Goslee Associates, 1100 Madison Avenue, New York, N.Y. 10021; 212-737-0252. Napkins and tableware as well as floral designs.

• Renny Designs for Entertaining, 27 East 62nd Street, New York, N.Y. 10021; 212-371-5354. A full-service company for entertaining, including dinnerware and linens.

Repair, carpets

• Beshar's, 49 East 53rd Street, New York, N.Y. 10022; 212-758-1400.

• Dildarian, 595 Madison Avenue, New York, N.Y. 10022; 212-288-4948.

• Pat Konecky, 500 West End Avenue, New York, N.Y. 10024; 212-874-1662.

Repair, china and glass

• Art Cut Glass Studio, 79 East 10th Street, New York, N.Y. 10003; 212-982-9580.

• Center Art Studio, 149 West 57th Street, New York, N.Y. 10019; 212-247-3550.

• Expert China Repairs, 231 East 50th Street, New York, N.Y. 10022; 212-355-7467.

• Gem Monogram and Cut Glass, 623 Broadway, New York, N.Y. 10013; 212-674-8960.

• Hess Repairs, 200 Park Avenue South, New York, N.Y. 10003; 212-260-2255.

• Mr. Fixit, 1300 Madison Avenue, New York, N.Y. 10028; 212-369-7775.

Repair, furniture

• Antique Furniture Workroom, 225 East 24th Street, New York, N.Y.

10010; 212-683-0551.

• Kurdan Building Contractors, 10-21 47th Road, Long Island City, N.Y. 11101; 212-729-7373.

• Sack Conservation Company, 15 East 57th Street, New York, N.Y. 10022; 212-753-6562.

• Max Schneider and Son Antiques, 225 East 24th Street, New York, N.Y. 10010; 212-369-2065.

• Sotheby's Restoration, 440 East 91st Street, New York, N.Y. 10028; 212-472-3463.

Repair, marble

• New York Marble Works, 1399 Park Avenue, New York, N.Y. 10028; 212-534-2242.

Repair, sewing machines

• Village Craftsmen, 57 Rockaway Avenue, Valley Stream, N.Y. 11580; 516-825-9371. Repairs sewing machines, specializing in home machines, and fabricates parts.

Repair, typewriters

• The U-Type-It Center, 60 West 39th Street, New York, N.Y. 10018; 212-354-6888. Rental and repair of typewriters.

Ron Rezek, see listing under "Lighting, designers."

Ribbons and Rolls, see listing under "Wrapping."

Gerrit Rietveld, furniture designer. For sources of reproductions of his designs, see pages 204 to 205.

M. Clark Robertson Studio, 401 Lafayette Street, New York, N.Y. 10003; 212-420-9804. Textile surface designer who prints and produces his own fabrics by silkscreen.

Rock-A-Way, 3523 Hull Avenue,

Bronx, N.Y. 10467; 212-654-5026. Antique and contemporary rocking pieces.

Robert L. Rodin, 116 West 29th Street, New York, N.Y. 10001; 212-244-0554. Architect, b.1951 in New York City. Studied at the Pratt Institute and the Polytechnic of Central London. Work is both commercial and residential. Rodin believes that designs should be "readable" and the effect understandable to anyone. See pages 212 to 213.

Mies van der Rohe, furniture designer. His work is available through designers and architects at Knoll International, 655 Madison Avenue, New York, N.Y. 10022; 212-826-2400.

Rookwood, P.O. Box 8924, Cincinnati, Ohio 45208; 513-321-6742. Retail source for American pottery.

Room Service Antiques, 1239 First Avenue, New York, N.Y. 10021; 212-879-0961. Old and new pieces, including some turn-of-the-century English oak tables and stenciled mirrors.

Rugs, see "Tapestries," "Carpets and carpeting," and "Kilims."

Scentsitivity, 39 East 65th Street, New York, N.Y. 10021; 212-988-2822. Gifts and indulgences geared to the senses, including potpourri, soaps, and perfumes.

Michael Schaible, see Bray-Schaible.

Second Hand Rose, 573 Hudson Street, New York, N.Y. 10014;

212-989-9776; and 131 Perry Street, New York, N.Y. 10014; 212-243-9522. Modern furniture, fabrics, and accessories from the 1920s to the 1950s.

Second Helping, 2768 Broadway, New York, N.Y. 10025; 212-866-0688. Second-generation New York kitchenware.

Paul Segal Architects Associates, 730 Fifth Avenue, New York, N.Y. 10022; 212-247-7440. Architect, b.1944 in New York City. The firm is composed of twenty-four designers and architects who do work on commercial, multifamily, and unusual buildings, as well as renovations in landmark buildings. See pages 48 to 53 and 92 to 97.

Shelton, Stortz, Mindel & Associates, 216 West 18th Street, New York, N.Y. 10011; 212-691-3962. Established in 1978, the firm consists of partners Peter Shelton, Robert Stortz, and Lee Mindel. The company provides architectural, interior, and graphic design work, as well as real estate development services. See pages 98 to 101.

Silver

• Charles H. Fuller, P.O. Box 4325 Main Station, San Francisco, Calif. 94101; or 1855 Market Street, San Francisco, Calif. 94103; 415-626-2300. Fuller, with an inventory of patterns dating from 1828, can help a customer locate discontinued silver-plate and sterling patterns by mail-order.

Siris-Coombs Architects, 2112 Broadway, New York, N.Y. 10023; 212-580-2220. Both Peter Coombs, b.1944, and Jane Siris, b.1946, received their Masters of Architecture from Columbia University, then spent five years at different

Peter Coombs and Jane Siris

firms before going into business as a team in 1976. They will take on a variety of design projects, including private and multifamily residences, commercial space, and construction and renovation. Their definition of good design is ''that which satisfies both the client's needs and tastes and the architect's desire to pursue an aesthetic and dynamic space through form and use of materials.'' See pages 54 to 56.

Skylights

• B.B. Plastics, 2015 Blake Street, Berkeley, Calif. 94704; 415-845-6527. Plexiglas bubble skylighting and ventilating bubbles.

Sointu Modern Design Store, 20 East 69th Street, New York, N.Y. 10021; 212-570-9449. Modern design classics, including avant-garde jewelry and accessories designed by Hans Appenzeller; vases and bowls of anodized aluminum; work by Erik Magnusen and International Contract Furnishings reproduction pieces designed by the Viennese architect Josef Hoffmann.

Sola Designs, 242 West 27th Street, New York, N.Y. 10001; 212-242-2224; and Ballek Road, Riegelsville, Pa. 18077; 215-838-0040. Louis Tregre designs, selects and produces items for the use of the elderly and people of all ages who do not possess full physical capabilities. Pieces include seating, tables, beds, and tableware.

Square One L.A., 8806 Beverly Boulevard, Los Angeles, Calif. 90048; 213-275-6683. Industrial objects and furniture, including metal shelving, slate marble, lacquered beds, circular staircases, fabrics by Uli, hand-painted screens by Mo and Lisa McDermott, and

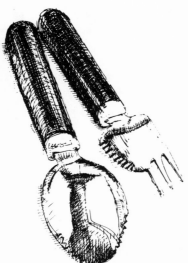

Knoon and knork,
Sola

stools. See also listings under ''Housewares.''

Stained glass

• Great American Salvage, 3 Main Street, Montpelier, Vt. 05602; 802-223-7711. Stocks three hundred stained-glass panels. Mail-order service with access to other sources.

• See also listings under ''Architectural details.''

Stainless steel flatware

Stainless steel used to be sterling silver's poor relation. But rising silver prices and sheer convenience have brought this easy-to-care-for and practical type of flatware out of the kitchen and into the dining room. Unlike sterling silver, which is made of nearly pure silver, or silver plate, in which a certain weight of silver is electroplated to a brass or copper alloy base, stainless steel is an iron-based material that is durable and rust-resistant. As its name implies, stainless will resist most acids and stains from foods such as eggs. Buying stainless steel flatware can be a confusing task. To judge quality, check if the finish is shiny or matte. The choice is a matter of taste, but there should be no blemishes on the surfaces or edges. In general, lighter pieces are cheaper as they contain less material and will bend more easily under pressure. A heavier piece is sturdier, but can be clumsy. All stainless steel has an iron base. Added to it is chrome or chrome and nickel, known as the 18/8 type. The best material for forks and spoons is a chrome and nickel variation because it is more rust-resistant. If a knife blade is sharp, it will probably have been made from the better-quality ma-

terial and will have the best cutting edge. Some names to look for in stainless steel flatware in terms of quality of material used as well as design include Stanley Roberts, Dansk International, Reed & Barton, H.E. Lauffer, Oneida, Trend Pacific, National Silver, Supreme Cutlery, Oxford Hall, Georg Jensen, Dalia, and Georgian House. Many large department stores, such as Bloomingdale's, B. Altman & Company, Macy's, and Abraham & Straus, carry a wide selection of stainless steel flatware at a range of prices. Other sources include:

• Lee Bailey at Henri Bendel, 10 West 57th Street, New York, N.Y. 10019; 212-247-1100.

• Manhattan Ad Hoc Housewares, 842 Lexington Avenue, New York, N.Y. 10021; 212-752-5488.

• Turpan Sanders, 386 West Broadway, New York, N.Y. 10011; 212-925-9040.

• Fortunoff's, 681 Fifth Avenue, New York, N.Y. 10022; 212-758-6660.

• Conran's, 160 East 54th Street, New York, N.Y. 10022; 212-371-2225.

Stairs

• Boston Design Corporation, 42 Plimpton Street, Boston, Mass. 02118; 617-426-5887 or 800-225-5584. Mail-order and showroom, with custom-worked spiral stairs and benches. See also pages 136 to 139.

John Stedila Design, 175 West 93rd Street, Penthouse A, New York, N.Y. 10025; 212-865-6611. Designer, b.1946 in Pennsylvania. Approaches each project ''space first, then furniture, then color.'' He is drawn to making space "as simple and open as possible," and never denies "a view or source of light." $15,000 minimum per room, but flexible. Partner is Tim Button. See pages 136 to 137.

Stenciling

Stenciling, a traditional decorative art, is enjoying a revival, especially in country interiors. There are many stenciling traditions and patterns to choose from, from Early American to Victorian, and most book stores stock a number of pattern and methodology books. Although stenciling is an art that many people can learn to do by themselves and be adept at, there are professional stencilers to hire who will adapt traditional patterns or create new ones to match a particular interior scheme. Listed below are some professional stenciling artists.

• Joanne Alderman, 307 West 92nd Street, New York, N.Y. 10025; 212-678-1177. Specialist in Early American stencils.

• The Clayton Store, Star Route, Southfield, Mass. 02159; 413-229-2621. Artists Neil and Sue Connell do custom stenciling.

• Pamela Friend, 590 King Street, Hanover, Mass. 02339; 617-878-7596. Custom cutting and painting of stencils, $150 to $500 a room.

• Itinerant Reproduction, Hinman Lane, Southbury, Conn. 06488; 203-264-8000. Lectures and workshops on Early American wall and floor stenciling, and availability of artists.

• Cile Lord, 42 East 12th Street, New York, N.Y. 10003; 212-228-6030. Stenciling of floors and walls.

• Virginia Teichner, P.O. Box 844, New Canaan, Conn. 06840; 203-355-1517. Stenciling and adapting patterns for an entire room can start at $750. For an example of this artist's work, see pages 226 to 229.

• Adele Bishop Stencil Workshops and Seminars, Box 557, Manchester, Vt. 05254; 802-362-3537. Write or call this group for information on stenciling seminars and workshops given throughout the country.

Robert A.M. Stern, 200 West 72nd Street, New York, N.Y. 10023; 212-799-9690. Born in 1939 in New York City. Attended the Yale School of Architecture. A leading postmodernist, Stern's practice consists of institutional, commercial, and residential work. See pages 30 to 33.

Robert Mallet-Stevens, French furniture designer. Reproductions of his designs are available from Furniture of the Twentieth Century.

Robert Stortz, see Shelton, Stortz, Mindel & Associates.

Carole Stupell, 61 East 57th Street, New York, N.Y. 10022; 212-260-3100. Store that specializes in home decorative accessories geared to table setting. See also listings under "Gift stores."

Charles Swerz and Associates, 202 West 40th Street, New York, N.Y. 10018; 212-921-7980. Both Charles Swerz, b.1948, and Jerry Van Deelen, b.1951, are designers who studied in California before founding their own firm in 1979. According to Swerz, the client should spend money on "space first, furnishings next — and lighting is also important." No minimum. "We don't turn people down because of dollars." See pages 172 to 177.

T

Tapestries

Tapestries, or woven wall hangings, are available in a wide variety of forms. Many craftspeople and artists can be commissioned to make tapestries to fit a certain space or to coordinate with an interior design scheme. Listed below are a number of galleries and artists who specialize in this craft. See also listings under "Craft galleries."

• ACA American Indian Arts, 25 East 73rd Street, New York, N.Y. 10021; 212-861-5533. Navajo rugs and wall hangings.

• Susan Lynne Berger, 463 West Street, New York, N.Y. 10014; 212-989-0232. Hooked rug tapestries.

• Hadler/Rodriguez Galleries, 38 East 57th Street, New York, N.Y. 10022; 212-752-7734. Contemporary fiber works.

• Renate Halpern Galleries, 147 West 57th Street, New York, N.Y. 10022; 212-988-9316. Retail and wholesale source for Oriental rugs, tapestries, and textiles.

• Roger Middleton, 707 Carroll Street, Brooklyn, N.Y. 11215; 212-638-8262. Navajo weavings.

• Tell Tale Totes and Contemporary Tapestries, 199 Lincoln Road, Brooklyn, N.Y. 11225; 212-284-0370. Custom-designed tapestries by Marie Wilson.

Telephones

• The Phone Booth, 12 East 53rd Street, New York, N.Y. 10022; 212-751-8310. Phone systems,

Charles Swerz and Jerry Van Deelen

Tent,
Moss Tent Works

David Sanders
and Gregory Turpan

cordless phones, and answering machines.

• Phone Songs, 17 East 96th Street, New York, N.Y. 10028; 212-691-3346. Nine prerecorded songs appropriate for answering machines in both businesses and residences. Nationally marketed and available in most New York City department stores.

• Phone Center Stores:

One Liberty Plaza, New York, N.Y. 10048; 212-406-1392.

162 West 23rd Street, New York, N.Y. 10011; 212-741-2450.

269 Amsterdam Avenue, New York, N.Y. 10023; 212-496-9895.

1095 Avenue of the Americas, New York, N.Y. 10036; 212-391-1059.

210 East 86th Street, New York, N.Y. 10028; 212-988-8699.

585 Second Avenue, New York, N.Y. 10010; 212-679-5462.

• Telecord 25, P.O. Box 698, Malibu, Calif. 90265. Extension cord that fits most phones with clip-in cords and wall jacks. Comes in nine colors and costs $11.95 plus postage.

Tents

• Moss Tent Works, Camden, Me. 04841; 207-236-8368. Sculpture tents. See also listing for ''Future Tents.''

The Place For Antiques, 993 Second Avenue, New York, N.Y. 10022; 212-475-6596. Adirondack twig furniture. See''Rustic Furniture,'' pages 218 to 219, and listings under ''Americana, antiques'' and ''Americana, new.''

Things Antique, 250 West 77th Street, New York, N.Y. 10023; 212-799-0755. Specializes in re-

stored, turn-of-the-century furniture, including an extensive array of curved-top Saratoga and flat-top trunks that range in cost from $85 to $150 apiece. See also listings under ''Americana, Antiques.''

Tiffany & Company, 727 Fifth Avenue, New York, N.Y. 10022; 212-755-8000. French porcelain, earthenware, crystal, sterling silver, imported linens. Stores in Atlanta, Houston, Beverly Hills, San Francisco, and Chicago.

Tile

Apart from the sources for tile given on pages 182 to 183, listed below are a number of other tile suppliers in the New York area that offer quarry and ceramic tile, domestic and imported.

• American Oleon Tile Company, 150 East 58th Street, New York, N.Y. 10022; 212-688-1177. To-the-trade showroom for popular, basic tile, now available in a wide range of pastel colors.

• Ceramica Mia, 405 East 51st Street, New York, N.Y. 10022; 212-759-2339.

• Country Floors, 300 East 61st Street, New York, N.Y. 10021; 212-758-7414.

• Design Technics Ceramics, 160 East 56th Street, New York, N.Y. 10022; 212-355-3183. Wholesale source for ceramics, including lamps, tiles for floors and walls, and dinnerware.

• Elon, 964 Third Avenue, New York, N.Y. 10022; 212-759-6996. A showroom of handmade Mexican tiles, including leathery terra cotta tiles, patterned and solid-colored tiles. Ceramic lavatories, faucets, and accessories.

Tile, handmade

Many artists and craftspeople make and decorate tile by hand; some can match fabric or custom-make tiles to be used as decorative borders.

• Design Tiles, 500 Chestnut Street, Mifflinburg, Pa. 17844; 717-966-3373. Hand-painted ceramic tiles designed and produced by Andrea West.

• Hastings Tile and Il Bagno Collection. Showroom: 201 East 57th Street, New York, N.Y. 10022; 212-755-2710; Business office: 410 Lakeville Road, Lake Success, N.Y. 11042; 516-328-8600. Wholesale and retail source for hand-crafted and hand-painted ceramic tiles, elegant Italian bathroom fixtures, and imported kitchens from Europe.

• Hearthstone Tile Company, 10 St. John Place, Port Washington, N.Y. 11050; 516-944-6964. Handmade tiles by Brenda Bertim. Prices range from $7 to $50 per tile.

• Terra Designs, 211 Jockey Hollow Road, Bernardsville, N.J. 07924; 201-766-3577. Manufactures Pre-Columbian- and primitive Americana-style tiles, and custom-designed ceramic tiles.

• Tile Selection by Amaru, 150 East 58th Street, New York, N.Y. 10022; 212-755-3818 or 516-487-4750. Hand-painted Italian ceramic and designer monocatura.

Tools, see Brookstone and Garrett Wade, listed under ''Catalogs.''

Topeo, see listing under ''Fifties.''

Townhouse Collection, 145 East 72nd Street, New York, N.Y. 10021; 212-988-6937. Crystal vases, candleholders. See also listings under ''Gift stores.''

Peter Townsend, see listing for Una Architectural Studios. See pages 132 to 135.

Trompe l'oeil

This method of faking it with paint is an increasingly popular interior decorating process. Listed below are a number of artists and muralists to supplement listings on pages 188 to 189.

• Jean-Pierre Heim and Christine Feuillate, 241 West 36th Street, New York, N.Y. 10036; 212-239-0076, 724-7400, or 947-5386. Interior design and architecture; interior and exterior perspective.

• Richard Neas, 157 East 71st Street, New York, N.Y. 10021; 212-772-1878. Artist who specializes in trompe l'oeil.

• See also pages 184 to 189.

• See also listings under "Walls, painted."

Turpan Sanders, see listings under "Housewares," and "Glassware."

Typewriters

• The U-Type-It Center, 60 West 39th Street, New York, N.Y. 10018; 212-354-6888. Rental and repair of typewriters; $8.50 per day for an IBM Selectric. Word processing machines are also available.

U

Umbra Shades, 2388 Midland Avenue, Scarborough, Ontario, Canada; 416-299-0088. Paper and vinyl shades that are easy to install.

Umbrellas

• Zip-Jack Industries, 678 Central Park Avenue, Yonkers, N.Y. 10704; 914-423-5000 or 212-299-0288. Manufacturers of the Zip-Jack custom umbrella, an indoor or outdoor, water-repellent, mildew-resistant, unbleached boat canvas and wood umbrella. Available with either a round or square top, and four or eight ribs.

Una Architectural Studios, 1 White Street, New York, N.Y. 10013; 212-966-6855. Peter Townsend, partner, b. 1948. Prefers custom residential work and commercial jobs, both retail stores and office buildings. Influenced most importantly by the city, and by the way he sees "people and space interact." See pages 132 to 135.

Unica Trading, 192 Lexington Avenue, New York, N.Y. 10016; 212-685-5890. Mainly wholesale source for imported rustic, provincial, one-of-a-kind furniture, as well as baskets.

Union Products, Leominster, Mass. 01453; 617-537-1631. Lawn and garden products, including planters, decorative plastic animal sculptures.

Upholstery

Interior designers and decorators tend to guard their reliable upholstery sources with some secrecy. Listed below are some that will deal both with the trade and with the general public.

• Guild Furniture, 30 West 36th Street, New York, N.Y. 10018; 212-695-3266. Cushions and frames for banquettes.

• Imperial Leather Furniture Company, 315 West 47th Street, New York, N.Y. 10036; 212-246-1150. Cushions and coverings for banquettes.

• Steven Jonas, 30 West 26th

Street, New York, N.Y. 10010; 212-685-5610. Wall coverings, draperies, bedspreads, and upholstery.

• Starlight Upholstery, 336 East 75th Street, New York, N.Y. 10021; 212-879-4361. Cushions, fabric, and bedding for banquettes.

• See pages 208 to 209.

V

The Vermont Country Store, Route 100, Weston, Vt. 05161; 802-824-6932; and Route 103, Rockingham, Vt. 05161. Country home accessories, door bells, kitchen gadgets, dusters, seat cushions, candies and condiments, whole grains.

Jane Victor Associates, 64 University Place, Suite 402, New York, N.Y. 10003; 212-254-5199. Jane Victor and Rudy Yanes, partners. Yanes, b. 1946, attended the Fashion Institute of Design and Merchandising in Los Angeles. Victor, b. 1941, studied at New York University and the Pratt Institute. Their work is both residential and commercial. See pages 62 to 63.

Victorian Collectibles, 6916 North Santa Monica Boulevard, Fox Point, Wis. 53217; 414-352-6910. Nineteenth- and early-twentieth-century Victorian wall coverings, including ceiling canvases.

Video Masters, RD 2, Box 313, Yorktown Heights, N.Y. 10598; 914-248-5189. Video inventory system includes visual record of household or business contents on color videotape; exterior views,

Market umbrella,
Zip-Jack Industries

pans of each room, close-up views, documentation of papers.

Vignelli Associates, 410 East 62nd Street, New York, N.Y. 10021; 212-593-1416. A company established in New York in 1971 by Massimo and Lella Vignelli. Their design work includes corporate identity and graphic programs; transportation and architectural graphics; books, magazines, and newspapers; exhibitions and interiors; and, through Vignelli Designs, furniture and a variety of products. See pages 156 to 159.

Kevin Walz

W

Wall hangings

• Greenberg Tapestry, 580 Eighth Avenue, New York, N.Y. 10018; 212-840-1112. Barbara R. Greenberg produces simple abstract wall hangings and free-hanging pieces made from sisal linen and wool that she dyes. Works on commission, accommodating design to individual space.

• See also listings under "Tapestries."

Wall systems

• R.V. Cole, 16 East 30th Street, New York, N.Y. 10016; 212-686-6840; and Montauk Highway, Wainscott, N.Y. 11975; 516-537-3144. Trundle, loft beds, and wall systems.

• Custom Art Furniture, 225 East 24th Street, New York, N.Y. 10010; 212-684-4465. Portable modular wall systems.

• See also listings under "Closets."

Walls, painted

• Wallworks, Box 427, Bedford, New York, N.Y. 10506; 914-234-7969. Norman and Marguerite Deltufo produce murals and graphic art, including landscapes, seascapes, and silhouettes. They custom design for both interiors and exteriors. Prices vary depending on number of doors and windows. Estimates and color sketches for each client.

• See also page 188 for a listing of trompe l'oeil artists, many of whom do painted murals.

Kevin Walz Design, 143 West 20th Street, New York, N.Y. 10011; 212-242-7177. Interior designer, b.1950. Works from a conceptual point of view, with attention to detail and spatial problem-solving. Strives for clean lines and warm tones: "I've only used gray industrial carpeting once." See pages 102 to 105.

Whimsical Walls, 136 Quinn Road, Briarcliff Manor, N.Y. 10510; 914-941-3686. Painted walls for children's rooms. See "Children, furniture and accessories, Motif Designs."

Windows

• Elegant Manufacturing Company, 137-47 Northern Boulevard, Queens, N.Y. 11354; 212-358-2440. A source for venetian blinds and shades, vertical blinds and shades, radiator covers, replacement windows and doors, storm windows and doors, and vanities.

• Sol-R-Veil, 60 West 18th Street, New York, N.Y. 10011; 212-924-7200. A division of General Draperies. A shading material designed to be used on the interior and exterior of window systems. The shade blocks heat in the summer and insulates in the winter.

Wine accessories

• The Wine Enthusiast, P.O. Box 63, Chappaqua, N.Y. 10514; 914-238-9799. Accessories for oenophiles, including corkscrews and wine racks.

• The Wine Glass, made by Epic Products, P.O. Box 7861, Newport Beach, Calif. 92660; 714-641-8194. An unbreakable wine glass made of high strength acrylic.

Stanley Wisniewolski, 11-29 Catherine Street, Brooklyn, N.Y. 11211; 212-388-5454. Artist.

Wolfman-Gold & Good Company, see listings under "Housewares" and "Glassware." See also pages 214 to 217.

Thomas K. Woodard, American Antiques and Quilts, see listing under "Americana, antiques." See also pages 226 to 229.

Woodwork

• Barewood, 141 Atlantic Avenue, Brooklyn, N.Y. 11201; 212-875-3833. A woodworking plant that produces mantels, paneling, and a large selection of doors. Craftsmen refinish, modify, and frame doors.

Wrapping

There are those among us who can get the gift and the wrapping and put it all together. For those who need a little help, these services below can gift wrap for special occasions.

• The Bag Lady, 111 East Cabot Lane, Westbury, N.Y. 11590; 516-334-1495. Founded by Madeline Perney. Manufactures and distributes shimmering silver gift bags. Available by mail-order only.

• Ribbons and Rolls, 190 Columbus
Avenue, New York, N.Y. 10023;
212-362-2482.

• Annie Wrapper, 956 Lexington
Avenue, New York, N.Y. 10021;
212-535-7903.

Samuel Yellin Metalworkers, 5520
Arch Street, Philadelphia, Pa.
19139; 215-472-3122. Large
metalwork, including ironwork for
commercial, municipal, and individual jobs.

Zabar's, see listing under ''Housewares.''

Zip-Jack Industries, see listing
under ''Umbrellas.''

Index

Suzanne Slesin, the assistant editor and a reporter for The Home Section of *The New York Times* is a former home furnishings editor at *New York* and *Esquire* magazines. She is the co-author of *High-Tech: The Industrial Style and Source Book for the Home,* and *French Style.* Her articles on home design have appeared in many magazines— *House & Garden, Industrial Design, Maison de Marie-Claire, Domus,* and *Abitare,* as well as in *The New York Times Magazine.*

Tom Bodkin, an award-winning graphic designer, is the art director of the Travel section of *The New York Times.* Formerly the art director of The Home Section of *The New York Times,* he has also been a designer at CBS and the art director of Avant-Garde Media, Inc.